ANALYSING TEXTS

General Editor: Nicholas Marsh

Chaucer: The Canterbury Tales *Gail Ashton*

Shakespeare: The Tragedies *Nicholas Marsh*

Virginia Woolf: The Novels *Nicholas Marsh*

Jane Austen: The Novels *Nicholas Marsh*

Thomas Hardy: The Novels *Norman Page*

Further titles are in preparation

Analysing Texts
Series Standing Order ISBN 0–333–73260–X
(*outside North America only*)

You can receive future titles in this series as they are published by placing a standing order. Please contact your bookseller or, in case of difficulty, write to us at the address below with your name and address, the title of the series and the ISBN quoted above.

Customer Services Department, Macmillan Distribution Ltd
Houndmills, Basingstoke, Hampshire RG21 6XS, England

Shakespeare:
The Tragedies

NICHOLAS MARSH

Published by
PALGRAVE
Houndmills, Basingstoke, Hampshire RG21 6XS and
175 Fifth Avenue, New York, N. Y. 10010
Companies and representatives throughout the world

PALGRAVE is the new global academic imprint of
St. Martin's Press LLC Scholarly and Reference Division and
Palgrave Publishers Ltd (formerly Macmillan Press Ltd).

ISBN 0–333–73930–2 hardcover ✓
ISBN 0–333–67406–5 paperback

This book is printed on paper suitable for recycling and made from fully managed and sustained forest sources.

A catalogue record for this book is available from the British Library.

Cataloging-in-Publication data is available from the Library of Congress

ISBN 0–312–21372–7 cloth
ISBN 0–312–21373–5 paper

10   9   8   7   6   5   4   3
08   07   06   05   04   03   02   01

Printed in China

For Benji

Contents

General Editor's Preface

This series is dedicated to one clear belief: that we can all enjoy, understand and analyse literature for ourselves, provided we know how to do it. How can we build on close understanding of a short passage, and develop our insight into the whole work? What features do we expect to find in a text? Why do we study style in so much detail? In demystifying the study of literature, these are only some of the questions the *Analysing Texts* series addresses and answers.

The books in this series will not do all the work for you, but will provide you with the tools, and show you how to use them. Here, you will find samples of close, detailed analysis, with an explanation of the analytical techniques utilised. At the end of each chapter there are useful suggestions for further work you can do to practise, develop and hone the skills demonstrated and build confidence in you own analytical ability.

An author's individuality shows in the way they write: every work they produce bears the hallmark of that writer's personal 'style'. In the main part of each book we concentrate therefore on analysing the particular flavour and concerns of one author's work, and explain the features of their writing in connection with major themes. In Part 2 there are chapters about the author's life and work, assessing their contribution to developments in literature; and a sample of critics' views are summarised and discussed in comparison with each other. Some suggestions for further reading provide a bridge towards further critical research.

Analysing Texts is designed to stimulate and encourage your critical and analytic faculty, to develop your personal insight into the author's work and individual style, and to provide you with the skills and techniques to enjoy at first hand the excitement of discovering the richness of the text.

NICHOLAS MARSH

A Note on Editions

References to act, scene and line numbers in the four tragedies we study in this volume are to *The Arden Edition of the Works of William Shakespeare*, published by Routledge. In the Arden series, *Hamlet* is edited by Harold Jenkins (1982), *Othello* is edited by M. R. Ridley (1958), and *King Lear* and *Macbeth* are both edited by Kenneth Muir (1972 and 1951 respectively). Act, scene and line numbers from other works by Shakespeare are taken from *William Shakespeare: The Complete Works,* edited by Peter Alexander (Collins, London and Glasgow, 1951).

PART 1

ANALYSING SHAKESPEARE'S TRAGEDIES

Introduction: Analysing Shakespeare's Poetry

I have avoided technical terms as much as possible in this book; but some metrical analysis, and one or two other terms, are useful. So we should have some knowledge of the form of Shakespeare's poetry before we start.

Blank Verse

In these plays, most of the text is written in **blank verse**. Blank verse has no rhyme, and ten-syllable lines. Experts disagree about whether blank verse has a meter – a regular pattern of stresses – or not. Those who say that it is metrical regard many of Shakespeare's lines as 'irregular'. Others say that it has no set meter, but some of the lines have a 'regular iambic meter'. Yet another group says that the natural stress-pattern in the English language is 'iambic'; so there is an 'iambic' background, even where there is no set meter.

We will not take sides in this argument. It is useful to notice when the stresses in Shakespeare's poetry do not form any pattern, and we will often call these rhythms 'irregular'. It is equally useful to notice when there is a strong 'iambic' pattern. The next section explains the few technicalities involved.

Iambic Pentameter, Caesurae, Couplets

An 'iamb' or 'iambic foot' is a unit consisting of two syllables with the stress on the second syllable. So the word 'report' is an iamb because we never put the stress on the first syllable and say '*re*port'; we always stress the second syllable and say 're*port*'.

Five 'iambs' in succession make a line of poetry called **iambic pentameter**. For example:

> An honest mind and plain, he must speak truth.
>
> *(King Lear,* 2, ii, 96)

If you say this aloud, you naturally stress 'hon-', 'mind', 'plain', 'must' and 'truth'. If you forget the words and listen to the rhythm, it sounds like 'de-*dum* de-*dum* de-*dum* de-*dum* de-*dum*'. That is the sound that a regular line of iambic pentameter makes. When we point out meter in our analyses, we will print the stresses in italics, so our example would look like this: 'an *hon*est *mind* and *plain*, he *must* speak *truth*'.

Each iambic unit of two syllables is called a 'foot', so there are five 'feet' in a pentameter line. We will sometimes comment when one of the feet is 'reversed'. This means that the first syllable in one of the feet is stressed, instead of the second. For example, three lines after the one quoted above, Cornwall says '*Har*bour more *craft* and *more* cor*rupt*er *ends*'. This sounds like '*dum*-de de-*dum* de-*dum* de-*dum* de-*dum*' because we say '*har*bour' not 'har*bour*'.

Even our example of a regular line is not perfect, however. Notice that 'speak' is not stressed in the iambic pattern; but when we say the line aloud, the final three syllables are almost equally stressed. There is a heavier, more frequent beat at the end of the line. That is why it sounds dogmatic and powerful.

Pauses are extremely important when analysing rhythm: we will often look at the punctuation, and discuss the phrasing of a passage. Pauses often come near the middle of a line. If a pause occurs between the fourth and seventh syllables of the line, it can be called a **caesura** (plural **caesurae**). I use this term because the alternative is a clumsy phrase: 'pause in the middle of the line'. So, there is a caesura after 'plain' in our example from *King Lear*. I have also chosen to avoid the clumsy phrases 'line with a punctuation mark at the end of it' and 'line with no punctuation mark at the end of it'. We will use the short, self-evident terms 'end-stopped line' and 'run-on line' to describe these two phenomena.

In Shakespeare's tragedies most of the text is in blank verse.

However, we will come across two other kinds of writing as well. Some scenes or parts of scenes are written in **prose**. It is often worth noticing when Shakespeare shifts from poetry to prose or back again, because it can indicate a change of tone in the drama. For example, the prose sections usually, but not always, involve characters from the lower ranks of society. On the other hand, as you pursue your Shakespeare studies you will find that some passages are printed as poetry in one edition, and as prose in another. This happens when different editors cannot agree, so we will be careful not to draw too many conclusions from such changes.

The other kind of writing we will meet occurs when two adjacent lines rhyme. When this happens, the pair of rhyming lines is called a **couplet**. Shakespeare sometimes writes a couplet for the final lines of a scene, an act or an important speech. His couplets are usually also in regular iambic meter. Couplets often produce an effect of balance between the two lines, and they lend themselves to neat statements or to irony in the final line or half-line. Shakespeare uses them to express a concluding statement: a condensed summing-up of what has been happening. For example, at the end of Act 1 of *Hamlet*, Hamlet summarises his feelings about meeting the Ghost and his duty to revenge his father, in this couplet:

> The time is out of joint. O cursed spite,
> That ever I was born to set it right.
> (*Hamlet*, 1, v, 196–7)

Some of Shakespeare's early plays were written almost entirely in couplets, and even in the mature tragedies he occasionally uses couplets for a whole speech. Another variation on this form happens when four lines rhyme alternately (i.e. the first with the third, the second with the fourth).

Imagery

We pay close attention to imagery in all of the extracts we analyse, and Chapter 7 concentrates on imagery. So it is important, at the start, to clarify what 'imagery' is. We do not call it 'imagery' when the words make a picture in your head. We only call a word or a group of words an 'image' if they express a comparison between something in the play and something imaginary which is there for the sake of the comparison. For example, when Hamlet says that the sky is:

> . . . this majestical roof fretted with golden fire . . .
> (*Hamlet*, 2, ii, 301)

we know that the sky is not really a roof, and the stars are not really gold paint or flames. The sky and stars are compared to a gilded roof.

There are two kinds of image which have different names. If an image is stated in explicit language (such as 'man . . . how *like* an angel' in line 306 of the same scene, where 'like' expresses the comparison), it is called a **simile**. If we understand the comparison but none of the words explain that a comparison is happening (as in our example of 'this . . . roof', when we know that Hamlet is talking about the sky but the words do not explain this), the image is called a **metaphor**.

1

Openings

We will take an extract from each of the four tragedies we are studying, in each chapter of Part I. We will begin by looking closely at these samples from the texts, finding out as much as we can by analysing how they are written. Remember that these works are 'wholes' in the sense that everything about them contributes to the meaning they convey: it is just as much there in the style – the way they are written – as in the subject-matter. So we can take a sample and analyse the style in detail, confident that beginning in this way will bring us insights into the meaning and artistic purpose of the whole text. We are particularly interested in any features we find that are common to all four plays.

This 'group of works' was written for the theatre, and our approach should take this into account consciously: it is both important and extremely helpful to imagine a performance of the play in a theatre, with audience, actors and actresses. Plays exist in performance, with sight and sound and in space and time, as well as on the page. They spring into existence during the first minute of the first act. The dramatist has been given a set space and time, and the magical power to create a world within those limits. The vital question for us as we study his intentions is: what sort of a world has he chosen to create, and why? We will find out a lot about the answer to this question by looking at the first vital minutes of the performance. Imagine that we are sitting in the audience. The lights in the auditorium dim, and the people around us become quiet. The curtain rises (or, in many modern theatres and in Shakespeare's time, the stage is lit and the actors enter). What happens?

* * *

Here is the opening of *Hamlet*:

SCENE I.
Elsinore. A platform before the castle.
FRANCISCO *at his post. Enter to him* BARNARDO.

Bar.	Who's there?	
Fran.	Nay, answer me; stand, and unfold yourself.	
Bar.	Long live the King!	
Fran.	Barnardo?	
Bar.	He.	5
Fran.	You come most carefully upon your hour.	
Bar.	'Tis now struck twelve; get thee to bed, Francisco.	
Fran.	For this relief much thanks; 'tis bitter cold,	
	And I am sick at heart.	
Bar.	Have you had quiet guard?	10
Fran.	Not a mouse stirring.	
Bar.	Well, good night.	
	If you do meet Horatio and Marcellus,	
	The rivals of my watch, bid them make haste.	
Fran.	I think I hear them.	

Enter HORATIO *and* MARCELLUS

	Stand, ho! Who is there?	15
Hor.	Friends to this ground.	
Mar.	And liegemen to the Dane.	
Fran.	Give you good night.	
Mar.	O, farewell, honest soldier, who hath reliev'd you?	
Fran.	Barnardo hath my place. Give you good night.	*[Exit.*
Mar.	Holla! Barnardo!	20
Bar.	Say, what, is Horatio there?	
Hor.	A piece of him.	
Bar.	Welcome, Horatio; welcome, good Marcellus.	
Mar.	What, has this thing appear'd again to-night?	

| *Bar.* | I have seen nothing. | 25 |

Mar. Horatio says 'tis but our fantasy,
And will not let belief take hold of him
Touching this dreaded sight, twice seen of us;
Therefore I have entreated him along
With us to watch the minutes of this night,   30
That if again this apparition come,
He may approve our eyes and speak to it.

Hor. Tush, tush, 'twill not appear.

Bar.   Sit down awhile,
And let us once again assail your ears,
That are so fortified against our story,   35
What we two nights have seen.

Hor.   Well, sit we down,
And let us hear Barnardo speak of this.

Bar. Last night of all,
When yond same star that's westward from the pole,
Had made his course t'illume that part of heaven   40
Where now it burns, Marcellus and myself,
The bell then beating one—

                          Enter GHOST.

Mar. Peace, break thee off. Look where it comes again.

                                        (*Hamlet*, 1, i, 1–43)

What are the outstanding features of this opening sequence? The characters are mounting guard on the battlements of Elsinore castle, at night, and the opening line is a guard's challenge: 'Who's there?' An atmosphere of military tension is immediately established. With military tension goes danger, emphasised by their cautious responses to each other ('Nay, answer me; stand, and unfold yourself' and 'Stand, ho! Who is there?') and their expressions of gratitude and relief when they recognise each other: 'Welcome . . . welcome'. Being alone on the battlements is frightening – at the end of his watch Francisco says 'For this relief much thanks' because he is 'sick at heart', and Barnardo does not want to be alone for long ('bid them make haste').

Darkness isolates people from each other. More than a quarter of this extract is devoted to questioning and establishing the identities of others. The introductory exchanges, between Barnardo and Francisco, become a conversation; but when the other two characters arrive and Francisco talks to them, we are reminded of the thick darkness again: Marcellus, although he is talking to Francisco, still cannot see Barnardo and does not realise that he is close by ('Holla! Barnardo!').

Darkness, military tension, fear and uncertainty: these are our outstanding impressions of the extract. Our next task is to look more closely, using a variety of literary approaches, to follow up this impression and see whether we can find further insights into the 'world' of *Hamlet*. In our effort to imagine the performance, we can look at the physical structure of the scene, the grouping and movement of the characters. At the start there are two, separate, then they join each other. On the entry of another pair, Francisco leaves Barnardo and joins them so the groups are three and one. Next, Francisco leaves and the other two join Barnardo, but the lines suggest that they come into his view one by one rather than together. There are only very short times of stillness (for example, Francisco's and Barnardo's exchange between meeting and parting occupies about twenty seconds) before movement fragments the characters and dialogue again. Finally, after another fifteen seconds, Barnardo's story is interrupted by the arrival of the Ghost. The scene seems designed to show the characters' desire to be in company and settle down (both Barnardo and Horatio emphasise 'Sit down' and 'sit we down') in conflict with conditions and events that break them up, interrupt and isolate them.

So far, we have imagined the first minutes of *Hamlet*, paying attention to its effect in performance. Now we can take a more conventional 'literary' approach. What are the outstanding features of the style in this passage? We are looking for noticeable characteristics of rhythm, phrasing, diction, imagery and uses of language. This is a poetic drama, so we may begin by describing the rhythms. It quickly becomes clear that the opening exchange consists of unusually short phrases. In the first twelve lines there is an average of three words to each punctuation break, and the lines are not poetry until lines 6–8 when the two guards actually meet, which are written as regular iambic pentameter. There is a contrast, then, between uncertain verbal fragments and the formal, metrical exchange when they meet. The same contrast happens in reverse after the regularity of lines 13 and 14, when the exchanges come in half-lines and the blank verse remains disjointed and disturbed until Marcellus begins to speak at line 26.

His speech (ll.26–32) does establish a steadier rhythm and form, so that when Barnardo begins to tell them about the Ghost, there is room for Shakespeare to vary the pace significantly, building suspense by the use of one very long dependent clause (twenty-four syllables) and two shorter ones (both six syllables). The sentence-structure delays Barnardo's statement, creating suspense. We never reach the eagerly awaited main clause because the Ghost enters and conversation is shattered again. So, for the second time since the play began, we have heard scattered, fragmented language gradually becoming more continuous and articulate, allowing the characters to communicate their experiences, then being fragmented again by an unexpected event. It is reasonable to bring together what we have learned from our first impressions, the scene's physical structure, and these poetic features, thus: the opening few minutes of *Hamlet* show characters struggling to achieve stability and to express an understanding of their world, and a force which repeatedly shatters their efforts, working counter to the characters' desires. Our analysis has brought us to a significant realisation about the tragic world Shakespeare creates: humanity desires, and struggles to establish, order; but the world's conditions or 'fate' deny such desires, bringing disorder and showing the futility of the characters' efforts.

This insight has come from analysing the dramatic effect and the form of the opening scene; we have still hardly noticed what the characters say. Our next task is to look at the language. In this extract, there are several words and phrases that carry metaphorical meanings. The first is 'unfold' in line 2, soon followed by Francisco's 'sick at heart' and 'Not a mouse stirring'. Dialogue becomes literal again until Horatio speaks for the second time and refers to a 'piece' of himself. Barnardo brings in the first extended metaphor, appropriately a military image in which the guards 'assail your [Horatio's] ears' which 'are so fortified' against their story. The odd one out from these images is the rather common, colloquial 'Not a mouse stirring'. All of the other metaphors express the nature of a person. People can 'unfold' themselves or be 'a piece' of themselves; they can be 'sick' but in their emotions, not medically but 'at heart'; and they can erect barriers and battle against belief, being 'assailed' but 'fortified'. In all of these ideas, the common element is a view of human beings as divided within themselves. People consist of different pieces, some of which may be hidden, absent, or heavily defended. The imagery, then, conveys fragmented human beings. Two deductions from this analysis are worth noting. First, the characters show the opposite of harmony and singleness of purpose in themselves. Second, Shakespeare has already raised the unanswerable question 'what is a man?' and gone further: can we know what we are? Are we anything except what our actions make us? Can our actions make us anything, or are we victims of fate? What are thoughts, what is will, and how do they fit into a universe that ignores our struggles?

You may think our deductions go too far – after all, they are only based on a few brief metaphors from forty lines of *Hamlet*. Yet the image of a man unfolding himself does call into question the basic relationships within the personality, between thought, action, appearance and hidden soul, because the image could not be expressed if these questions were not asked. These are fundamental questions about our existence: uncertainty, and rival metaphors for what we are, are a noticeable motif at the start of *Hamlet*.

Finally, the element of 'wrongness' in the world of *Hamlet* is there from the first word, which comes from the wrong man. Francisco, standing guard, does not challenge the approaching figure in the dark. Instead, and shockingly, Barnardo issues the guard's challenge 'Who's there?'. They know that this is wrong: Francisco tries to restore the proper order by replying 'Nay, answer me; stand, and unfold yourself'. Barnardo's reply to this question dislocates the situation further. He says 'Long live the King': that is, he declares his loyalty instead of giving his name. Horatio and Marcellus do the same thing when they are challenged. Evidently, a declaration of loyalty makes a safe greeting; but as an answer to 'Who is there?' it is oblique and inadequate.

* * *

The opening scene of *Hamlet* has made a very rewarding extract for study. We now turn to the opening of *King Lear* and compare the two.

SCENE I.

A state room in King Lear's palace.

Enter KENT, GLOUCESTER, *and* EDMUND.

Kent. I thought the King had more affected the Duke of Albany than Cornwall.

Glou. It did always seem so to us; but now, in the division of the kingdom, it appears not which of the Dukes he values most; for equalities are so weigh'd that curiosity in neither can make choice of either's moiety.

Kent. Is not this your son, my Lord?

Glou. His breeding, Sir, hath been at my charge: I have so often blush'd to acknowledge him, that now I am braz'd to't.

Kent. I cannot conceive you.

Glou. Sir, this young fellow's mother could; whereupon she grew round-womb'd, and had, indeed, sir, a son for her cradle ere she had a husband for her bed. Do you smell a fault?

Kent. I cannot wish the fault undone, the issue of it being so proper.

Glou. But I have a son, Sir, by order of law, some year elder than this, who yet is no dearer in my account: though this knave came something saucily to the world before he was sent for, yet was his mother fair; there was good sport at his making, and the whoreson must be acknowledged. Do you know this noble gentleman, Edmund?

Edm. No, my Lord.

Glou. My Lord of Kent: remember him hereafter as my honourable friend.

Edm. My services to your Lordship.

Kent.   I must love you, and sue to know you better.
Edm.   Sir, I shall study deserving.   30
Glou.   He hath been out nine years, and away he shall
           again. The King is coming.
    Sennet. Enter one bearing a coronet, KING LEAR, CORNWALL,
   ALBANY, GONERIL, REGAN, CORDELIA, *and attendants.*
Lear.   Attend the Lords of France and Burgundy,
           Gloucester.
Glou.   I shall, my Liege.   *[Exeunt Gloucester and Edmund.*
                                   (*King Lear*, 1, i, 1–34)

What happens in the theatre? The inky darkness and military
tension of the start of *Hamlet* are not here. Instead the setting is a
'state room' where three more or less aristocratic characters talk in a
calm manner. The characters mention names and events. By the end
of the extract we know the names of all three, but mentions of 'the
King' and 'the division of the kingdom' leave us full of questions.

At first glance, then, this play begins very differently from
Hamlet. The two opening scenes do share some dramatic elements,
however. First, the question of identity arises again when Kent asks
to be introduced to Edmund. From that moment, the details of who
and what Edmund is dominate until the King enters, filling lines
7–32 of the scene. Second, the insecurity about perception and
reality that we noticed in *Hamlet* is also present here. The language
at the start of *King Lear* emphasises a fundamental doubt: although
these characters are able to see, we quickly realise that they are
unable to know, or rely on, what they see. The first two words are 'I
thought' – an admission of a previous, mistaken interpretation of
the King's feelings. In Gloucester's reply we hear 'did always seem',
'it appears not', and a suggestion of two Dukes frantically seeking
for a meaning, in vain: 'curiosity in neither can make choice . . .'.
Soon, Gloucester is heard explaining Edmund's illegitimacy in very
plain language, yet finishing with the oddly phrased: 'Do you
smell a fault?'. The sense of people deceived, looking for a false construction of reality, and sniffing around for a strong sinful 'smell'
behind the appearances of the court, undermines the audience's
confidence: shifting truths and perceptions, an unreliable façade,

and a hint of common grossness are our first impressions from this scene.

What features of language and style occur at the start of *King Lear*? First and most obviously, this play does not begin in poetry: these characters are speaking prose. There is a strong iambic cadence in the King's first command ('At*tend* the *Lords* of *France* and *Bur*gun*dy*)'; otherwise there is no rhythmic regularity at all. What, then, can we notice? Gloucester speaks much more, and at greater length, than do Kent and Edmund. Kent's longest speech is thirteen words, while Gloucester makes four much longer speeches of between twenty-two and sixty-two words, all within this brief extract.

There is also a strong contrast between styles of speech. First, look at Kent's and Edmund's sentences. Kent begins the play with a neat comparative construction, not wasting words. Then he asks a polite question. Notice in particular that four of Kent's five sentences begin with the pronoun 'I'. They are direct statements from himself: 'I thought', 'I cannot', 'I cannot', 'I must'. This habit of beginning with himself emphasises Kent's independence. His statements do not grammatically depend on the previous line: they could stand alone, complete. Edmund speaks hardly at all, and only responds to the other two.

Gloucester's style is in sharp contrast. Look at lines 3–6. The first phrase sets the subject-matter, echoing Kent but using a less direct construction ('it did seem to us' rather than 'I thought'). The second part of the sentence, however, meanders and grows clumsy from the attempt to include more explanation ('in the division of the Kingdom') and to envisage both Dukes engaging in the same activity from opposite standpoints – a comparison Gloucester's constructions barely cope with ('in neither . . . of either's moiety'). Gloucester's sentences, then, seem to grow over-full and uncontrolled. They start from something mentioned in the dialogue, but we cannot predict where they will end. In addition, the punctuation includes several semi-colons and colons used loosely as moments of thought-transition rather than to aid any 'structure' in the sentence. Look, for example, at lines 19–21: '. . . is no dearer in my account: though this knave came something saucily to the world . . .'. The colon after 'account' does not denote consequence, or any logical connection between the ideas before and after it; instead, it seems to mark the moment when Gloucester forgets about his legitimate son Edgar, and his thoughts start to flow towards the true object of the sentence, which is to remember the sexual pleasure he enjoyed with Edmund's mother ('there was good sport at his making').

In this way, Gloucester's speeches resemble surges of muddled thoughts, not reasoned statements contributing to the discussion, and the contrast between his 'voice' and Kent's direct terseness is the sharpest stylistic feature of the extract. It is supported by ambiguity in some key words, which has the effect of reminding the audience that meaning and truth are complicated: the single apparent meaning of a word is not its whole meaning. Kent uses the word 'affected' in the first line. The emotional word sits uneasily in a dry political statement. Gloucester's 'values', in his reply, adds to the impression of a judgement made on irrational grounds (is Lear 'pricing' the Dukes according to his feelings for them, and measuring out the kingdom according to their 'value'?). These two words set up resonances of possible alternative meaning; but when Gloucester admits Edmund's breeding has been at his 'charge', the two meanings (it has cost him money; he has been accused of being Edmund's father) are equally possible – and we cannot know which one is in Gloucester's mind. Ambiguity then grows into *double entendre* with Kent's 'conceive', which Gloucester manipulates as a lewd pun. In the first ten lines, then, the slight resonance of doubt about the meaning of words which was introduced in 'affected' (l.1) has mushroomed into a lewd pun on 'conceive' (ll.10–12). Later in the extract there are further questionable words and phrases, such as Gloucester's 'account' (estimation? expense?), Kent's reference to Edmund as 'proper' (morally or physically 'proper'?), and Edmund's smooth 'I shall study deserving' (how do you do that, and if you do, are you sincere or insincere?). The audience is now educated to sense more than one level of meaning in the characters' words, and therefore in their thoughts and lives.

Apart from the isolated 'smell a fault', the images in this extract do not stand out; but we should notice that there is already a group of three metaphorical words used to suggest a confusion of personal and financial values: 'values' (l.5), 'charge' (l.8) and 'account' (l.19) seem to begin a theme of images about money and personal value, and we may expect these metaphors to continue and develop through the rest of the play.

As with *Hamlet*, we have left discussion of the scene's subject-matter until last.

Kent and Gloucester begin by discussing the King's intentions: Lear's thoughts and actions are of supreme importance in his kingdom, evidently. These two noblemen, and the Dukes of Cornwall and Albany, anxiously await Lear's decision. The majority of the extract, on the other hand, turns on the disturbing and shameful subject of Edmund's identity. Gloucester is emotionally involved in this subject: he has 'blush'd' and is now 'braz'd to't', and he is full of embarrassment, apologising twice for Edmund's illegitimacy and awkwardly attempting to make light of his sin in 'Do you smell a fault?'. Yet his memories of sexual pleasure with Edmund's mother ('there was good sport at his making') still excite and drive his thoughts, even now. Throughout the contortions of Gloucester's mind, Edmund himself remains unexplainable. Kent coins the contradiction neatly, as we would expect: 'I cannot wish the fault undone, the issue of it being so proper'. Gloucester runs helplessly around the moral mess he is in, and ends grudgingly: 'the whoreson must be acknowledged'. The dialogue, then, raises but does not answer these questions: is Edmund good or bad? Was his conception and birth a sin or not a sin, or a sin excused by the outcome? The subject of Edmund's identity and nature seems to swell uncontrollably, taking over from the fruitless discussion of court news with which the play began.

This subject-matter, and the form, are both reminiscent of the opening of *Hamlet*. In *Hamlet* there was a tension between the stability the characters desired, and the frightening onset of fragmenting disorder dramatised in the form of dark night, and the Ghost. The characters were striving to establish order, but this was repeatedly dashed to pieces. In *King Lear* a similar conflict seems to exist, between superficial politeness and the orderliness of the court, with the King's power supreme, and chaotic excuses for sin, confusion of values, with insecurity about perception and truth, which surge up in Gloucester's speeches and overwhelm the political discussion before it can develop. In other words, the contrast we have noted between Gloucester's and Kent's styles of speech conveys a conflict between smooth surface and seething interior, which reminds us of the structure of ideas at the start of *Hamlet*.

Also, in *Hamlet* we noticed fundamental questions about humanity. The opening of *King Lear* also raises questions about the nature of Man. In this case, the other characters strive and fail to explain the identity of Edmund. In the process, the audience is driven to ask: are people commodities, to be priced? Can sin bring good, and if so, is it not sin? How can we understand intention, achievement, and nature in humankind? These questions receive no answer; but the problem is held up to us vividly, and changes with each new angle of view. We experience a strong feeling of the insoluble complexity of Man's nature.

The complexity only increases on re-reading. This is largely due to an irony which is not apparent until later in the play: the superficial smoothness of Kent's speeches does not express order, but blind moral confusion (see, for example, 'I cannot wish the fault undone'). Edmund's brief politeness is not order: later, he is revealed as a vicious hypocrite. This irony, only a gentle hint in the opening scene, undermines the contrast of styles. The more we take notice, the more any vestige of superficial orderliness dissolves, and complexity envelops all characters and their language, however neatly they express themselves.

*   *   *

The opening minutes of *Othello* happen thus:

SCENE I.

Venice. A street.

Enter IAGO *and* RODERIGO.

Rod.   Tush, never tell me, I take it much unkindly
       That thou, Iago, who hast had my purse,
       As if the strings were thine, shouldst know of this.

Iago.   'Sblood, but you will not hear me.

	If ever I did dream of such a matter,	5
	Abhor me.	
Rod.	Thou told'st me, thou didst hold him in thy hate.	
Iago.	Despise me if I do not: three great ones of the city,	
	In personal suit to make me his lieutenant,	
	Oft capp'd to him, and by the faith of man,	10
	I know my price, I am worth no worse a place.	
	But he, as loving his own pride and purposes,	
	Evades them, with a bombast circumstance,	
	Horribly stuff'd with epithets of war:	
	And in conclusion,	15
	Nonsuits my mediators: for 'Certes,' says he,	
	'I have already chosen my officer,'	
	And what was he?	
	Forsooth, a great arithmetician,	
	One Michael Cassio, a Florentine,	20
	A fellow almost damn'd in a fair wife,	
	That never set squadron in the field,	
	Nor the devision of a battle knows,	
	More than a spinster, unless the bookish theoric,	
	Wherein the toged consuls can propose	25
	As masterly as he: mere prattle without practice	
	Is all his soldiership: but he, sir, had the election,	
	And I, of whom his eyes had seen the proof,	
	At Rhodes, at Cyprus, and on other grounds,	
	Christian and heathen, must be lee'd, and calm'd,	30
	By debitor and creditor, this counter-caster:	
	He, in good time, must his lieutenant be,	
	And I, God bless the mark, his worship's ancient.	
Rod.	By heaven I rather would have been his hangman.	
Iago.	But there's no remedy, 'tis the curse of service,	35
	Preferment goes by letter and affection,	
	Not by the old gradation, where each second	
	Stood heir to the first: now sir, be judge yourself,	
	Whether I in any just term am affin'd	
	To love the Moor.	40

(*Othello*, 1, i, 1–40)

What happens in the theatre when this play starts? The scene is 'Venice. A street'. Later in the scene, Iago and Roderigo are not recognised by Desdemona's father, so we know that – as in *Hamlet* – it is the middle of the night and very dark. As with *King Lear* and *Hamlet*, the play begins with subordinate characters. They are soldiers and courtiers, not kings and generals, and *Othello* is like *King Lear* in that the opening dialogue discusses the hero's power to make important decisions. In this case, Othello has decided to appoint Cassio as his second-in-command, and Iago is full of resentment.

Both of the men on stage are angry. Roderigo starts with the petulant 'Tush', and Iago's first word is an oath ''Sblood'. Within six lines, the conflict between them gives way, however, and Iago dominates, railing venomously against Othello. Sitting in the audience, we reel from the shock of so much naked hatred and venom, so suddenly displayed at the start of the play. Later in the same scene, Iago's coarseness to Desdemona's father is a further assault on the audience's sensitivity. From the first moments, then, this play attacks our delicacy: the scene is dark, and the ideas, emotions and words are angry, often offensive.

Analysis of the language and poetry enhance this impression. Strong words of discord and hatred come thick and fast in lines 1–8: 'Tush', 'unkindly', ''Sblood', 'Abhor', 'hate', 'Despise'. The diction becomes more complex during Iago's long speech, but words with the spitting force of expletives continue to appear: 'stuff'd', 'Forsooth', 'damn'd', 'prattle'. Iago quickly adopts a tone of sarcasm brimming with contempt. For example, he describes Othello's pompous way of speaking as 'bombast circumstance', and pours scorn on Cassio by calling him an 'arithmetician' and a 'Florentine'. His scorn likens the 'bookish theoric' to 'a spinster' (Cassio's lack of experience in soldiering is like a spinster's lack of marital experience) or to politicians, the 'toged consuls' who sit and debate while others risk their lives in battle; and Cassio's academic studies are again derided in 'debitor and creditor, this counter-caster'.

The extract is in blank verse. The first eight lines have a broken rhythm (shown by the frequent punctuation), conveying angry bursts of talk. In Iago's speech the pace varies considerably. For example, lines 15–18 are broken into short phrases, and the blank

verse is interrupted by two irregular half-lines, as he tells how
Othello rejected him. Lines 21–7, on the other hand, consist of
longer phrases, five of which are the full length of a poetic line or
longer: the poetry gushes and there is some regular iambic beat (e.g.
'That *never* *set* a *squad*ron *in* the *field*). These features increase the
pace of the poetry, conveying the rapid flow of Iago's contempt for
Cassio.

Iago's sentences may remind us of the loose, emotional structure
of Gloucester's diction in *King Lear*. Between lines 8 and 33 there
are only two sentences: one of four lines, the other a vast structure
which hangs loosely upon colons and a question-mark, in five long
sections, each one almost a paragraph in its own right. It is often difficult to see the structure of a long sentence clearly. In such circumstances it is helpful to summarise the sentence as briefly as possible,
cutting out the detail of the original so that you can see the basic
framework. Here is a summary of Iago's vast sentence:

'Othello said he had appointed someone, Michael Cassio, who
has no practical experience: but he has the job, and I am passed over:
he is lieutenant, and I am Othello's ancient.'

The summary shows that Iago repeats his statement of Othello's
injustice. The colons do not stand for logic in the sentence's structure, but (as with Gloucester) denote the beginning of a new movement in the character's thoughts. So, the section beginning
'Forsooth' (l.19) and leading to 'all his soldiership' (l.27) has a consistent tone of contempt and becomes increasingly insulting of
Cassio, while the next section, beginning 'but he, sir' (l.27) and
going as far as the colon after 'counter-caster' (l.31) has a different
tone, one of bitter complaint.

Each section of Iago's sentence, on the other hand, has an internal
'shape' in which successive phrases build upon each other towards a
higher pitch of hostility. The effect of the speech as a whole, then, is
of a succession of swellings of hatred and bitterness, only loosely
restrained within the confines of language. Iago's second speech
(ll.35–40) is similar in structure, being a single sentence changing
direction at the colon after 'first' (l.38). It is a shorter and more purposeful sentence, however, which shows that Iago has not lost
control of himself. Lines 38–40 actually answer Roderigo's implied

question of line 7, returning us abruptly to the original dispute between them.

There are many images within this extract. Iago has been holding the 'strings' of Roderigo's 'purse', did not 'dream' of Othello courting Desdemona (which is the subject of their argument), had his supporters who 'capp'd' to Othello, and knows his 'price'. The 'bombast' (padding) of Othello's speech is 'stuff'd' with military terms, and a legal image occurs in 'Nonsuits', while Cassio is like a 'spinster' and 'toged consuls' who will 'prattle' (like a child). Iago himself is 'lee'd' (has had the wind taken out of his sails by a competitor sailing to windward of him) and therefore *be-*'calm'd' by Cassio, who is an elementary accountant, a 'counter-caster' who calculates with beads on an abacus.

These images come in the form of rapid metaphors, the only consistency being between Cassio as 'arithmetician' (l.19) and 'counter-caster' (l.31). However, we should notice the kinds of ideas these metaphors conjure up for us during the opening minutes of the play. First, a contemptible artificiality is strongly evoked by 'capp'd', 'bombast', 'stuff'd', and the pretentiousness of 'arithmetician', 'bookish theoric', 'toged consuls', 'prattle' and 'counter-caster'. Second, the idea of a person having commercial value, a 'price', appears here and reminds us of *King Lear*. Finally, there is a sense of power and manipulation on several levels in Iago holding the 'strings' of Roderigo's 'purse', 'great ones' who 'capp'd' or begged favours from Othello, and Cassio stealing Iago's wind. In the world of *Othello*, then, the imagery implies that each character is in a dependent or manipulative relation to others. The emphasis is on taking from people, using people, and begging, withholding or granting favours.

The subject-matter of *Othello's* opening is the injustice, or wrongness, of the world. Iago states that pretentiousness is preferred over honest experience. There is, therefore, a similarity between the content of this scene and the artificial court etiquette we found in *King Lear* or the dangerous 'something wrong' with the world which was already apparent in the first minutes of *Hamlet*. In this play, however, the subject-matter is overwhelmingly negative: almost every phrase conveys injustice, lack of value, wrongness. Only Iago's idea that he knows his own 'price', and the passing reference to his real military service 'At Rhodes, at Cyprus', interrupt negative expressions of contempt and hostility.

*   *   *

It is becoming increasingly clear that we will draw further conclusions about the tragedies from our examination of their opening minutes. For example, confusion has figured, in one form or another, in all the openings we have looked at. Before we pursue these ideas, however, let us look at the opening minutes of *Macbeth*:

SCENE I.
An open place.
Thunder and lightning. Enter three WITCHES.

1 Witch.	When shall we three meet again?
	In thunder, lightning, or in rain?
2 Witch.	When the hurlyburly's done,
	When the battle's lost and won.
3 Witch.	That will be ere the set of sun.
1 Witch.	Where the place?
2 Witch.	Upon the heath.
3 Witch.	There to meet with Macbeth.
1 Witch.	I come, Graymalkin!
2 Witch.	Paddock calls.
3 Witch.	Anon!
All.	Fair is foul, and foul is fair:
	Hover through the fog and filthy air. [*Exeunt.*

5

10

SCENE II.
A camp.
Alarum within. Enter KING DUNCAN, MALCOLM, DONALBAIN, LENOX, *with Attendants, meeting a bleeding Captain.*

Dun.	What bloody man is that? He can report,
	As seemeth by his plight, of the revolt
	The newest state.
Mal.	This is the Sergeant,

	Who, like a good and hardy soldier, fought	
	'Gainst my captivity.—Hail, brave friend!	5
	Say to the King the knowledge of the broil,	
	As thou didst leave it.	

Cap. Doubtful it stood;
As two spent swimmers, that do cling together
And choke their art. The merciless Macdonwald
(Worthy to be a rebel, for to that   10
The multiplying villainies of nature
Do swarm upon him) from the western isles
Of Kernes and Gallowglasses is supplied;
And Fortune, on his damned quarrel smiling,
Show'd like a rebel's whore: but all's too weak;   15
For brave Macbeth (well he deserves that name),
Disdaining Fortune, with his brandish'd steel,
Which smok'd with bloody execution,
Like Valour's minion, carv'd out his passage,
Till he fac'd the slave;   20
Which ne'er shook hands, nor bade farewell to him,
Till he unseam'd him from the nave to th'chops,
And fix'd his head upon our battlements.

Dun. O valiant cousin! worthy gentleman!

Cap. As whence the sun 'gins his reflection,   25
Shipwracking storms and direful thunders break,
So from that spring, whence comfort seem'd to come,
Discomfort swells. Mark, King of Scotland, mark:
No sooner justice had, with valour arm'd,
Compell'd these skipping Kernes to trust their heels,   30
But the Norweyan Lord, surveying vantage,
With furbish'd arms, and new supplies of men,
Began a fresh assault.

Dun. Dismay'd not this
Our captains, Macbeth and Banquo?

Cap. Yes;
As sparrows eagles, or the hare the lion.   35
If I say sooth, I must report they were
As cannons overcharg'd with double cracks;

So they
Doubly redoubled strokes upon the foe:
Except they meant to bathe in reeking wounds,   40
Or memorize another Golgotha,
I cannot tell—
But I am faint, my gashes cry for help.

Dun. So well thy words become thee, as thy wounds:
They smack of honour both.—Go, get him surgeons.   45
[*Exit Captain, attended.*
(*Macbeth*, 1, i, entire, and 1, ii, 1–45)

What is it like in the theatre? From the first moment, *Macbeth* lifts the audience out of normality and into a different and terrifying world. The first sound is thunder, and the first sight, lightning. On stage are three witches, characters who belong in our childhood nightmares – they are a frightening supernatural stereotype we instantly recognise. The impact of the short first scene, then, is absolute: by the time these three hags have agreed to meet again, the audience knows that the world of this play is different from the world of everyday life. The rules of everyday life do not apply either, because this play's world contains magic and supernatural beings.

At the same time, there is a series of disturbing words and ideas: 'thunder', 'lightning' and 'rain', 'hurlyburly' and 'battle', 'foul', 'fog' and 'filthy air', all occur within twelve lines; the names of the witches' familiar spirits, 'Graymalkin' and 'Paddock', are outlandish; and we suffer an onslaught of opposites which attacks our normal understanding of words. This begins with a battle being 'lost and won' and becomes a denial of meaning, in 'Fair is foul, and foul is fair'.

The witches speak in short, rhyming iambic lines until line 7, and the scene ends with a regular couplet. This bouncy rhythm may remind us of spells or incantations. It certainly seems to enhance the effect of senselessness in the language. The content of the scene is nothing. We will meet the witches again in Scene iii, when they become important within the play. The first scene is entirely unnecessary – all they do is appear and agree to meet later. Why, then, did Shakespeare include it? The answer can only be that he judged it vital to shock the audience at the start, to provide an immediate and violent jolt into the world of *Macbeth*.

The second scene begins some thirty seconds after the start of the play and brings more familiar conditions: a King, two Princes, a Lord and a messenger from the battle (the Captain) discuss the war. However, this scene is still far from normality. First, it begins with an 'Alarum' (the noise of a battle), and the Captain is bleeding to death from his wounds throughout our extract. Second, the King demands news from the wounded man before sending for surgeons. The audience sees a man covered in blood, who gasps through a lengthy account of the battle, while four others take no action to save his life. The second scene makes the world of *Macbeth* more recognisable, then, but emphasises disorder and brutality: blood, battle and carelessness of human life.

The language of this scene is dense, full of effective words, metaphors and similes. There are frequent terms denoting wildness in both man and nature: 'bloody', 'spent', 'cling', 'choke', 'swarm', 'brandish'd', 'smok'd', 'bloody execution', 'carv'd', 'unseam'd', 'fix'd', 'Shipwracking storms', 'direful thunders', 'spring', 'swells', 'redoubled strokes', 'bathe', 'reeking wounds', 'faint', 'gashes cry'. Many of these are metaphors comparing the power of natural forces to the men and armies described (for example, the Norwegian attack is likened to a storm following fair weather, and Macdonwald's villainies are swarming insects). This is a vivid style, and creates conditions for Shakespeare to use imagery freely.

What are the images in the extract from Scene ii? First, the two armies are likened to exhausted swimmers, both drowning; then, Macdonwald's sins 'swarm' upon him before the Goddess Fortune is introduced like a 'whore', smiling on Macdonwald but disdained by Macbeth who is dedicated to a purer God, Valour. Macbeth 'carv'd' his way, presumably hacking enemy soldiers as he would hack undergrowth to make a path through woods (although 'carve' also reminds us of carving meat), until, reaching Macdonwald, he 'unseam'd' him (like a tailor), or split him open from belly to chin. Victory, followed by a new attack, cause the Captain to explain how sunshine and storms originate in the same place or flow from the same 'spring'. Finally, Macbeth and Banquo are eagles or lions, or

double-loaded cannons, in contrast to their enemies who are sparrows or hares, and the Captain finds two ideas to represent their
fighting (they want to 'bathe in reeking wounds' and create a new
'Golgotha'). The final metaphor sees the Captain's wounds personi-
fied, as they 'cry for help'.

Is there a common thread in these images? First, as we have
already remarked, there are several images of natural forces. The
forces of nature will be a recurrent metaphor in this play for wild
and destructive actions of men. Second, there are some everyday and
vulgar references. For example, the word 'carve' brings dining to our
minds, 'unseam'd' belongs with the tailor, and the warriors will wash
or 'bathe' in wounds.

The nature images impress us with the vast power of the elements
and thus inflate the brutalities of men, making them indistinguish-
able from the violence of the natural world. Thus, the whole world
of the play, rather than only the characters, is filled with brutality.
The other images, of everyday life, bring trivial domestic matters
shockingly together with the most gory horrors: 'unseam'd' refers to
disembowelling, and 'bathe' is coupled with 'reeking wounds'.

The Captain employs an expressive, varied style, and his sentences
help to create the effectiveness of his tale. His first sentence is a brief
summary, then he embarks upon a very long structure in two parts.
The first half (up to the colon after 'whore' (l.15)) emphasises
Macdonwald's wicked power. The second half builds through successive delaying phrases such as 'Disdaining Fortune' and 'Like Valour's
minion' to a powerful climax when Macbeth defeats the enemy. The
triumphant final line has a regular iambic beat: 'And *fix'd* his *head*
up*on* our *battlements*'. The whole speech, until the final two lines, is
marked by interjected phrases. Dramatically, this suggests the
wounded Captain's gasping delivery, but it also conveys growing
energy as the climax of the speech comes nearer. His second speech
is also strongly constructed, all designed to lead up to the short final
line: 'Began a fresh assault'. During the third speech, however, he
comes to a sudden stop: the Captain breaks off with a half-line at 'I
cannot tell—', and finally asks for help.

This scene tells the story of a battle and is full of the butchery of
war. However, there are two comments which contrast with the gory

tale so sharply that they seem to belong to a different world. First, Macbeth's most horrific acts bring forth 'O valiant cousin! worthy gentleman!' Second, the Captain's open wounds, and his violent tale, are praised: 'So well thy words become thee, as thy wounds: / They smack of honour both'. The contrast is between the Captain and King Duncan. Here, as in *King Lear*, we find the artificially cour- teous language of the court ('valiant', 'worthy gentleman', 'become', 'honour'). In this play, the horrors of war are so dominant that Duncan's fine words already sound fatuous and ineffectual. Finally, the solution Duncan offers is hopelessly inadequate: 'Go, get him surgeons' is the first mention of medicine and doctors in the play. It is already apparent that no doctor will be able to staunch the floods of blood which already wash over this play. Brutality and gore are already out of control, then, in the world of *Macbeth*. Civilised values such as honour and worthiness, and the attempts of an orderly society to repair the damage by calling surgeons, already appear feeble, silly or doomed.

Conclusions

1. We have found that there is something 'wrong' in all of the four
   worlds we meet in the opening minutes of these plays. In *Hamlet*
   life is fragmentary and suffers at the hands of an unpredictable
   fate; in *King Lear* people cannot know what is really happening,
   and are in a moral confusion; in *Othello* the world is unjust,
   rewarding false pretention over experience; in *Macbeth* evil
   witches presage horror, and people are already killing, maiming
   and spilling blood. None of these worlds is ordered according to
   civilised or moral principles.

   Our analyses of dramatic effect and style have made our
   understanding more detailed and precise than this, however: we
   can also suggest how these worlds are going 'wrong' and how
   Shakespeare creates this insight. In all four of the plays, there is a
   tension between two forces which are in contrast to each other,
   or which fight against each other in conflict. In *Hamlet* we found
   the desire for understanding and stability helpless against the

blows of an unpredictable fate; and this conflict was embodied in the style which repeatedly attempted to establish poetic expression, only to be dashed to pieces by events. In *King Lear* courteous exchanges and political discussion are brushed aside by an upswelling of sin, shame, sexuality and moral confusion. Again, the contrast between styles – Kent's terseness as against the loosely constructed surge of Gloucester's speech – embodies the forces that are in conflict within that world. In *Othello* artificial and theoretical knowledge are pitted against real experience in a world where favours are cynically sought and unjustly granted. Here again the style reveals the true state of the world: Iago's venom attacks Othello and ridicules Cassio, its power dominating the play. In *Macbeth* brutality and gore engulf the drama, in contrast to Duncan's honourable platitudes; and the clash of two styles renders the King's authority ridiculous and ineffectual.

There is something 'wrong' in each play, then; and in each case we find an unequal conflict. Shakespeare's writing conveys the power of chaotic, disorderly forces, suggesting that their victory over civilisation and order is inevitable. The explosion of negative forces is at different stages at the start of the different plays. For example, in *King Lear* Gloucester's unsettled personality is merely ominous and we sense an approaching breakdown of order; but in *Macbeth* the world is already in disorder: the language of honour glorifies butchery, and horror spreads into everyday life. The dramatic and linguistic structure of these plays, on the other hand, is essentially the same in each case.

We can therefore draw a provisional conclusion that we have found two kinds of language in the opening extracts, embodying forces that we can think of as respectively chaotic and negative, and orderly. We will look for these features in the extracts we analyse in later chapters.

2. All four plays raise unanswerable questions about humanity: what is a man? Is there any system of words or knowledge which will enable us to understand or know either others or ourselves? Dramatically, these doubts are presented as characters who are insecure about the facts of the world around them, or unsure of their interpretations of reality. The most obvious presentation of

this feature occurs in the confusing darkness of *Hamlet*'s opening, where a 'piece' of Horatio comes in among fearful questions and disjointed answers concerning identities. However, the different truths debated by Iago and Roderigo in *Othello*, confusing news from the battle in *Macbeth*, and unresolved questions about the King's intentions and Edmund's nature in *King Lear*, all provoke such fundamental questions. We may therefore expect these plays to become investigations into the nature of Man.

3. Our close analysis reveals that language often creates contradictions (for example, between 'fair' and 'foul' in *Macbeth*) or is ambiguous (such as 'charge' and 'conceive' in *King Lear*). Language, in fact, seems to be failing: it carries little reliable meaning and darkens understanding. We should pursue this insight in future chapters, therefore. Is there any system of meaning that can succeed in expressing a truth, or can represent an actual experience? If language cannot contain experience, is this similar to the basic conflicts discussed in (1) above, where an orderly system strives to contain chaos but inevitably fails?

4. Although these plays all express an explosion of disorder, each one also conveys a strong but more or less corrupt structure in society. Thus, in *Hamlet* the only security lies in parrot declarations of loyalty: there is much disorder, but the brute necessity of war cows society. In *King Lear* the King's power is supreme, but unpredictable – a mystery to guessing Dukes and courtiers. In *Othello* each person manipulates or is manipulated in an all-embracing political dance of exploitation. In *Macbeth* King Duncan's authority is false: strength and brutality create an order of the victorious and the dead. These social structures have one common feature: they are all corrupt distortions of a civilised state.

Methods of Analysis

The following analytical approaches have been applied to the extracts in this chapter:

1. *The text as drama.* Make a conscious effort to imagine how the scene appears on stage. Ask what effect it would have on an audience. Think about the grouping and movement of the characters, and the setting, sound effects and other theatrical elements which contribute to the dramatic structure of the scene. These elements are not always apparent if you merely read the text. For example, the Captain's open wounds in *Macbeth* are only mentioned at his entry and exit. They disappear from the text during the scene; but they are constantly present to an audience because we see him bleeding throughout the scene.

2. *Language.* Look for words and phrases which stand out. When you have selected them, ask whether they have qualities in common. They may fall into groups that you can classify. Try to group them as similar kinds of words, or as having a meaning or emotion in common.

3. *Imagery.* Images add figurative ideas to our experience as we hear or read the play. Notice the images, and think about them in the same way as you think about the language: look for what images have in common. Do the images fall into groups, or is there one recurring kind of image? Analysing imagery often helps us to perceive the structure and development of ideas in the play.

4. *Poetry.* These four tragedies are all blank verse plays; but the form of Shakespeare's writing varies within the plays. He writes prose, blank verse and some irregular poetry. Look for half-lines, changes from prose to verse or vice versa, patches of regular iambic meter, and couplets. These features usually express character or tone, or mark times of upset or change in the scene.

5. *Rhythm or pace.* Notice the punctuation that divides the language into phrases. You will find places where phrases seem short and broken, other places where phrases are much longer and the speaker's speed increases. Explain how these variations in pace relate to the character or the subject-matter of the speech.

6. *Sentences.* Look at the sentences. First, notice how long or short they are; then describe their structure. This is often a revealing guide to the structure of a character's ideas.

7. *Subject-matter.* Decide what the scene is about. This may be no more than what happens during the scene (for example, we said

that the second scene of *Macbeth* is about the story of a battle); or there may be a subject which dominates what characters think and talk about (for example, Iago's long speeches are about what he sees as injustice in the world).

These are useful points to focus on, but not separate items: as you analyse, you will find that each aspect of the play adds to your developing understanding, contributing to a 'whole view'. Notice that our analysis has shown this: when we come to consider the subject-matter, many of the points we find are already obvious from the earlier parts of the analysis; or we discover that subject-matter and style fit each other exactly. Our aim is to progressively develop this 'whole view', not to pigeon-hole each aspect of style separately.

These approaches make a list of clear tasks that you can carry out when analysing an extract on your own. Using the suggested work below, you can practise using analysis yourself, building your insight into the tragedy you are studying.

Suggested Work

At the end of our first chapter I suggest that you build directly onto the analysis we have just carried out, and take the next part of each play as an extract for detailed analysis.

In *Hamlet* look at 1, i, 44–82, which gives the Ghost's first appearance and exit, the sentries' reactions, and Marcellus's question about imminent war. In *King Lear* study 1, i, 35–119. This is a long extract to take for detailed analysis; but as it deals with Lear's question and his three daughters' answers, it would go against sense to stop before all three daughters have responded. In *Othello* analyse 1, i, 40-81. Iago and Roderigo prepare to wake Brabantio; and within this section Iago declares his self-interest and deception: 'I am not what I am'. In *Macbeth* study the remainder of Act 1, Scene ii, in which Duncan disposes of the old Thane of Cawdor and gives the title to Macbeth.

These analyses will further develop what we have found in the opening minutes of each play, and can be regarded as a direct continuation of what has been done in this chapter. In *King Lear* the passage will also present much new and complex material, but you should also note how the features we have already identified are still present. For example, the insecurity about language (does it express any truth, or nothing?) is a prominent concern in his daughters' answers to Lear.

2

Endings

We have examined the first minutes of each tragedy, and found 'wrongness': forces of disorder had exploded or threatened to explode, and the restraints of civilisation were portrayed as weak, unable to prevent disaster from overwhelming the world of the play. Language was breaking down, proving deceptive or inadequate to express experience. In this chapter we will analyse the final minutes of each play: how is the audience left when tragedy has come to an end?

*　　*　　*

Here is the end of *Hamlet*:

Hor.   Not from his mouth,
　　　Had it th'ability of life to thank you.
　　　He never gave commandment for their death.
　　　But since, so jump upon this bloody question,　　　　380
　　　You from the Polack wars and you from England
　　　Are here arriv'd, give order that these bodies
　　　High on a stage be placed to the view,
　　　And let me speak to th'yet unknowing world
　　　How these things came about. So shall you hear　　　385
　　　Of carnal, bloody, and unnatural acts,
　　　Of accidental judgments, casual slaughters,
　　　Of deaths put on by cunning and forc'd cause,

	And, in this upshot, purposes mistook	
	Fall'n on th'inventors' heads. All this can I	390
	Truly deliver.	
Fort.	Let us haste to hear it,	
	And call the noblest to the audience.	
	For me, with sorrow I embrace my fortune.	
	I have some rights of memory in this kingdom,	
	Which now to claim my vantage doth invite me.	395
Hor.	Of that I shall have also cause to speak,	
	And from his mouth whose voice will draw on more.	
	But let this same be presently perform'd	
	Even while men's minds are wild, lest more mischance	
	On plots and errors happen.	
Fort.	Let four captains	400
	Bear Hamlet like a soldier to the stage,	
	For he was likely, had he been put on,	
	To have prov'd most royal; and for his passage,	
	The soldier's music and the rite of war	
	Speak loudly for him.	405
	Take up the bodies. Such a sight as this	
	Becomes the field, but here shows much amiss.	
	Go, bid the soldiers shoot.	

Exeunt marching, [bearing off the bodies,]
after which a peal of ordnance is shot off.
(*Hamlet*, 5, ii, 377–408)

There are four bodies on stage, those of Claudius, Gertrude, Laertes and Hamlet. Horatio and Osric are near to Hamlet. Fortinbras has marched in with the English Ambassadors, 'with drum, colours, and Attendants'. In the final minutes of the play the surviving characters are static. The only movement on stage is formal, ceremonial, as 'four captains' lift Hamlet's body to carry it to a platform, and other soldiers begin to remove the other bodies. These orderly movements and the strong military structure ('drum, colours', 'Bear Hamlet like a soldier', and 'Go, bid the soldiers shoot') contrast with the frightened stumbling movements of Act 1, Scene i. The bodies are to be placed 'High on a stage . . . to the view' and Fortinbras invites 'the noblest to the audience'. Clear sight, light and openness are also in total contrast to the darkness of the earlier scene.

The language adds to these impressions, denoting orderliness, reconciliation and ceremony: 'commandment', 'give order', 'Truly deliver', 'noblest', 'embrace', 'rights' and 'claim', 'cause', 'presently perform'd', 'most royal', 'The soldier's music and the rite of war' and 'Becomes'. This language reminds us of discipline, diplomacy and courtrooms – places of order and decision. Notice also that the style is more literary and more distant. Earlier, Hamlet thought it would be 'sport' to have Claudius 'Hoist with his own petard' and wanted to 'Blow them [his enemies] at the moon' (3, iv, 208–11). Now, the same thought is expressed by Horatio as: 'purposes mistook / Fall'n on th'inventors' heads'. The physical energy of 'Blow' and 'Hoist', and Hamlet's image of gunpowder, has become a calmer language as abstract 'purposes' are 'Fall'n'. In the same way, Hamlet's death is glossed by the polite euphemism 'passage' (l.403). The language, then, shows that civilised order is back in control, and the wild experiences of raw life and death are kept at a distance.

There are descriptions of the frightful tragedy that has occurred. Horatio mentions 'carnal, bloody, and unnatural acts', 'accidental judgments, casual slaughters', 'deaths put on by cunning, and forced cause' in this 'bloody question'. Notice, however, the legal terms 'judgments', 'cause' and 'question'. His language tells us that savage events are over: they are now a matter for discussion and judgment. Horatio believes that explanation will overcome chaos: when people understand, they will accept, and the tragedy will not be a threat to order any more. Men's minds are 'wild' but understanding will calm them; 'mischance / On plots and errors' could happen, but understanding will prevent this.

Rhythmically, the whole passage has a measured evenness. The two half-lines (lines 405 and 408) are purely indications to the performers, one giving time for Fortinbras to turn and order his officers to 'Take up the bodies', the other echoing final line of the play. The majority of the poetry, however, has even phrasing, and much of it is dominated by a steady iambic beat (for example 'Bear *Ham*let *like* a *sol*dier *to* the *stage*' and the line following, or most of lines 384–8). The characters finish their speeches to each other. There is no interruption or riposte: they allow each other to finish, taking turns to speak and behaving with formal courtesy. Finally, Fortinbras's opinion is expressed in a rhyming couplet (ll.406–7), underlining the feeling that the bodies, and with them the entire disturbing tragedy, will now be cleared away. Such sights 'become the field', and will soon be put back where they belong. To sum up, various elements in the style of this passage emphasise that order and control will be restored.

Order, then, is restored. Chaos is put back into its cage. However, a brief look at the content of the passage reveals that our experience of the ending of *Hamlet* is much more complex than this. Notice, for example, that Horatio seeks to excuse the murder of Rosencrantz and Guildenstern, suggesting that Hamlet's action was 'forc'd cause' or in self-defence. We remember Hamlet saying, without remorse, 'They are not near my conscience' (5, ii, 58). This irony reminds us that Horatio's story will be what stories always are: a re-shaping and selective version of what happened. It will calm men's minds and help to restore order, but it will not be the exact truth. We may feel both relief and regret that we are returning to a world of convenient, superficial half-truths. It is inevitable that this should happen, and the audience is relieved to be distanced from Hamlet's attempts to express an inexpressible agony. On the other hand, we wince at Horatio's bland confidence: 'All this can I / Truly deliver'. Moral ambiguity also disquiets us: Fortinbras will take advantage of disaster, opportunistically claiming the vacant throne of Denmark. He expresses this as a paradox: 'with sorrow I embrace my fortune'. Fortinbras may sincerely feel his 'sorrow', but the audience senses a cynical irony again. Politics must go on, and Fortinbras is politician enough to put in his claim quickly (about a minute after discovering the bodies) and to mention his 'rights of memory' in support of that claim.

These ironies remind us that when order is restored, it comes at the cost of many qualities we admire: truth, humility and moral rightness. With order comes half-truth, bland arrogance, and a compromise between ambition and morality.

*   *   *

Here is the ending of *King Lear*:

Edg.	He faints! My Lord, my Lord!	310
Kent.	Break, heart; I prithee, break!	
Edg.	Look up, my Lord.	
Kent.	Vex not his ghost: O! Let him pass; he hates him	
	That would upon the rack of this tough world	
	Stretch him out longer.	
Edg.	He is gone, indeed.	
Kent.	The wonder is he hath endur'd so long:	315
	He but usurp'd his life.	
Alb.	Bear them from hence. Our present business	
	Is general woe. [*To Kent and Edgar.*] Friends of my soul, you twain	
	Rule in this realm, and the gor'd state sustain.	
Kent.	I have a journey, sir, shortly to go;	320
	My master calls me, I must not say no.	
Edg.	The weight of this sad time we must obey;	
	Speak what we feel, not what we ought to say.	
	The oldest hath borne most: we that are young	
	Shall never see so much, nor live so long.	325

[*Exeunt, with a dead march.*
(*King Lear*, 5, iii, 310–25)

King Lear has carried Cordelia's body onto the stage, and dies while looking at her face. The bodies of Goneril and Regan are on stage, and there are several people present including Edgar, Albany and Kent. There has been a succession of rushing entries and exits throughout the final actions of the tragedy. When Lear himself dies, the scene becomes static: our extract then has four bodies on the stage, several officers and attendants, and three surviving characters (Edgar, Kent and Albany) who begin to discuss the government of the kingdom in the future.

Both language and poetry in this extract show an abrupt change at line 318. Before Albany's sentence 'Our present business / Is general woe', the phrases are short and broken. Many are only one or two words (such as 'Break, heart; I prithee, break!'), and the only longer phrase contains an image of the world as a torturer's rack, on which Lear has been stretched and died – an image of agony. After line 318, the pace becomes more measured with strongly end-stopped lines and a pause at the middle of each line (except l.322), giving symmetry to the characters' speech. Before line 318 we hear 'faints', 'break' (twice), 'Vex', 'ghost', 'hates', 'rack' and 'this tough world', 'Stretch him out', 'endur'd' and 'usurp'd'. This language denotes pain and violence; the words are all short and many of the consonants are hard. It is a spiky, painful language. After line 318 this diction virtually disappears, although there is one echo in 'gor'd state'. Instead, we hear more harmonious sounds, and the expression of 'woe' is gentler and softer: 'Rule in this realm', 'sustain', 'journey', 'Speak what we feel', 'oldest hath borne most' and so on. The predominance of softer consonants such as *m, n, b, w* and *r*, and the long vowel-sounds in words like 'realm' and 'borne' give a gentler tone to the language. Notice also that Kent refers to his own death as a journey he will be called to by his 'master', and that Edgar refers to a hanging, two stabbings, a death from poison and another from a broken heart with the melancholy, vague phrase 'this sad time' (l.322).

The poetry changes entirely at the same point. From line 319 onwards, there are rhyming couplets following iambic meter. The final couplet contrasts young and old with a symmetrical doubled construction in the final line ('Shall (never see so much), nor (live so long)'). It is like the neat concluding couplet of a sonnet. Clearly, Shakespeare intends us to hear calmness and regular harmony in the final eight lines of the play.

Like *Hamlet*, then, *King Lear* ends with a noticeable restoration of harmony in language and poetry, and a period of stage stillness after the violent movement of the tragic climax. The content of this extract, however, does not go as far towards restoring order as that in *Hamlet*. Where Fortinbras assumed the kingship quickly, supported by Horatio and Hamlet's dying voice, here all three survivors are reluctant to assume the responsibilities of a king. Albany suggests the other two, but Kent declines the offer; and Edgar, in his final speech, postpones his answer: 'The weight of this sad time we must obey' shows that grief is still too strong for him to think about the future. Albany's feelings are the same ('Our present business / Is general woe'), and Kent's outlook is towards his own death.

In this play the sharp pains of tragedy remain until almost the final seconds. Kent calls on his own heart to break and powerfully expresses the agony of Lear's suffering: his image of the 'rack of this tough world' is painful, and is similar to Lear's own 'but I am bound / Upon a wheel of fire, that mine own tears / Do scald like molten lead' (4, vii, 46–8). In *King Lear*, then, pain and grief linger, over-shadowing the end, despite a strong resurgence of calmness and order in the style. As in *Hamlet*, irony hints that the new age will not be fully honest when it comes. Edgar says that during 'this sad time' they must 'Speak what we feel, not what we ought to say'. This implies that he will cease to express his feelings honestly when the period of mourning comes to an end. Soon, when political life re-starts, people will revert to saying 'what [they] ought to say' and hiding their true feelings.

* * *

Let us turn to the final minute of *Othello*:

Cas.	This did I fear, but thought he had no weapon,
	For he was great of heart.
Lod.	[*to Iago*] O Spartan dog,

More fell than anguish, hunger, or the sea,
Look on the tragic lodging of this bed:
This is thy work, the object poisons sight,   365
Let it be hid: Gratiano, keep the house,
And seize upon the fortunes of the Moor,
For they succeed to you: to you, lord governor,
Remains the censure of this hellish villain,
The time, the place, the torture: O, enforce it!   370
Myself will straight aboard, and to the state
This heavy act with heavy heart relate.   [*Exeunt.*
(*Othello*, 5, ii, 361–72)

The stage is crowded at the climax of *Othello*: Lodovico, Montano, officers, Iago as a prisoner and the wounded Cassio in a chair are all on stage around a bed on which lie the bodies of Desdemona and Othello. Emilia's body is also on stage. The final movement, however, was Othello's suicide, and the characters seem to remain still for the duration of our extract. Lodovico's speech differs from the final words of *King Lear* and *Hamlet*. There is no sense of a general announcement, like Fortinbras's, or Edgar's and Albany's, speeches. He directs his speech at Iago, then to Gratiano and finally to Cassio. Also, Lodovico begins to speak in violent hatred (ll.362–5), and this erupts again in lines 369 and 370. Both of the other final discussions we have studied expressed agreement between the survivors. Dramatically, then, this is a sudden and much less settled ending than the other two.

Lodovico's style does not revert to calmness or harmony, either. His final lines give us 'anguish', 'tragic', 'the object poisons sight', 'seize', 'hellish villain', 'torture', 'enforce', 'heavy act'. The poetry shows energy, with a variety of rhythm and pace between such measured formality as 'to you, lord governor, / Remains the censure of this hellish villain', and the chopped phrases of fury in the next line when his feelings about Iago erupt again: 'The time, the place, the torture: O, enforce it!' (ll.369–70). Only the final couplet displays the regularity and balanced neatness of a conclusion. Again, as in *King Lear*, the final line has the symmetry of a doubled construction, this time with the added formality of repetition and inversion: 'This heavy act with heavy heart relate'.

This ending, then, shows different characteristics from those we have found in the other plays. The subject-matter, on the other hand, leads our thoughts to consider similar questions. The sadness of tragedy is present in the form of Othello's and Desdemona's bodies; but the horror of what has happened is still alive in the person of Iago, now a prisoner. Lodovico has not yet managed to deal with the problem of Iago's evil. He is in two minds. At first, he wants to punish Iago by forcing him to 'Look on' those he has killed. In a moment, however, he suffers a revulsion of feeling: the bodies 'poison sight' and he orders 'Let it be hid'. Finally he shows that Iago's existence is still an unbearable provocation, and he longs to inflict pain upon the villain (l.370). The authority of the Venetian state, represented by Lodovico, is not calm. It seeks an impossible revenge on the chaotic villainy that has fuelled tragedy. The tragedy itself is too painful to look at, and will be hidden or cleared out of sight. This conclusion reminds us of the double-edged ironies we have already found: Fortinbras will take his political opportunity, and Horatio will re-write history; after a period of mourning, Edgar will politically say 'what we ought to say'. In all three cases, the painful knowledge of tragedy will not be resolved: it will be sent into a distant memory, and avoided.

Earlier in the final scene of *Othello*, Iago spoke for the last time:

> Demand me nothing, what you know, you know,
> From this time forth I never will speak word.
>   (5, ii, 304–5)

Lodovico's speech underlines the truth of this: 'what you know, you know'. They know the chilling truth of Iago's evil, and more deeply they know that he released a destructive power which originated within Othello and is therefore present within all men. This is still destructive knowledge, disturbing the final lines of the play. Iago's final utterance reminds us that the truths revealed by tragedy are beyond the scope of language. Words cannot express them, so further words are not necessary.

*   *   *

Finally, we turn to the ending of *Macbeth*:

SCENE IX.
Within the castle.
Retreat. Flourish. Enter, with drum and colours, MALCOLM, *old*
SIWARD, ROSSE, *Thanes, and Soldiers.*

Mal.	I would the friends we miss were safe arriv'd.
Siw.	Some must go off; and yet, by these I see,
	So great a day as this is cheaply bought.
Mal.	Macduff is missing, and your noble son.
Rosse.	Your son, my Lord, has paid a soldier's debt:

                                                                    5

He only liv'd but till he was a man;
The which no sooner had his prowess confirm'd,
In the unshrinking station where he fought,
But like a man he died.

Siw.   Then he is dead?

Rosse.   Ay, and brought off the field. Your cause of sorrow   10
Must not be measur'd by his worth, for then
It hath no end.

Siw.   Had he his hurts before?

Rosse.   Ay, on the front.

Siw.   Why then, God's soldier be he!
Had I as many sons as I have hairs,
I would not wish them to a fairer death: 15
And so, his knell is knoll'd.

Mal.   He's worth more sorrow,
And that I'll spend for him.

Siw.   He's worth no more;
They say he parted well and paid his score:
And so, God be with him!—Here comes newer comfort.

        Re-enter MACDUFF, *with* MACBETH's *head.*

Macd.   Hail, King! for so thou art. Behold, where stands   20
Th'usurper's cursed head: the time is free.
I see thee compass'd with thy kingdom's pearl,
That speak my salutation in their minds;
Whose voices I desire aloud with mine,—   24
Hail, King of Scotland!

All.   Hail, King of Scotland!   [*Flourish.*

Mal.   We shall not spend a large expanse of time,
Before we reckon with your several loves,
And make us even with you. My Thanes and kinsmen,
Henceforth be Earls; the first that ever Scotland
In such an honour nam'd. What's more to do,   30
Which would be planted newly with the time,—
As calling home our exil'd friends abroad,
That fled the snares of watchful tyranny;
Producing forth the cruel ministers
Of this dead butcher, and his fiend-like Queen,   35

Who, as 'tis thought, by self and violent hands
Took off her life;—this, and what needful else
That calls upon us, by the grace of Grace,
We will perform in measure, time, and place.
So thanks to all at once, and to each one,   40
Whom we invite to see us crown'd at Scone.

> [*Flourish. Exeunt.*
> (*Macbeth*, 5, ix, entire)

The scene is an interior, 'Within the castle' in contrast to the climax of the tragedy which takes place outside on a battlefield. Malcolm and his nobles are all on stage. Dramatically, then, this is a peaceful final scene and a relief from the wildness of all that precedes it. Soldiers are present, and the scene begins with 'drum and colours': as in the final minutes of *Hamlet*, there is an emphasis on military order and discipline. When Macduff enters, he brings with him a shocking object: Macbeth's head. This is a physical intrusion of the tragedy's brutality into Malcolm's orderly final scene, and remains on stage until the end.

The language is varied and flexible; but notice that the vocabulary of chivalrous ideals is used confidently here. Remember that Duncan's 'valiant' and 'worthy' sounded absurd in the bloodbath of Act 1, Scene ii. Here, 'prowess', 'unshrinking station', 'God's soldier', 'a fairer death' are spoken with confidence and harmonise with the characters and surroundings. A courtly, ceremonial diction is also surfacing after the tragedy: 'compass'd', 'salutation', 'Henceforth'; and we notice that Malcolm passes from the pronoun 'I' (ll.1, 17) to using the royal plural 'we' in his final speech. Malcolm's speech (ll.26–41) is quite regular, leading to two couplets in grand and formal style that conclude the play. Poetic analysis shows that Malcolm's equilibrium is disturbed during the course of this speech, however. An iambic rhythm, well-established in lines 30–4, is stopped by heavy, unremitting stresses: 'this dead butcher' and 'fiend-like Queen'. The meter then takes two more lines to recover from this disturbance. Clearly, memories of Macbeth's gory, brutal reign, disturb the calm of Malcolm's victory, and this is reflected by the sudden energies disrupting the rhythm.

What imagery do we find here? First, there are frequent references to commerce: victories, life, death, sorrows and human quality are all connected to a recurrent metaphor of bargains and price. Victory is 'cheaply bought' (l.3), although Siward's son 'has paid a soldier's debt' (l.5), but if sorrow is 'measur'd by his worth', it will be infinite (l.11). He is 'worth more sorrow' which Malcolm will 'spend' (ll.16–17); but he is 'worth no more' as he has 'paid his score' (ll.17–18). When Malcolm begins to organise the kingdom, he says he will not 'spend . . . expanse' of time, but will 'reckon' and 'make us even' (ll.26–8). These metaphors create a strong sense that the value of everything is being calculated. Gains and losses are being assessed and added up to form a balance-sheet, showing an overall profit. Malcolm underlines this impression of a careful orderliness in his accounts, when he says that all 'needful' things 'We will perform in measure, time, and place'.

Second, there are two positive images, suggesting precious values and hope. One is a jewellery reference (when Macduff sees Malcolm 'compass'd with thy kingdom's pearl' (l.22)), and the other brings to mind natural growth: 'Which would be planted newly' (l.31).

Everything about the dramatic effect and style of this scene, then, suggests conclusions similar to those we have reached about *Hamlet* and *King Lear*: that order will be restored, and that survivors rapidly distance themselves from, and seek to forget, the unpalatable truths of tragedy.

The subject-matter agrees, and is in sharp contrast to the opening of the play. In this scene, Rosse and Siward put forward two views of human 'worth'. Rosse says that it 'hath no end', against Siward who claims that his son's death is 'worth no more' sorrow as he 'paid his score'. However, Rosse only mentions infinite worth after saying that we 'Must not' use it as a measure; and Malcolm takes a middle course, saying he is 'worth more' but by implication not an infinite amount. Proportion is the subject of this discussion, and the great imponderables of life and death are brought firmly into proportion by the insistent commercial metaphors the characters use. This is entirely different from the opening scenes. There, apparently endless bloody destruction distorted the world's proportions.

As in the other three endings we have looked at, the audience is encouraged to be critical of this peace and harmony, because there are lingering reminders of the tragedy. The most vivid is Macbeth's head, brought on and displayed by Macduff. The courtiers' hand-some words about victory and cost cannot make the severed head vanish, or erase the physical truth: battles are about cutting people up. There are also jarring moments, when we suspect irony because the dialogue seems too superficial. This impression is difficult to pin down, but I suggest three moments that I find hard to accept at face value: first, Siward's reaction to news of his son's death (can anybody really be this pompous at such a moment?); second, Malcolm pro-moting his Thanes to become Earls (no more than a change of name, an empty gesture); and finally, the near-doggerel sound and anti-climactic final rhyme of the final couplet. Surely something important, like 'crown'd', should be the last word. What matters is that he will be King, not the name of the town; yet the meter and rhyme make Malcolm foolishly emphasise 'Scone'.

These features remind us that political order and language are not adequate: the restoration of order is a relief from tragic pain, but also demands that we accept its half-truths and shallow calculations. As Rosse observes, we 'must not' consider the infinite value of an indi-vidual, for if we do, sorrow that 'hath no end' will be our lot. If, on the other hand, the kingdom is to be put back into order, such things have to be forgotten or ignored.

Conclusions

1. In Chapter 1 we picked out conflict between chaos and order, and an actual or impending explosion of chaos, which would inevitably destroy all order. Now we can say more about this con-flict, for each play ends with a final settlement between the forces which were opposed. The endings all show a restoration of mea-sured calmness in pace and rhythm, together with increasing for-mality of diction, with words and phrases often drawn from legal, commercial or court vocabularies. Another feature of this style is euphemism or distance about disturbing events (for example, Hamlet's death becomes his 'passage'). This style coincides with

actually establishing order after tragedy. Even in *Othello*, where the conflict is still volatile at the end, there are examples of this orderly writing. The opposing force of chaos, which appeared irresistible at the start of each play, seems to have become a painful memory of suffering or horror – memory of the tragic climax which has just occurred. It is typically expressed by vivid physical metaphors, and in rough language with short and jagged-sounding words (we remember 'break', 'rack' and 'vex' from *King Lear*). It occasionally tears through the smooth surface of the other, harmonious style. The conflict is now in a final phase: the unbearable pain and unthinkable truths of tragedy are being put back beneath the surface, and a smooth but superficial order is pushing them into distance and out of memory. *Hamlet* and *Macbeth* take this process quite a long way. In *King Lear* and *Othello*, on the other hand, the process of healing has barely begun, but will take place in the future.

2. The audience is not able to accept restored order at face value. Ironies and intrusions of tragic pain continue to remind us that order, and its language, are shallow and use half-truths. We are conscious of the price we pay for being relieved of tragic pain, therefore, and the conflict in these final scenes highlights the paradox between order and tragedy. There is a dilemma: tragedy is utterly demanding, destructive and therefore impractical; yet order is deceitful, artificial and calculatingly unemotional. The conflict we have analysed, then, expresses a fundamental human dilemma.

3. The tragedies' openings raised the question: what is a man? Such questions are still implicit in the plays' endings, but not prominent. However, in each case the tragedy has produced too much knowledge about humankind, and this excessive experience of Man's nature disturbs the ending. For example, Iago's villainy, Macbeth's brutality and Lear's suffering are all problems the survivors have to deal with, as are the confusing destructions and 'unnatural acts' in Hamlet's tragedy. Most of the survivors indicate that they wish to deal with these insights by placing them at a distance, and by artificially beautifying them with ceremony.

4. Language was failing to contain or express experience in the

plays' openings. It is worth noting that these final scenes all show a rejection of the true depth of tragic experience, in favour of inadequately shallow language. Our fundamental dilemma (see (2) above) applies again: language is a system that is unable to contain or express the full range of human experience; but perhaps it is preferable to universal destruction - perhaps it *must* be restored.

5. The distorted social order presented at the start of each play has been exploded by tragic destruction. However, the endings are all more or less unsatisfactory restorations of order. Edgar's 'what we ought to say', Horatio's biased account of Hamlet, and Malcolm's political gestures all suggest one truth. Order is, perhaps, renewed, and the best that can be established after destruction. However, it is potentially corrupt and will inevitably be corrupted. As in (2) and (4) above, we face a dilemma.

These conclusions show that tragedy presents us with the fundamental choices of existence on several levels – individual, social and political – and puts them in the form of paradoxes that cannot be resolved.

Methods of Analysis

In this chapter we have based our approach on the same methods used in Chapter 1. We have developed our analytical approach in two ways, however:

1. We have allowed some of the barriers between different aspects of analysis to become more flexible. So the idea that we plod through language, poetry, imagery, sentences, content, and so on, each in its own separate paragraph, has developed into something more sophisticated. For example, Malcolm's language and imagery in the final speech of *Macbeth* both contribute to the prominent feature of his style: insistent emphasis on measurement and calculation. It was more natural to analyse and discuss these two aspects of style together, since they work together. As

you become more practised at the business of analysing Shakespeare, you will take the most natural, flexible approach more and more often.

2. We consciously used the conclusions from the first chapter. After analysing another set of extracts, make a methodical comparison between your new conclusions and those reached earlier. This enables you to find further insights, and begin to articulate points about the development, content and 'shape' of a whole play.

Suggested Work

Look at the climax of the tragedy you have to study, immediately preceding the ending. Use the conclusions to this chapter as a basis for your ideas, use the same methods of analysis, and look for contrasts between the climax and the ending.

In *Hamlet* study 5, ii, 319–63, from Laertes's confession to Hamlet's death. In *King Lear* you can look at 5, iii, 256–310, from Lear's re-entry carrying Cordelia's body, to his own death. In *Othello* study from the entry of Lodovico and Venetian authority, as far as Othello's final speech and suicide (5, ii, 284–357). In *Macbeth* the tragic hero's final meeting with Macduff, and his death, is a separate scene (5, viii) of thirty-four lines, which you can analyse in its entirety.

3

The Hero

In this chapter we will approach the tragic heroes by analysing one major speech from each. We will concentrate on the speeches themselves, making no attempt to study a whole character. A thorough analysis of one of the heroes can be done by looking at further extracts (speeches spoken by the hero and about him) from the particular play you are concentrating on, repeating the approach shown in this chapter. Our aim is to discover how Shakespeare creates tragic character: can we recognise how words and drama combine to characterise the hero, and are there any features they, or their speeches, all have in common?

All the same, we will refer to other parts of the plays to develop a sense of context around our detailed work. This happened in Chapter 2, when we remarked that Lear used an image of torture earlier in the play, similar to Kent's image of a 'rack' which was in the analysed extract.

Bear in mind that we have found conflict between order and a chaotic destructive force in Chapter 1; and we found out more about this conflict in Chapter 2. Some such conflict may also exist within the character of each hero: does the tragic process which happens in the world of the play also happen on a personal level, within the tragic hero?

* * *

The following speech is spoken by Othello after Iago has hinted at adultery between his wife, Desdemona, and Cassio. Othello is alone:

Oth.   This fellow's of exceeding honesty,
        And knows all qualities, with a learned spirit,
        Of human dealing: if I do prove her haggard,
        Though that her jesses were my dear heart-strings,   265
        I'ld whistle her off, and let her down the wind,
        To prey at fortune. Haply, for I am black,
        And have not those soft parts of conversation
        That chamberers have, or for I am declin'd
        Into the vale of years,—yet that's not much—   270
        She's gone, I am abus'd, and my relief
        Must be to loathe her: O curse of marriage,
        That we can call these delicate creatures ours,
        And not their appetites! I had rather be a toad,
        And live upon the vapour in a dungeon,   275
        Than keep a corner in a thing I love,
        For others' uses: yet 'tis the plague of great ones,
        Prerogativ'd are they less than the base,
        'Tis destiny, unshunnable, like death:
        Even then this forked plague is fated to us,   280
        When we do quicken: Desdemona comes,
        If she be false, O, then heaven mocks itself,
        I'll not believe it.
            Enter DESDEMONA *and* EMILIA.
                            (*Othello*, 3, iii, 262–83)

Othello is thinking about the possibility that his wife is unfaithful. His thoughts consist of reasons for and against being suspicious of her. Iago's 'honesty' and 'learned spirit' make Othello inclined to believe him; but Desdemona's appearance makes his love and trust return – if she is false, 'then heaven mocks itself, / I'll not believe it'. In between these contrary views, Othello dwells on arguments which make her adultery plausible: his colour, lack of refined manners and age all persuade him that Iago must be right. Dramatically, then, we hear a man veering between love and jealousy, explaining the thoughts which are pushing him one way or the other. Dramatic irony is strong: we know Iago's dishonesty, while Othello thinks he is honest; and we know that Desdemona is loyal. Irony makes the audience feel fear and pity: we fear that Othello will never see through Iago, and will believe in his wife's guilt; and we pity him for the agony his ignorance brings. The dramatic irony creates a strong sense of 'if only': if only he knew what we know.

The speech is dense and complex, full of rapid movements of thought and changes of mood. In this situation we begin by sorting out rhythm and sentence-structure, hoping to find a shape in the speech, which will help us analyse further. If we can look at the speech in sections rather than as a complicated whole, it will be easier to clarify what is going on in Othello. There is a regular rhythm up to the colon after 'dealing' (l.264); 'if I do *prove* her *hagg*ard' interrupts this and the pace increases suddenly in line 265. Othello's first sentence, then, falls into two distinct halves, the first measured and the second disturbed. His second sentence begins with irregular phrasing, ranging from one word ('Haply') to eleven words between pauses. The pace is very broken, then suddenly races, then breaks again with two dashes around the short '—yet that's not much—' and the sentence itself breaks off unfinished. This, then, is a very jumpy and disturbed passage. Next, two powerful stresses at the start of line 271 ('She's gone') mark an outcry of new emotion, and much of lines 272–6 runs fast with a nearly regular iambic beat (e.g. 'That *we* can *call* these *de*licate *crea*tures *ours*') as far as the colon after 'uses'. Then the rhythm changes again, becoming irregular and containing words which are too awkard to fit any metrical pattern ('Prerogativ'd', 'unshunnable'), and the irregularity continues until the colon after 'quicken' (l.281). '*Desdemona comes*' re-establishes an iambic pattern which continues to the end of the speech except for the single outstanding exclamation 'O' in line 282. We have found six rhythmic sections, then. Now we can look at what Othello says, to see whether his thoughts come in six movements in the speech, changing when the rhythm does.

First, he thinks of Iago's honesty and knowledge (up to 'dealing', line 264), of Desdemona as a hawk (as far as 'fortune', line 267), of his own weaknesses (as far as 'much', line 270), of jealous beliefs and the pain he feels (as far as 'uses', line 277), and of betrayal in general (until 'quicken', line 281); then Desdemona appears and his love returns. There are six episodes of thought and feeling in this speech, then. We can call them six internal states of Othello. Now look at each more closely, noticing language and imagery. We hope to understand how the relationships between them, and the way Othello's mind moves from one to another, build the character of the tragic hero.

Othello uses courteous language to describe Iago: 'exceeding honesty', 'qualities', 'learned spirit' and 'human dealing'. These bring to mind the best qualities in human nature. When his mind turns to Desdemona, Othello's diction is transformed: 'haggard', 'jesses', 'whistle her off' and 'let her down the wind' to 'prey' all contribute to the metaphor of Desdemona as a hawk, a half-trained but basically wild bird of prey. The contrast is between Iago as 'human' and Desdemona as belonging in the animal kingdom, conveyed by literary words applied to Iago, such as 'qualities' and 'learned', and the rougher more elemental sounds in 'haggard', 'jesses' and 'whistle'. This analysis helps us to understand how the inside of Othello's mind is structured. He interprets reality in terms of a contrast between the higher civilised achievements of humanity, which he admires, and a primitive, low world of non-human creatures, birds and beasts, which he finds disgusting. He places Iago in the human, civilised world, and Desdemona is relegated to a place of primitive wildness, scarcely tamed.

The next episode complicates matters. There are civilised values of 'honesty', where Iago 'knows' with a 'learned spirit'; but Othello now describes 'chamberers' who have 'soft parts of conversation', and contrasts himself because he is 'black'. The longer and more sophisticated words now apply to high-society seducers, whom he calls 'chamberers', and his contempt for them is clear. In this case the gloss of human society is negative, in contrast to Othello's honest monosyllable 'black'. In the same movement of thought, however, he refers to being old in an elaborate and decorative style: 'I am declin'd / Into the vale of years'. In this section of the speech, then, the simple conflict between human civilisation and primitive passion becomes complicated: there is dishonest, evil sophistication ('chamberers'); and there are honest facts – like Othello's age – which deserve pretty euphemisms.

Othello does not complete these thoughts. He breaks off to cry out against being betrayed: 'She's gone, I am abus'd'. In the development of this episode, he settles the structure of his ideas. He admires the beauty of women ('these delicate creatures') but does not believe in its value: it is undermined by the word 'appetites', the primitive truth underlying a deceitfully fine appearance. Othello then brings forward two negative prospects: first, to 'be a toad, / And live upon the vapour in a dungeon', and second, to 'keep a corner in a thing I love, / For others' uses'. Both of these are expressed in plain, even coarse language (for example, Desdemona is 'a thing I love' with a 'corner' in her) showing the revulsion Othello feels. So, he is equally horrified by two possible outcomes: first, to descend to an animal level ('be a toad'), and second, to accept and take part in the hypocrisy of false appearances ('keep a corner'. . . etc.). By implication, then, he searches for a third option: to be 'honest' and to 'know' with a 'learned spirit'. He wishes to be truly, not falsely, human.

The fifth section is a generalisation about betrayal. Othello suggests that it is universal 'like death' and inevitable from the moment of our birth ('fated . . . When we do quicken'); and he states that 'great ones' are more vulnerable than the 'base'. Betrayal itself is a 'plague', and later 'this forked plague'. The outstanding word in this section is 'Prerogativ'd', a long, quasi-legal term denoting the formal privileges of those in the highest rank in society. Othello's statement does not make clear sense: if sexual betrayal is universal, it must happen to everybody. Why, then, are 'great ones' more vulnerable to it? The answer reveals Othello's feelings: his statement does not make *logical* sense, but within the structure of his thoughts it makes *emotional* sense. Othello is shocked by the vast gulf between fine appearances and a repulsive hidden truth. Emotionally, it is the distance between a person so high, a 'great one', and the lowness of primitive sexuality that shocks Othello. It is less horrifying in the case of a 'base' man, because he is lower in the order of things, nearer to primitive sexuality in any case. So betrayal of a base man does not offend Othello's feelings so painfully. Othello's way of perceiving the world, what we could call the structure of his senses, depends on a firm concept of high and low, of the civilised and the primitive, in nature. This is his system for understanding the world around him. Now, he is reeling from the shock of a new thought – that high only seems high, but is really low. So, he reverses the usual order by giving more 'prerogative' (a word belonging to royalty) to the 'base' and less to the 'great'. This bitterly misplaced word, then, shows how the shock of suspecting Desdemona is turning Othello's perceptions of the world upside-down.

When he sees Desdemona, Othello enters the sixth and final mental experience of this speech. The idea that the high and the base may be one and the same in reality has set his mind in turmoil. But Desdemona is so beautiful, and the thought of her betrayal so horrible, that the gulf between them becomes immeasurable to him. He has been used to placing experiences onto a sort of scale in his mind, but this experience goes off the scale at both ends. His mind is unable to make these ideas fit anywhere within the structure of his thoughts, and so it seems there is no sense in the universe, that 'heaven mocks itself'. The shock of this thought may be shown by the exclamation 'O' which stands outside the iambic beat of line 282; it is so monstrous to Othello that he recoils from it: 'I'll not believe it'.

Notice that we had to begin by finding an overall 'shape' in this complicated, densely detailed speech. Then we were able to think of different sections in the speech, one by one. Finally, we used a variety of analytical skills (looking at language, imagery, rhythm and sound) to help us describe the successive sections.

What have we discovered? Certainly, conflict between civilised order and primitive sexuality is a prominent feature within Othello's character, just as it is a feature of the whole world of the play. Uncertainty is also there: Othello cannot trust appearances, and cannot perceive reality as it is. He relies on Iago who 'knows' and is 'learned', but suspects the sophisticated 'chamberers' of Venetian society, including his sophisticated wife, of not being what they pretend to be. The situation provokes questions about humanity: are people merely beasts dressed up? Is it possible to 'know' about another person? Othello needs answers to these questions urgently, to settle his suspicion of Desdemona. In this sense his character constitutes an investigation into the nature of humankind. Finally, Othello's experience is too great for his capacity. It becomes too huge and too intense, passing beyond the ability of his thoughts to comprehend, and beyond the ability of words to express. So, he comes to paradox and contradictions reminiscent, for example, of the witches' 'Fair is foul' at the start of *Macbeth*. In this speech he strives to express the enormity of his experience: 'O, then heaven mocks itself'. It is a magnificent phrase, but the words defeat meaning.

How has Shakespeare created this man? We have found a series of sections, each one expressing a different state within Othello. Thought and emotion are simultaneous: for example, the thought that sophisticated appearances are sham accompanies sharp pain in relation to Desdemona. Emotional experience therefore modifies Othello's perception of the whole world, so the personal is, at the same moment, universal: 'If she be false, O, then heaven mocks itself'. The effect is that the most intimate questions of individual character expand into enormous significance; and the universe is brought intimately close. The different states Othello passes through reveal a range of different elements in his character. For example, in this speech we find rationalisation ('This fellow's of exceeding honesty' and 'Haply, for I am black'), emotional outburst ('She's gone, I am abus'd') and reflection (''tis the plague of great ones'). The relationships between these different states build our sense of the 'whole' character. We learn the range of his thoughts and feelings from the range of the internal states he experiences.

It is important to notice that Othello's feelings are fast-moving: they change all the time, modified by new experiences (such as Desdemona's arrival) or by new thoughts (sophistication is admired in Iago, repellent in a 'chamberer'). This movement has an emotional logic, as we found in Othello's remarks about 'great ones'. It would be foolish, therefore, to impose a static idea onto one of Shakespeare's tragic characters. Beware of statements which rely on mind-concepts: 'conscious' and 'subconscious' are misleading. So are all statements which pretend to distinguish what he 'thinks' from what he 'really feels', or which rely on opposites such as 'reason' and 'passion'. We have found that the character does not work in that way. The different elements are simultaneous, and integrated. 'What he thinks, he really feels, and vice versa' is a more accurate account than any divisive, static concepts of character.

*   *   *

We have already made significant progress. Now let us look at *Hamlet*. The strolling players have arrived at Elsinore. Hamlet welcomes them and asks their leader to perform a speech about the fall of Troy in which the Queen, Hecuba, watches Pyrrhus butcher her family. Hamlet is eventually left alone on stage.

Ham.	Oh what a rogue and peasant slave am I!	
	Is it not monstrous that this player here,	545
	But in a fiction, in a dream of passion,	
	Could force his soul so to his own conceit	
	That from her working all his visage wann'd;	
	Tears in his eyes, distraction in his aspect,	
	A broken voice, and his whole function suiting	550
	With forms to his conceit? And all for nothing!	
	For Hecuba!	
	What's Hecuba to him, or he to her,	
	That he should weep for her? What would he do,	
	Had he the motive and the cue for passion	555
	That I have? He would drown the stage with tears,	
	And cleave the general ear with horrid speech,	
	Make mad the guilty and appal the free,	
	Confound the ignorant, and amaze indeed	
	The very faculties of eyes and ears.	560
	Yet I,	
	A dull and muddy-mettled rascal, peak	
	Like John-a-dreams, unpregnant of my cause,	
	And can say nothing—no, not for a king,	
	Upon whose property and most dear life	565
	A damn'd defeat was made. Am I a coward?	
	Who calls me villain, breaks my pate across,	
	Plucks off my beard and blows it in my face,	

Tweaks me by the nose, gives me the lie i'th'throat,
As deep as to the lungs—who does me this?   570
Ha!
'Swounds, I should take it: for it cannot be
But I am pigeon-liver'd and lack gall
To make oppression bitter, or ere this
I should ha' fatted all the region kites   575
With this slave's offal. Bloody, bawdy villain!
Remorseless, treacherous, lecherous, kindless villain!
Why, what an ass am I! This is most brave,
That I, the son of a dear father murder'd,
Prompted to my revenge by heaven and hell,   580
Must like a whore unpack my heart with words
And fall a-cursing like a very drab,
A scullion! Fie upon't! Foh!
About, my brains. Hum—I have heard
That guilty creatures sitting at a play   585
Have, by the very cunning of the scene,
Been struck so to the soul that presently
They have proclaim'd their malefactions.
For murder, though it have no tongue, will speak
With most miraculous organ. I'll have these players   590
Play something like the murder of my father
Before mine uncle. I'll observe his looks;
I'll tent him to the quick. If a do blench,
I know my course. The spirit that I have seen
May be a devil, and the devil hath power   595
T'assume a pleasing shape, yea, and perhaps,
Out of my weakness and my melancholy,
As he is very potent with such spirits,
Abuses me to damn me. I'll have grounds
More relative than this. The play's the thing   600
Wherein I'll catch the conscience of the King.   [*Exit*
                            (*Hamlet*, 2, ii, 544–601)

This is another long and complicated speech, but we can see at a
glance that it is constructed in a series of sections separated by the

very short lines 'For Hecuba!', 'Yet I', 'Ha!' and 'A scullion! Fie upon't! Foh!'. There is also a clear change of thoughts between Hamlet's furious 'lecherous, kindless villain!' and his self-questioning 'Why, what an ass am I!', that is, between lines 577 and 578. Can we summarise the subject of each section? The speech begins with the statement that Hamlet thinks himself a 'rogue and peasant slave', then lines 545–52 as far as 'For Hecuba!' describe the Player's performance. Lines 553–60 contrast the Player and Hamlet, and imagine what the Player would be like if he had a real motive. Lines 561–70 focus on Hamlet's failure to take revenge against Claudius, developing a series of insults against himself and culminating in the exclamation 'Ha!'. In lines 572–7 Hamlet begins by stating that he should accept criticism because he ought to have killed Claudius, and his language becomes increasingly violent until 'kindless villain!' (l.577). At this point he stops himself, and berates himself for using words instead of actions, like a cursing 'scullion!' (ll.578–83). In line 584 Hamlet orders his brain to go 'About', and a new thought is introduced. He has heard that a play can affect guilty people, bringing them to confess their crimes. This idea is explained in clear, measured rhythm (from line 584 to 'organ' in line 590). Hamlet then briefly explains his plan to test Claudius's guilt with a play, ending with the stern statement of his vengeful purpose: 'I know my course' (ll.590–4). Finally, he raises doubts about the Ghost (it may be 'a devil') and himself (he could be deceived because of his 'weakness' and 'melancholy'), and ends with a couplet stating what he has decided (from line 594 to the end of the speech). There seem to be eight states of thought, or eight sections, in this speech. The first line and the final couplet do not belong to larger 'sections' of the speech: they seem to be opening and closing statements, like a framework at each end of Hamlet's more detailed meditation.

Like Othello, Shakespeare conveys Hamlet to us by means of a number of internal states; but his opening line, 'O what a rogue and peasant slave am I!' immediately establishes that his sense of order has suffered a shock. The thought that he, a prince, is equivalent to a 'peasant slave' is outrageous. We recognise, as with Othello, a man whose orderly system of perception has been shattered. The first section has an excited tone enhanced by the emphasis on the first syllable of the line in 'Is', 'But' and 'Tears', and the uneven length of phrases, from half-lines to the amazed rush in lines 547–8. This section is a single rhetorical question which contains, packed into its structure, seven examples and one outright statement ('And all for nothing!'). The impression is of Hamlet's highly charged mind in which all the complexities of what he sees are included in what is 'monstrous'. His language contains tension between the physical words describing what the Player does, 'force' and 'working', with the natural outcome of this in 'wann'd', 'Tears', 'broken voice', on the one hand, and abstract terms, some rather academic, such as 'fiction', 'dream', 'function', 'forms' and 'conceit' (twice). This tension conveys Hamlet's thought: the insubstantial motive (for acting is pretence), giving rise to powerful physical effects, is 'monstrous'. So, from realising disorder in the first line, Hamlet's mind now perceives another form of dislocation: there is no correspondence between causes and effects, interior truth and appearance. Hamlet mentions a 'conceit', which is an idea developed to a sophisticated level, and this, together with the contrast in language, hints at an even more disturbing thought – that something real (such as the physical tears of the Player) can be created out of nothingness. This is a new intensity of appearance–reality disturbance: the appearance is not deceptive, it is real; but there is nothing behind it and it exists for no reason. These ideas are all governed by the significant adjective 'monstrous' which means both unnatural and disproportioned. 'For Hecuba!' is an outraged cry, and the short line poetically creates an echoing silence as if to challenge the audience to answer the rhetorical question 'Is it not monstrous . . . ?'.

The second section compares the Player to Hamlet himself, and we notice a logical development of thought. However, as the series of questions about the Player, with their jolting, irregular rhythm, gives way to Hamlet's own situation, the rhythm and phrasing become more regular and the language more sonorous. Compare, for example, the short, chopped syllables of 'What's Hecuba to him, or he to her' (l.553) with the long vowels and open consonants we find in 'And cleave the general ear with horrid speech' (l.557). It is as if describing the effect of real passion releases something in Hamlet, allowing his language to roll, flow and crescendo. He even includes the intensifiers 'indeed' and 'very', building to the fine final phrase 'faculties of eyes and ears' and completing an iambic meter.

This is an internal, emotional development. It suggests that Hamlet is temporarily in a more harmonious state within himself. The sense of a logical link between the first two sections is reduced, for we see that the state Hamlet reaches here meets an emotional need, a reaction against the horror of dislocation he experienced from seeing the Player's performance. Ironically, the idea of the insubstantial cause creating a physical effect occurs again: 'speech' will 'cleave'. Hamlet's movement from state to state, then, can be likened to Othello's: it is a dynamic process, simultaneously emotional and intellectual.

The third section, beginning 'Yet I', is much more broken into pieces of thought and language. Notice that the constructions are also more condensed and knotty (for example, 'unpregnant of my cause' and 'Upon whose property . . . A damn'd defeat was made'). Hamlet uses concrete metaphors for his baseness, suggesting lead ('dull . . . mettled') and 'muddy'; then he develops another series of rhetorical questions: 'Who calls me villain . . . ?'. The answer, of course, is nobody except himself. This series of questions takes us through 'pate', 'beard', 'nose', 'throat' and 'lungs', the progress entering Hamlet's body and ending at his inner organs.

If we compare this to the earlier rhetorical questions about the Player, we can see that the situation is reversed: there the actor had no cause but abundance of effect, while here there is ample cause (Hamlet *is* a coward) but nobody is attacking him – there is no effect. Hamlet is struggling with a senseless situation again, where there is no relationship between the inside (essence) and the outside (its show, or effect); his outrage is again expressed as a series of unanswerable questions, culminating in the single-syllable line 'Ha!', where the rhythm allows almost a whole line's silence to emphasise that there is no answer to this absurdity.

The next section (ll.572–7) begins deep inside Hamlet: the idea of inner organs is carried on from 'lungs' as he is 'pigeon-liver'd' and lacks 'gall'. Now, in Hamlet's mind, the wrongness exists inside himself where the normal physical organs are deficient or missing. Hamlet again condenses constructions ('lack gall / To make oppression bitter') when describing himself, and the rhythm is still disturbed until 'or ere this' when his mind and emotions swing around to contemplate his hated uncle. Suddenly the iambic meter beats steadily ('I *should* ha' *fatt*ed *all* the *reg*ion *kites*'), and the image of disembowelling Claudius (emptying out his 'offal') ironically completes the contemplation of inner organs Hamlet began inside himself. Emotionally, then, this section completes a journey of feelings that began in the previous one. His revulsion against his own insides is directly transferred onto the image of kites feeding on his enemy's bowels. Intellectually these two sections are also a sequence, although not in an expected order. Hamlet effectively says: 'I am a coward. Am I a coward? I am a coward, or – revenge!'. The effect of this development shows us that the pain of thinking about himself can only be escaped or resolved by filling his mind with the hated idea of Claudius.

The climactic 'kindless villain!' rings in the air. Hamlet hears his own fury, which reminds him that he has not done anything yet, and in lines 578–83 he berates himself again for his lack of activity. These lines are irregular and jerky in rhythm, and the construction is also fragmented. The main sentence comes in little pieces: 'That I', then another two clauses, then 'Must', and another interruption before 'unpack my heart'. The strongest words are 'whore', 'drab' and 'scullion', three insults to himself which balance the earlier list of insulting words for Claudius. Elements of Hamlet's earlier states reappear. First, to call himself a 'whore' not only echoes 'rogue and peasant slave', making a nonsense of social order – it goes further, suggesting a wrongness in nature itself, if Prince Hamlet is a woman. Additionally, Hamlet's perception of emptiness reaches a new insight. Remember that he was shocked at words acted or without true motive in the Player's performance; then his own real motive lacked expression or action. Here, he sees himself 'unpack my heart with words': he accuses himself of using words to dissipate emotion. So, language is not merely unreliable; it can be destructive, reducing the emotion that caused it. Words can be a substitute for action that leaves total emptiness – emotion used up, consumed in the words, and the words used up, meaning nothing after they are spoken.

The five sections we have looked at so far show a complex process unfolding within Hamlet. The disorder he perceives makes him investigate action, motive and speech in himself and the Player, and these elements of a human being appear in different relationships in the different sections, each time with an unnatural gulf (such as between motive and speech in the Player in the first section) or lack (such as 'But I . . . lack gall') inhibiting the proper functions of a person. Meanwhile, his emotions unfold in a series of turns, focusing within himself, then externally upon Claudius, then within himself again. Each focus leads to revulsion. Thinking about his own inaction and emptiness repels him, so he fills himself with hatred of Claudius; focusing on Claudius reminds him of his inaction, which inspires his self-hatred again.

The sixth section begins with a conscious effort to escape this vicious circle, as Hamlet orders his thoughts to change tack: 'About, my brains'. The rhythm and language are calmer, and the construction easier, more conversational, as Hamlet explains his reason (ll.584–90) and his plan (ll.590–4). There is another image of Claudius wounded, in which Hamlet probes the wound and watches to see whether Claudius will flinch. These two logical sections culminate in a determined, decisive tone with four equally stressed sounds: 'I know my course'.

The final section (ll.594–9) contrasts again. The sentence contains three thoughts, but they are added to each other loosely as Hamlet thinks of them, using the conjunction 'and'. They are not constructed, but occur one after another within the hero's mind, and the rhythm runs fast for each thought, then pauses, then runs again. The tone of this section, then, is weaker and more random than that in the preceding sections six and seven. It is as if Hamlet feels the need for more reasons to justify his plan, and finds them quickly as they occur to his mind. When he has done this, his mind becomes settled: the final couplet closes the speech with a regular iambic beat and powerful rhyme, all the formal hallmarks of a decisive intention.

Analysing Hamlet's speech has confirmed our grasp of how Shakespeare creates the hero's character. The speech divides into episodes which we have called 'sections'. They express internal states of simultaneous thought and feeling, and one episode often gives way to the next for emotional rather than intellectual reasons. For example, it is painful for Hamlet to think about his own failure to act. He turns to hating Claudius to stop his pain, not because reason leads his thoughts that way. We understand the internal 'structure' of the hero's personality by understanding these 'states' and their relationship to each other. There are dynamic shifts and changes, so static explanations of the hero's character will be unhelpful.

The two heroes we have examined so far share a common experience: both face shocks which we have called a 'gulf', 'gap' or 'lack', 'dislocation' or 'disproportion'. They have a mental system they are used to relying on, which helps them to make sense of the world. Tragic experience attacks this system, destroying its structure. Both of them react to this shock with outrage. They are disturbed, it is 'monstrous', their emotions and their language are unable to cope with it. Can we further define what 'it' is?

'It' occurs when logical ways of thinking about the world break down. Things are without cause, or without effect. Appearance does not match reality and nothing makes any sense. In Othello's case, Desdemona was at once too perfect and too base to imagine; in Hamlet's case, everything is too empty and unexplainable to bear. In short, the world becomes senseless, ridiculous, 'absurd'. It is this experience of the 'absurdity' or lack of coherence in the world around them that drives the tragic heroes' emotions and thoughts. In the speeches we have looked at, they either twist and turn to avoid meeting the 'absurd', or they are unable to cope with it, and they fail to express it in words. Shakespeare's poetry creates this failure of language in the form of insoluble paradoxes (see 'heaven mocks itself' from *Othello*) or sudden changes of direction (see 'About, my brains' from *Hamlet*). In the speech we are about to analyse, from *King Lear*, his sentences break off unfinished, and this conveys his failure to express the tragic thought completely. We can make use of the word 'absurd' to describe this element of Shakespeare's tragedy. So, it is absurd to see a woman so perfect and so base (*Othello*); and it is absurd to have tears without motives, motives without action, or words without either (*Hamlet*). We will develop this idea further in our analyses of *King Lear* and *Macbeth*.

*   *   *

In *King Lear* his daughters Goneril and Regan argue that their servants can look after Lear, so he does not 'need' knights of his own. Goneril says 'What need you five-and-twenty, ten, or five', and Regan adds 'What need one?'. Lear replies, arguing that there are human 'needs' which are more than merely practical:

Lear.   O! reason not the need; our basest beggars
      Are in the poorest thing superfluous:
      Allow not nature more than nature needs,
      Man's life is cheap as beast's. Thou art a lady;   265
      If only to go warm were gorgeous,
      Why, nature needs not what thou gorgeous wear'st,
      Which scarcely keeps thee warm. But, for true need,—
      You Heavens, give me that patience, patience I need!—
      You see me here, you Gods, a poor old man,   270
      As full of grief as age; wretched in both!
      If it be you that stirs these daughters' hearts
      Against their father, fool me not so much
      To bear it tamely; touch me with noble anger,
      And let not women's weapons, water-drops,   275
      Stain my man's cheeks! No, you unnatural hags,
      I will have such revenges on you both
      That all the world shall—I will do such things,
      What they are, yet I know not, but they shall be
      The terrors of the earth. You think I'll weep;   280
      No, I'll not weep:
      I have full cause of weeping, [*Storm heard at a distance.*] but
        this heart
      Shall break into a hundred thousand flaws
      Or ere I'll weep. O Fool! I shall go mad.
              [*Exeunt Lear, Gloucester, Gentleman, and Fool.*
              (*King Lear*, 2, iv, 262–84)

We begin with rhythm and sentences again, hoping to find the episodes in the speech. First, lines 263–8 have a consistent style: words like 'superfluous', 'gorgeous', and terms of theoretical argument such as 'nature', 'scarcely' and 'Allow', bring a debating tone, and there is much repetition to develop Lear's point: 'need', 'warm', 'nature' and 'gorgeous' all occur twice. Lear's constructions are literary and ornamental, such as the inversion 'Are in the poorest thing superfluous', or the subjunctive 'If only . . . were gorgeous'. The poetry flows fairly steadily (despite 'why' in parenthesis) until a major interruption in lines 268 and 269: 'But, for true need,— / You Heavens, give me that patience, patience I need!—'. Punctuation breaks up the verse as Lear's line of thought breaks off, and his speech changes direction. A second section lasts until 'Stain my man's cheeks' in line 276. The rhythm is less regular, with intermittent short and long phrases, and Lear's diction is more physical, with short verbs in plain constructions such as 'fool me', 'bear it', 'touch me' and 'let not'. Lear launches into a new direction with 'No, you unnatural hags'. This section is even more disturbed in structure and rhythm (the construction is interrupted twice), and focuses on revenge against his daughters. The fourth and final section concerns 'weep' or 'weeping', which appears four times in poetry which seems written in fragments from the half-line (l.281) to the three separate pieces of the final line: 'Or ere I'll weep. O Fool! I shall go mad'. This speech has four sections, then.

The first section argues about 'need' in two sentences which are logically consistent: beggars have more than their natural 'needs'; as a lady, you do not 'need' your fine clothes. We have commented on Lear's patterned and even style in this section, but the content also deserves attention. Lear rejects a practical philosophy that can see nothing higher than material needs because it would destroy human order, leaving all people on the same level, no better than dressed-up animals: 'Man's life is cheap as beast's'. Clearly, then, a negative, materialist view threatens Lear's orderly mental structure, the way he sees the world. We remember that Edmund articulated the materialist view in his speech beginning 'Thou, Nature, art my goddess' (1, ii, 1).

In the second section Lear begins to develop his argument, defining 'true need'. We expect him to tell us what human beings need which makes them more and higher than animals. At this point, however, he breaks off: 'You Heavens, give me that patience, patience I need!' bursts through the sentence-structure and chops up the flow of the poetry: it is an emotional explosion which leaves Lear overwhelmed by self-pity, incapable of pursuing his argument (ll.270–1). This is a new internal state, where his thoughts are driven by emotion; and the language changes from a patterned literary style to a rougher, more direct diction. Words and phrases begin to sound harsh and spitting ('wretched', 'stirs these daughters' hearts / Against' and 'stain my man's cheeks'), and the verbs are single-syllable actions. Lear's view of the world has changed completely, also. He imagines hostile Gods, responsible for his suffering, and begs them not to make him cry like a woman. This episode, then, shows increasingly disturbed and violent language as Lear is overcome by the possibility that the universe is all wrong: the Gods may be hostile and unjust. In addition, Lear is so insecure that he cannot be sure of his own identity: he fears his 'man's cheeks' will be stained by 'women's weapons' (tears), and this undermines his masculine idea of himself. Mastered by a surge of self-pity, fear and fury, Lear finds that the structured order he is used to believing in is crumbling. For the Gods to be pitiless, making sport with our suffering, or for a man to become a woman – in Lear's mind these are so shocking that it seems the world has gone mad: they are 'absurd'.

Lear's reaction to this threat is immediate: he floods himself with anger. The third section threatens revenge, abusing his daughters as 'unnatural hags' and building up a reckless speed ('I will have such revenges on you both / That all the world shall') before his sentence breaks off again, and he fails to express or imagine suitable punishment for them. Lear eventually finds a grand phrase to describe their punishment, 'The terrors of the earth'. This expresses the world-shattering significance of their argument to Lear's feelings; but it does not specify what he will do to them. Ironically, it reveals his lack of power.

These violent swings of mood, and two shattered sentences, have created the turmoil within Lear. His outrage, self-pity and impotent anger reflect an inability to comprehend two things which attack the foundations of his belief: first, how can daughters reject a father? (this is 'unnatural'), and second, how can he, a King, be powerless? In the final section of the speech, Lear's internal conflicts and his inability to resolve them are dramatically presented as short, alternating, repetitive phrases: they expect him to weep, he will not weep, he should weep, but he won't weep, his heart will break first. The only escape from this conflict is the prospect of madness: 'O Fool! I shall go mad'. The storm '*heard at a distance*' in line 282 dramatically coincides with the storm in Lear's heart, prefiguring the storm on the heath and Lear's madness in the next act. So, the tragic forces tearing the hero apart are expanded as external phenomena: individual tragedy rocks the world.

There is little imagery in this speech. There are some incidental uses of metaphor (such as '*touch* me with noble anger') but only two noticeable images: tears are 'women's weapons', and his heart is brittle, made of glass or precious stone, so hard that it will shatter 'into a hundred thousand flaws' rather than soften. This expresses Lear's reaction against 'feminine' softness, and the disastrous consequence of his obduracy: the shattering of his heart, his coming madness.

The way Shakespeare has created Lear shows many of the features already noted in *Othello* and *Hamlet*. The speech is a series of internal states, emotionally dynamic and revealing how his orderly perceptions are being shattered. Disorder expands until it seems to fill the universe (in Lear's case, the Gods are cruel); and he finds his experience impossible to express – both 'true need' and his vengeful fantasies are beyond language, beyond coherence. In this speech we find two further elements, however, which add detail to our idea of 'absurdity'. First, a materialist philosophy of 'nature' brings on Lear's horror, attacking his sense of values; and second, one direct consequence of tragic experience can be madness: when the universe is without proportion, words or sense, the hero's mind may reflect that senselessness, in the form of madness.

*   *   *

In *Macbeth*, following the murder of Duncan, the hero plots to kill Banquo. Macbeth is alone on the stage:

Macb.   To be thus is nothing, but to be safely thus:
          Our fears in Banquo

Stick deep, and in his royalty of nature
Reigns that which would be fear'd: 'tis much he dares; 50
And, to that dauntless temper of his mind,
He hath a wisdom that doth guide his valour
To act in safety. There is none but he
Whose being I do fear: and under him
My Genius is rebuk'd; as, it is said, 55
Mark Antony's was by Caesar. He chid the Sisters
When first they put the name of King upon me,
And bade them speak to him; then, prophet-like,
They hail'd him father to a line of kings:
Upon my head they plac'd a fruitless crown, 60
And put a barren sceptre in my gripe,
Thence to be wrench'd with an unlineal hand,
No son of mine succeeding. If't be so,
For Banquo's issue have I fil'd my mind;
For them the gracious Duncan have I murther'd; 65
Put rancours in the vessel of my peace,
Only for them; and mine eternal jewel
Given to the common Enemy of man,
To make them kings, the seed of Banquo kings!
Rather than so, come, fate, into the list, 70
And champion me to th'utterance!

(*Macbeth*, 3, i, 47–71)

This time we are able to find the speech's sections in the simplest way. There are no outstandingly broken 'crises' in the verse or breaks in the hero's constructions, so the sentences themselves are likely to reveal the structure. The first section of this speech describes Banquo's qualities (up to 'to act in safety', line 53); next, Macbeth develops a comparison between himself and Banquo, as far as mentioning 'Mark Antony' and 'Caesar'. The third section remembers the witches' prophecy, an example of how Banquo manages to eclipse Macbeth, and this vein continues as far as 'No son of mine succeeding' in line 63. A new structure and a new section then begin with 'If't be so', which is completed at 'the seed of Banquo kings!', line 69. The final two lines express Macbeth's determination to prevent such a future.

The first section begins with a distinction between Macbeth's position and his security. We remember him wishing that 'but this blow / Might be the be-all and the end-all' (1, vii, 4–5), and his present wish 'to be safely thus' echoes that hopeless desire. The second line, a half-line, ends on the name 'Banquo', and the subsequent gap in rhythm makes the name resonate. We can think of the word 'Banquo' as a mental and emotional action: by saying the name, Macbeth names and defines his fears, which were vague and many before. The remainder of the first section is filled with words of quality and admiration: 'royalty', 'Reigns', 'dauntless', 'wisdom', 'valour'. These build an impression of Banquo's noble nature, which is completed in the second section by comparing him to Caesar.

Lines 53–6, from 'There is none' to 'Caesar', seem to form a new section, because Macbeth moves into a different state. He began by voicing his general insecurity, then named his fear as Banquo. Now, 'There is none but he / Whose being I do fear'. Notice that this is not logical: to fear Banquo is not the same as feeling no other fears. It is an emotional change: Macbeth confines his fears to Banquo, perhaps because they are too shapeless and too many for him to cope with otherwise. This section is uneasy, each of three clauses starting and ending in the middle of a poetic line, and the breaks awkwardly heavy, a colon, a semi-colon and a full-stop. The subject-matter becomes an ambiguous comparison between himself as Mark Antony and Banquo as Caesar, in which he endows himself with Antony's famous generosity and nobility, but hands Banquo as Caesar the eventual victory. If we remember Macbeth's bloodthirsty crimes, Antony seems an inappropriate comparison. It is a wish rather than a fact: Macbeth wishes he were as noble as Antony, for that would remove his fear and guilt.

In the third section, beginning 'He chid the Sisters', Macbeth remembers Act 1, Scene iii, when the witches prophesied that Banquo should found a long line of kings. In lines 60 and 61 the rhythm is suddenly regular ('Up*on* my *head* they *plac'd* a *fruit*less crown*' etc.), and the lines are end-stopped, increasing the fluency of the poetry. This change coincides with a change of focus as Macbeth concentrates on himself. For the rest of the speech 'my', 'I' and 'mine' are the central pronouns.

The fourth section concentrates entirely on Macbeth, and gives four accounts of the crime he has committed. He says 'I fil'd my mind', 'murther'd', 'Put rancours in the vessel of my peace' and 'mine eternal jewel / Given to the common Enemy of man', all on behalf of Banquo's heirs. The final two versions are religious images – polluting a sacramental cup and surrendering to the Devil. The section is structured around semi-colons, into four parallel statements. The first two begin with the refrain 'For Banquo's issue' and 'For them', the last two end with 'Only for them' and 'To make them kings', and this in turn is echoed: 'the seed of Banquo kings!'. As a whole, this section has symmetry and repetition of form, then. The refrain harps on Macbeth's futility: he cannot achieve security, and his actions count for nothing. This is emphasised by the image for his soul, 'eternal jewel', in contrast to the 'common' Devil. We are reminded of Othello's disbelief – Desdemona was too beautiful and too base, at once. Here, Macbeth has given something too valuable, for nothing; and the disproportion between what he has given and the nothing he has in return makes life seem senseless, or 'absurd'. This is the tragic truth Macbeth cannot bear, which leads him to drown it out with thunderous self-assertion in the final two lines.

Macbeth speaks in defiant tone: 'come, fate,' are rhythmically isolated, single strong calls. He would rather give up his life ('to th'utterance') battling for or against fate. The ambiguity is in 'champion me': does it mean 'fight on my side', as it should, or 'be a champion against me in a fight to the death', as the sense and the situation demands? The irony remains, showing that Macbeth cannot resolve his central dilemma about prophecy: is fate with him, or against him?

We can understand how Shakespeare has built Macbeth, then. There are different states of thought and feeling in this speech; and the emotional drives to limit and name his fears, and to contradict the witches' prophecy, move Macbeth from state to state. On the other hand, this hero differs from the other three. He has no simple, single set of beliefs. Instead, his morals and perceptions are a kind of anarchy, and the speech conveys competing vestiges of three value-systems, those of Duncan, the witches, and Macbeth himself, none of which can assert itself in his mind. For example, Macbeth uses idealistic words to describe Banquo, and these are connected with 'gracious', applied to Duncan. In this system of values, Macbeth has given his soul to 'the common Enemy of man', and Duncan's chivalrous qualities are 'royal'. The witches, on the other hand, present temptation and insecurity: Macbeth cannot read their favour or their prophecies, so theirs is a perplexing influence which the hero tries to grasp but is unable to cope with. Finally, Macbeth himself relies on action: 'to be safely thus' and 'There is none but he / Whose being I do fear' convey a simple belief in cause and effect, and self-reliance – remove the man, remove the fear – which eventually leads him to challenge fate, willing to fight to the death.

Even in this chaotic situation, Macbeth recoils from the 'absurd'. He finds it unbearable to think that his life is futile. The first time this thought comes is in 'To be thus is nothing', and we see him evade the horror of this idea by channelling all his fears into fear of Banquo. The second time Macbeth recoils, it is from the idea that his own actions have been fruitless: his actions have been for Banquo, not for himself. Macbeth sets himself against fate, opposing his own strength against the value-systems of Duncan and the witches, in an attempt to smother the thought of his own futility. Ironically, his confusion undermines his challenge: he does not know which side fate will be on, and he expresses his foreboding that the fight will lead to his own destruction, 'to th'utterance'.

The ironies in this speech go further. Macbeth's admiration of Banquo, his comparison of himself to Antony, and his consciousness of having murdered the 'gracious' Duncan, suggest that 'royal' order is attractive to him: he has a desire to undo the past, restore the rightful state of things, and have his own noble, loyal character back. But his own brutality competes with this desire – so he can complain outrageously that Banquo's heirs will 'wrench' the sceptre from him with 'an unlineal hand' (l.62). The desire for order, for security, runs through the whole. Whether by a return to the past, or by a final act of bloodshed, Macbeth's heart needs to block out the chaos of competing values which threatens to show him the futility of his own actions.

Conclusions

1. The tragic hero is characterised by means of a series of 'internal states' where thought and feeling are simultaneous and integrated. The relationships between these states, which are expressed in 'sections' or episodes in the hero's speech, reveal the internal structure of the character's mind. Changes of rhythm, pace or diction, and sentence-structure, often reveal the transition from one episode to the next.

2. 'Order' or a system of values is always important. Typically the hero uses a structure of beliefs as a referent which helps him to interpret the world around him. Tragic experience appears as a challenge to, or contradiction of, these perceptual structures – something the hero faces which seems to shatter his mental structures, or seems to make them senseless. We have called this challenge the 'absurd' because its effect is to destroy meaning, purpose, order and proportion.

3. We can often see an emotional drive which causes the hero to move into a new state, so 'emotional logic' or dynamic forces within the characters are keys to understanding how they work. The heroes all react against the 'absurd' or tragic experience by attempting to evade it or to blot it out with other thoughts and feelings. Therefore, the emotional logic when the hero changes to a new internal state often reveals the pain of their tragic experience. Emotions flow and change, so static interpretations of the heroes are unhelpful.

4. In earlier chapters we have noticed that words fail to contain or express experience. This is particularly true of the 'absurd'. Shakespeare characteristically shows this by the use of paradoxes, broken sentences, and vague or empty rhetoric (such as Lear's threat, 'The terrors of the earth').

5. Imagery in the heroes' speeches often connects their internal experience of tragic chaos with a disruption of the universe, or external struggles between order and disorder (for example, Lear's imagination of hostile Gods, or Hamlet's threat to 'cleave the general ear with horrid speech').

Methods of Analysis

1. Look at the structure of sentences, or places where there is fragmented phrasing, in order to find where episodes of a speech
   begin and end. Then examine rhythm, diction, imagery and
   subject-matter in order to describe the character's internal state in
   each section.
2. Look at the relationships between the sections from the point of
   view of the heroes' reasoning and their emotional drives. Try to
   explain why the hero changes from one state to the next.
3. Pay particular attention to the hero's structural ideas about the
   world, and explain how some experience or realisation the hero
   faces, attacks his ideas, or threatens to deprive them of validity,
   rendering the world 'absurd' to the hero.

Suggested Work

At the beginning of this chapter I pointed out that we could not
attempt a full analysis of each tragic hero: our aim was limited to
analysing one major speech. Here are suggestions for how to build
upon the work done in this chapter, in order to further develop your
sense of the tragic hero's nature, and his function within the play.

The simple advice is to look at other major speeches of the character you have to study, using the approach demonstrated here. This
will enable you to build a fuller story of the hero's struggle against
tragic experience; and in this connection your aim is to find when
the hero first confronts the 'absurd' and when the hero finally faces
the destruction of his inner coherence. It will also furnish you with
further examples of imagery and dramatic effects which integrate the
microcosm (the struggle within the individual character) with larger
conflicts and disturbances in the wider world.

Begin this process of enlarging your detailed understanding of the
hero by analysing his first and last major speeches in the play:

Othello
1. Look at 1, ii, 17–28, when Othello declares his position strong

enough to counter Brabantio's complaint to the Duke. Othello's sense of justice and order is strong in this speech, but close analysis will reveal breaks in the development of his thoughts similar to those we have discussed in this chapter.

2. Look at 5, ii, 339–57, Othello's final speech when he describes how he wishes to be remembered. This is interesting as it shows an attempt to restore some coherence to his personality, following the tragedy.

Hamlet

1. Look at 1, ii, 76–86, when Hamlet answers his mother, already deeply disturbed about outward acting and show, and 'that within' which 'passes show'.
2. Look at 5, ii, 347–63, really two short speeches interrupted by Osric giving news of Fortinbras's arrival. You may be interested in how Hamlet's final lines relate to the 'ending' analysed in Chapter 2 above.

King Lear

1. Look at 1, i, 35–53, when Lear asks his daughters how much they love him.
2. Look at 5, iii, 304–10, where Lear grieves for Cordelia's death, and perhaps hopes that she might live, just before his own death. In this speech you will notice that the rawness of Lear's emotions and the violence of his inner conflict are still overwhelming, even at the end.

Macbeth

1. Look at 1, iii, 70–8, when Macbeth calls upon the witches to explain themselves.
2. Look at 5, viii, 27–34, Macbeth's final speech of defiance, following Macduff's announcement that he was not 'of woman born'. Macbeth's determination to oppose all enemies and the heavens, to the death, appeared at the end of the speech analysed in this chapter. It is expressed again in Act 5, but with some differences.

Many of these suggestions point you towards short speeches, where the hero expresses only one or two internal 'states'. In these cases you will be able to connect the feelings and ideas you discover with some element we have discussed in this chapter.

Note: as you further study the tragic hero, you will find it helpful to approach a whole scene in the same way as we have approached one speech: describe the different states of thought and feeling your character passes through, and explain how his reactions are caused, how and why he moves from state to state.

4

The Heroines

All four tragic heroes are men, and we have studied a major speech from each of them. In this chapter we will approach Shakespeare's heroines in the same way, by taking a major speech from each play as an example for analysis.

We bring questions with us, however – questions which have arisen during earlier chapters. In particular, three of the four heroes (Macbeth is the exception) express feelings about women that we should bear in mind during our coming study. Hamlet and Lear react to their experience of disorder by expressing insecurity about their maleness. Hamlet contemptuously applies chauvinist insults to himself, calling himself 'drab', 'whore' and 'scullion' for using words instead of taking action. By implication, he believes that men act and women curse. Lear is insecure about his will-power: he wants to be touched with 'noble anger' when he faces rejection by his daughters; but he is anxious lest 'women's weapons, water-drops' will stain his 'man's cheeks'. Lear's worries emphasise the weakness of women, and he clearly believes that women resort to tears as 'weapons'. Being effeminate would be unnatural and disastrous for both of these heroes, then. They react to the shock of disorder and dislocation in their worlds, and one of their anxieties is about gender: effeminacy takes its place amongst other monstrous and absurd shocks.

Othello talks of his wife as a possession. He realises that she can never be entirely owned or tamed, however; and this is a major part of the shock and disgust he feels. First, she is likened to a 'haggard' falcon, half-wild, and in the image his heart-strings are used as 'jesses' to keep her captive. Later in the speech Othello bemoans the fact that 'we can call these delicate creatures ours, / And not their appetites'. Clearly Othello desires complete, secure ownership of his wife; and he is terrified when he realises that such possession of a woman is not possible.

The heroes, then, have a strong sense of gender-identity. Hamlet and Lear believe that women are soft, weak and inconstant, and can only fight with words and tears. Othello wants Desdemona to be his property, an extension of himself, and her separate female existence frightens him. In this chapter we ask: are these male attitudes reflected in the women themselves on Shakespeare's stage? What other issues of gender will we meet in the process of studying the heroines? Another question arises because we bring with us a detailed understanding of how Shakespeare creates his heroes for the stage: does he create his heroines in the same way?

Before we embark on this investigation, however, we must take note of two dangers. We have to be cautious when we import modern ideas such as 'gender issues' and apply them to Shakespeare. First, if we allow 'gender issues' to dominate our thinking, we will be tempted to treat these characters as real women and to make unsupported assumptions about their society and the social pressures which form them. Remember that these heroines are only dramatic characters, not 'real' people. They only exist as far as Shakespeare has created them, and nothing of them exists outside the play. We can look for evidence of 'gender issues' in the text of the plays; but we can only discuss what is there, in the text, not what we might carelessly import from our modern consciousness. Be cautious, then, and avoid the realistic fallacy.

Second, we must be careful when we search for the causes of the heroines' behaviour. In many places, it will be tempting to say 'she is like this *because she is a woman*'. Only make this deduction if there is evidence in the text: does Shakespeare suggest that her gender is really a cause of her behaviour? Or, does he suggest other reasons for the way she behaves? There is an even more misleading form of this error: it can be tempting to analyse Shakespeare rather than his play. The error would be to say 'Shakespeare has made her like this *because that is what Shakespeare thinks women are like*'. Caution is important, then, and our rule must be to base all our ideas on analysis of the text, not on imported modern attitudes.

We will discuss these limits again at the end of the chapter, when we know what we have discovered about the four heroines. Now we can begin to study them.

* * *

In Act 4, Scene ii of *Othello* Desdemona asks Iago for advice: how can she regain Othello's love and trust?

Des.	O good Iago,	150

> What shall I do to win my lord again?
> Good friend, go to him, for, by this light of heaven,
> I know not how I lost him. Here I kneel:
> If e'er my will did trespass 'gainst his love
> Either in discourse of thought or actual deed,   155
> Or that mine eyes, mine ears, or any sense,
> Delighted them in any other form,
> Or that I do not yet, and ever did,
> And ever will (though he do shake me off
> To beggarly divorcement) love him dearly,   160
> Comfort forswear me! Unkindness may do much;
> And his unkindness may defeat my life,
> But never taint my love. I cannot say 'whore':
> It does abhor me now I speak the word;
> To do the act that might the addition earn   165
> Not the world's mass of vanity could make me.

> (*Othello*, 4, ii, 150–66)

The rhythm of this speech is much more even than that in any of the heroes' speeches. After line 152, nine of the remaining fourteen lines are regularly iambic. Such irregularities as there are denote emphasis, not a serious disturbance in the character. In lines 155–6 the stress falls on the first syllable of the line to emphasise 'Either' and 'Or'. In line 161 Desdemona exclaims unmetrically 'Comfort forswear me!', which is the climax of her structured eight-line sentence and carries natural emphasis. In line 163 the phrase 'I cannot say "whore"' disturbs the rhythm; and the two adjacent stresses, 'world's mass', in line 166 hold up the rhythm to give a suitable impression of vanity's vast bulk.

The speech is constructed as a series of statements in response to the initial question: 'How can I win Othello back? I do not know what I have done wrong, and I am not doing anything wrong (I love him). I may die from Othello's cruelty, but I will never do anything wrong (I will always love him).' The connection between these statements is logical and obvious: Desdemona's mind considers past, present and future in turn, but she returns the same clear answer in each case. There is, really, only one 'internal state' in the speech: she loves Othello. This love is expressed with absolute certainty: 'ever did, / And ever will . . . love him dearly', and 'may defeat my life, / But never taint my love'. Desdemona's language is as absolute as possible: we notice 'ever', 'ever' and 'never' in her declarations of love; there are also 'If e'er', 'any sense' and 'any other form'. Her love is stronger than 'life' and 'the world's mass' and she 'cannot' say 'whore' because it is against her nature: 'It does abhor me'. There is no sign, then, that Desdemona questions or feels a shock to her internal feelings and beliefs. She is distressed and feels helpless, but suffers no instability or conflict in her emotions.

Desdemona speaks an educated and expressive language. Her sentence from line 153 to line 161, for example, is formally constructed as an oath; and the three parallel sections of elaboration try to include all possibilities, in a style that reminds us of a legal clause: 'Or that mine eyes, mine ears, or any sense'. Words such as 'trespass', 'discourse', 'deed' and 'forswear' enhance this impression. Only the word 'whore' stands out: it is like an alien, a word that originated in a different place, in contrast to Desdemona's otherwise consistent style.

This is the nearest contact Desdemona has with the destructive turmoil that has transformed Othello himself. Remember that Othello used 'haggard' and 'creature' in his speech, and referred to a 'toad', 'plague', and so on. The word 'whore' belongs to his shock and disgust about base sexuality. What place does it occupy in Desdemona's speech? 'Whore' is isolated in quotation marks, and the surrounding sense underlines that it cannot become part of Desdemona: 'I cannot say "whore"'; to 'speak the word' goes against my nature or 'does abhor me'. Desdemona also states her ignorance of Othello's jealous passion: 'I know not how I lost him'. The tragic experience presented in the hero, then, causes the heroine to feel distressed and helpless; but she does not understand, and her personality remains unchanged by contact with tragedy. Desdemona is created as a limited character, then: Shakespeare has drawn the boundaries of her feelings and her nature very clearly, by her insistence on a single, absolute feeling, and the excluding fence she raises around the alien word 'whore'.

In *Othello* the heroine is characterised as a much simpler and more limited person than the hero. There is one further point which concerns her gender: Desdemona does not understand the complexities and conflicts of her husband's tragedy. In the distress she feels, she turns to a man (Iago) for help and advice. This suggests that she does not expect to understand for herself, but a man will be able to explain it to her. Remember, however, the warnings at the beginning of this chapter. It is tempting to say that Desdemona shows her helplessness and dependence on male advice *because she is a woman*. This theory supposes that she has grown up in a society that stereotypes women, and therefore lacks the self-confidence to rely on her own understanding. The evidence within the play, however, does not entirely support this idea: things are more complicated. For example, Desdemona is impressive in Act 1. Her marriage to Othello is a rebellion against her background; she is clear and firm when she defies her father's authority; and she declares herself fascinated by and eager to share Othello's masculine, military life. On the other hand, there is ample evidence from Othello himself, Iago, Roderigo and Cassio of repressive male attitudes towards women. Our conclusions must be cautious at this stage, therefore. All we know is that she has no conflict in her feelings, that she does not understand the destructive force which has hold of her husband, and that her response to the catastrophe in the hero is distress and helplessness.

*   *   *

In *Hamlet*, Ophelia suffers from Hamlet's wild and insulting behaviour during the 'nunnery' scene. After he has left, Ophelia speaks the following lines:

Oph.	O, what a noble mind is here o'erthrown!	
	The courtier's, soldier's, scholar's, eye, tongue, sword,	
	Th'expectancy and rose of the fair state,	
	The glass of fashion and the mould of form,	155
	Th'observ'd of all observers, quite, quite down!	
	And I, of ladies most deject and wretched,	
	That suck'd the honey of his music vows,	
	Now see that noble and most sovereign reason	
	Like sweet bells jangled out of tune and harsh,	160
	That unmatch'd form and feature of blown youth	
	Blasted with ecstasy. O woe is me	
	T'have seen what I have seen, see what I see.	

(Hamlet, 3, i, 152–63)

Ophelia's speech shows the same rhythmic features as Desdemona's. First, the majority of the speech follows an iambic beat. Second, there are a few examples of alterations to the rhythm to create emphasis or for obvious effect (such as 'eye, tongue, sword' in line 153, or 'quite, quite down' in line 156). Finally, there is one place where the rhythm is more complicated, interrupting the speech in the same way as Desdemona's 'I cannot say "whore"' interrupted hers. Ophelia's disturbance comes as a heavy opening stress on 'Blasted with ecstasy', which leads to a full-stop in the middle of the line. After this, the final one-and-a-half lines are metrical again, and have formal rhyme, making a couplet to conclude the speech.

Ophelia begins with an exclamation: 'O, what a noble mind is here o'erthrown!', and ends with the sentence 'O woe is me . . . ' etc. In between, her speech is in two sentences which treat the two sides of her experience in turn. First, she describes the change in Hamlet, the cause of her distress. Then she describes its effect, that she is a distressed witness of Hamlet's change. The structure of the speech is logical, then, its two halves related as cause and effect, and complementing each other.

Language and imagery in this speech emphasise admirable and ornamental things: 'courtier's, soldier's, scholar's', 'rose of the fair state', 'glass of fashion', 'mould of form' fill the first half; and 'the honey of his music vows', 'that noble and most sovereign reason', 'sweet bells' and 'unmatch'd form' are found in the second half. The images are of a flower, a looking-glass, honey, music and bells, all ideas which belong within a conventionally 'feminine' experience. Ophelia expresses Hamlet's change as 'quite, quite down!', as sweet bells 'jangled out of tune and harsh'; and in her final reference to a flower, as his 'blown' youth 'Blasted', contrasting his violent and irrational personality now with the harmonious and high qualities he used to show.

Ophelia's theme is order, which reminds us of elements we have found in the heroes' speeches: she is distressed that Hamlet, once so perfect, can have fallen so far into such discord. She experiences an irrational change in Hamlet, between his 'music vows' and 'jangled out of tune and harsh'. This contact with Hamlet's tragic conflicts has deeply affected her: like Desdemona, Ophelia seems unsure whether she will survive the forces she perceives destroying the hero. Desdemona said Othello's 'unkindness' may 'defeat my life'; Ophelia says 'O woe is me, / T'have seen what I have seen, see what I see'. She feels that this experience will darken the rest of her life. This heroine, then, shows greater understanding of the hero's state than Desdemona did. Her sense of the world's order is attacked by seeing him so distraught; and she has a foreboding that her life will suffer as a result of what she has seen.

On the other hand, there are complexities in Hamlet's behaviour that Ophelia does not face. First, she does not question appearances. Hamlet did not 'seem' to be 'Th'expectancy and rose of the fair state', and so on: to her, he *was* all the wonderful things she describes, and she still does not doubt this truth. So she does not question her own perceptions. Second, Hamlet has just subjected her to a degrading diatribe full of sexual disgust and gross innuendo, but Ophelia avoids his meaning: by saying that he is 'Blasted with ecstasy' she simplifies the truth, using the label 'insane' to block out the negative elements of Hamlet's change. The insistent beauty and sweetness of her diction and imagery also convey her determination to disregard what Hamlet has said to her. This beauty does not waver throughout the speech, except for the one contrasting word, 'Blasted'.

Finally, Ophelia is like Desdemona in her helplessness. The hero's tragedy makes her suffer, and may darken her future life, but there is no mention of her taking any action to prevent disaster or help Hamlet: her role is that of a passive, sympathetic observer who has 'seen' and will 'see'.

We have found, then, that Desdemona and Ophelia have a number of features in common. They both defend their minds against the degrading content of the hero's experience, avoiding too close a contact with it; and they both remain certain of their own mental structures, not questioning reality as they perceive it. In addition, both of them are distressed by the hero's behaviour and have forebodings about the future; and they are helpless, passive in the face of tragedy. The major difference between them is that Ophelia perceives the attack on order and proportion much more clearly than Desdemona. This is important: her perception of the gulf between what Hamlet was and what he now is shows that she feels the shock of what we have called 'absurdity', the shattering force of a tragic experience.

*   *   *

Now we turn to *King Lear*: here is Cordelia's speech to Lear when she has rescued him, and while she waits for him to wake:

Cor.	O my dear father! Restoration hang
	Thy medicine on my lips, and let this kiss
	Repair those violent harms that my two sisters
	Have in thy reverence made!
Kent.	Kind and dear Princess!
Cor.	Had you not been their father, these white flakes 30
	Did challenge pity of them. Was this a face
	To be oppos'd against the warring winds?
	To stand against the deep dread-bolted thunder?
	In the most terrible and nimble stroke

Of quick, cross lightning? to watch—poor *perdu!*—   35
With this thin helm? Mine enemy's dog,
Though he had bit me, should have stood that night
Against my fire. And wast thou fain, poor father,
To hovel thee with swine and rogues forlorn,
In short and musty straw? Alack, alack!   40
'Tis wonder that thy life and wits at once
Had not concluded all. He wakes; speak to him.

(King Lear, 4, vii, 26–42)

The rhythm and structure of this speech is less consistent than we have found with the other two heroines. Cordelia's distress and the bitterness of her anger are reflected in changes of rhythm and diction: her series of outraged questions (ll.31–6) culminate in fragmented short phrases, the broken rhythm that reveals disturbed emotion; this changes to fluent rapidity in lines 36–8, and the rhythm emphasises clipped, angry words such as 'dog' and 'bit'. Similarly, Cordelia's extreme distress brings broken phrasing followed by another rapid rush in 'Alack, alack! / 'Tis wonder that thy life and wits at once / Had not concluded all'. The speech, then, expresses the flow of powerful emotions of shock, pity and anger.

Cordelia's language is also more varied than the other heroines'. Remember the single outstanding word 'Blasted' from Ophelia, and Desdemona's revulsion from the word 'whore'. Cordelia's diction is not limited, but ranges from rather precious, self-consciously literary descriptions of Lear's ordeal, such as 'deep dread-bolted thunder', 'the most terrible and nimble stroke / Of quick, cross lightning' and the rather formal inversion 'rogues forlorn', to plain and coarse expressions of Cordelia's anger, such as 'Mine enemy's dog' and 'Though he had bit me'. In the context of the whole play, Cordelia's descriptions of the storm stand out as even more literary and artificial: we have heard Lear's violence and power, describing the same thing:

Blow, winds, and crack your cheeks! rage! blow!
You cataracts and hurricanoes, spout
Till you have drench'd our steeples, drown'd the cocks!

(King Lear, 3, ii, 1–3)

Her self-conscious descriptions convey to us that Cordelia only has a vague idea of the experience Lear has endured; but she is angry about her sisters' mistreatment of him, and expresses this in clear terms.

Although the language is varied and vivid, there is little imagery in Cordelia's speech. Her enemy's dog is used as an example, and lightning is described with living attributes, as 'nimble'; Lear's white hairs 'challenge pity' of her sisters, and his 'life and wits' might have combined to kill him: everything seems very alive, but the only clear metaphors she uses are of restoration, which will hang its 'medicine on my lips' so that her kiss can cure Lear, and her likening him in the storm to a sentry in a dangerous position, a '*perdu*'. These two ideas present a contrast between her healing care, and the danger Goneril and Regan exposed him to. They emphasise Cordelia in a feminine role, soothing and healing the hero's wounds.

Much of the content of this speech refers to ideas of order. For example, Cordelia is outraged that Lear, whose age should be respected, was treated worse than a dog; and her shock at the disruption of order is also conveyed when she imagines him in a 'hovel' with 'swine', 'rogues' and 'musty straw'. Her reaction to this shock, on the other hand, is a desire to protect him and care for him. In the context of the whole play, her attempt to restore him appears shallow: the audience knows that the 'violent harms' he has suffered are too deep to be cured by healing care alone, because he has faced truths she is unaware of. We have heard Lear say 'Take physic, Pomp; / Expose thyself to feel what wretches feel'; we have heard his analysis of 'The great image of Authority', and that 'When we are born, we cry that we are come / To this great stage of fools'. Yet Cordelia speaks naïvely of restoration. Her love for him is uncritical, and she talks about 'thy reverence' as if he had learned nothing about himself.

Cordelia, then, is similar to Ophelia: she is partly sensitive to the hero's suffering. She is also like Ophelia and Desdemona in that she perceives the catastrophic change tragic experience has wrought, but does not perceive any of the truths that tragedy reveals. Desdemona could not speak a degrading word; Ophelia did not question appearances; and Cordelia ignores all that Lear has learned about bare humanity, injustice and hypocrisy.

*   *   *

The last heroine to examine is Lady Macbeth. In Act 1 of *Macbeth* she receives a letter from her husband, telling her of the witches' prophecy. This speech is a soliloquy until Macbeth arrives; then she greets him:

Lady M.   The raven himself is hoarse,
    That croaks the fatal entrance of Duncan
    Under my battlements. Come, you Spirits   40
    That tend on mortal thoughts, unsex me here,
    And fill me, from the crown to the toe, top-full
    Of direst cruelty! make thick my blood,
    Stop up th'access and passage to remorse;
    That no compunctious visitings of Nature   45
    Shake my fell purpose, nor keep peace between
    Th'effect and it! Come to my woman's breasts,
    And take my milk for gall, you murth'ring ministers,
    Wherever in your sightless substances
    You wait on Nature's mischief! Come, thick Night, 50
    And pall thee in the dunnest smoke of Hell,
    That my keen knife see not the wound it makes,
    Nor Heaven peep through the blanket of the dark,
    To cry, 'Hold, hold!'
                Enter MACBETH.
                    Great Glamis! worthy Cawdor!
    Greater than both, by the all-hail hereafter!   55
    Thy letters have transported me beyond
    This ignorant present, and I feel now
    The future in the instant.
                            (*Macbeth*, 1, v, 38–58)

This speech is more energetic and volatile than the three already studied in this chapter. The rhythm is full of wild excitement: there are energetic stresses on verbs of action, at the start of lines (*'Shake my fell purpose'*, *'Stop up* th'access . . .'); several unstressed syllables often patter fast between stresses ('from the *crown* to the *toe*'); and paired stresses hang at the ends of some lines, making us wait to be plunged into the following line (*'top-full*' and *'thick Night'*). The pace of Lady Macbeth's speech changes constantly. Notice that even the final two lines slow down for three stresses on '*I feel now*' before she rapidly and suddenly ends: 'The *fut*ure *in* the *inst*ant'. This poetically imitates the compression of time into her present moment of excitement.

The opening sentence makes an ominous statement: the 'raven' is 'hoarse' and 'croaks' a 'fatal' arrival. The bird of death is associated with trappings of horror, then, before Lady Macbeth begins her long invocation, calling upon spirits to 'unsex' her. This invocation surges and builds continuously until line 50. Lines 50–4 continue the same idea, building up an invocation to 'Night' until its climax at 'To cry "Hold, hold!"'. Macbeth's entrance then gives rise to exclamations of greeting, and in the final sentence Lady Macbeth expresses the pitch of excitement she feels. The structure of this speech is not complex, then: it seems long and wild, but if we take away the opening and closing statements, the whole speech elaborates one idea, eagerly invoking the aid of 'you Spirits' and 'thick Night'.

Lady Macbeth's language and imagery are insistently physical, even sensual. Notice that the speech is about abstractions. Most of the terms discussed are concepts, standing for elements of the personality: sex, cruelty, remorse, compunction, and purpose. The verbs and metaphors, on the other hand, are full of action and very physical: 'fill me, from the crown to the toe', 'make thick my blood', 'Stop up th'access', 'Shake', 'take my milk for gall', 'pall thee in the dunnest smoke'. The verbs are all imperatives. This 'physicalising' language continues when she briefly refers to the actual act of murder, 'That my keen knife see not the wound it makes' (l.52), in which she imagines the steel knife alive and sentient. Finally, Heaven is imagined to 'peep through the blanket of the dark'. We can describe this as making the abstract concrete; and in her final statement Lady Macbeth asserts that her senses are so excited that she can 'feel now' things which are not there: 'The future'.

The 'Spirits' Lady Macbeth calls to her aid exist in 'sightless substances', however. Although her senses are so alive and acute, her speech is filled with the desire for blindness or darkness, so she calls on 'thick Night' to blot out her sight (l.50). The paradox of her heightened sensual excitement, coupled with a desire to freeze, block or otherwise prevent all feeling in herself, runs throughout the speech. The images include thickening her blood so it does not flow, and blocking up remorse and compunction. What, then, does she wish to become? She wishes to be all 'cruelty' or filled with 'gall', with an unshakeable 'fell purpose' like a knife which strikes blindly. In other words, she wishes to become unnatural, inhuman.

All of the above falls within the context of her demand: 'unsex me here' (l.41). The feminine qualities she wants to discard are compunction, 'milk' and remorse. By implication, the fixed creature with frozen senses who strikes without seeing, that she wishes to become, is what she imagines a man to be. Lady Macbeth's demand to be 'unsexed' is shocking, as is her bloodthirsty excitement and the graphic imagery she uses. On the other hand, the sexual stereotypes she expresses are rigidly conventional, and limit her understanding of the tragic action she is engaged in. For example, Macbeth himself faces complex, insoluble dilemmas. There are problems of action and its consequences ('if th'assassination / Could trammel up the consequence'); he fears that violence will breed violence ('we but teach / Bloody instructions') and his own actions will destroy him; and he not only worries about the injustice of the murder, but fears that heavenly powers will take side against the murderers and 'Will plead like angels, trumpet-tongu'd', causing discovery (these quotations are from his opening speech in Act 1, Scene vii). Lady Macbeth, on the other hand, believes in a 'man' who is an inhuman, remorseless automaton: 'When you durst do it, then you were a man' (1, vii, 49). It is these rigid stereotypes which divide Lady Macbeth from the complex dilemmas the hero experiences. Wild and shocking she may be; but her internal conflict is restricted to the single purpose of denying the softer emotions and shutting heaven's eyes.

This point may be clarified by comparing Lady Macbeth with Desdemona, Ophelia and Cordelia. Desdemona could not say 'whore': all the disgust in Othello's experience was thus closed off from her. Ophelia labelled Hamlet as mad, consequently shutting herself away from the degrading truths and half-truths he had uttered. Cordelia was angry, but had no idea what Lear has learned, or what his experience had been: her desire for 'restoration' prevented her from realising the true complexity of his tragedy. Lady Macbeth attempts to form herself, and Macbeth, into heartless, remorseless assassins, thus blocking out all complex considerations as if they are mere feminine weaknesses. Since she has adopted such a rigid structure of thought, she cannot perceive the dynamic forces and changes occurring within her husband.

The extraordinary hardness of Lady Macbeth's will has extraordinary consequences: in this speech she deliberately suppresses her own humanity. The content of her sleepwalking scene, later in the play (Act 5, Scene i), shows that the feelings she suppressed are still powerful in her unconscious mind. The emotionally connected, fragmented speeches she utters while asleep, full of changes of mood and revulsions of feeling, are reminiscent of the heroes' speeches we looked at in the last chapter. In Ophelia's mad scene (*Hamlet*, 4, v) there are fragmentary elements of the sexual theme Hamlet insulted her with in the 'nunnery' scene, suggesting an unconscious reaction to what he said, that surfaces in her distraction. Otherwise, Lady Macbeth is the only heroine whose mind Shakespeare characterises in this way, and in her case it only occurs while she is asleep.

*   *   *

What have we learned from these four studies? First, the conflict between order and chaos, which has been a constant element in all our investigations of Shakespearian tragedy, vitally affects the heroines just as it is present in every other aspect of the plays. Lady Macbeth is on the side of chaos – of a blind, indiscriminate destructiveness – and in her case the conflict is conveyed by the energy she puts into suppressing her other feelings. The other three experience the shock of disorder through their observation of the hero's transformation.

Second, gender stereotypes are an issue in these plays.

Desdemona's dependence on Iago for advice, Ophelia's helpless 'O woe is me', Cordelia's maternal feelings, and Lady Macbeth's rigid ideas of feminine and masculine attributes, all show stereotypes at work in the text and in the presentation of relationships to the audience. On the other hand, these sexual attitudes are a complex issue which the dramatist makes part of the play. Shakespeare does not resolve 'gender' in simple terms. We should remember that we have only studied four short speeches, and that there are other important female characters in the plays (Emilia in *Othello*, Gertrude in *Hamlet* and Goneril and Regan in *King Lear*). However, we can suggest a cautious conclusion. The four women we have looked at all accept the idea that women play a role secondary to the male. They observe, sympathise and suffer passively, or they nurture; but they do not think of women taking a central, active role in the world. Lady Macbeth wants to change her own role, but belief in the stereotypes still rules her mind. She cannot take action as a woman: she believes that she must lose her sex before she can act, so she concentrates on ensuring that her husband acts like a 'man'.

The most revealing feature we have found in common between all the heroines is the well-defined limitation in their minds. All four of the speeches we have examined develop a single idea and a single state of feeling. This means that Shakespeare's characterisation of the heroines, the way he creates their personalities on the stage, is simpler than the way he uses shifting internal states to convey the heroes. Structurally, these women are in contact with the central tragic experience of the play at second-hand: they respond to but do not participate in the hero's tragedy. We have seen above how the heroines have inner mental structures based on ideas of order, like the heroes; and their sense of order suffers a shock, the shock of the unexplained or the 'absurd'. But the heroines, unlike the heroes, do not have their beliefs shattered. Desdemona and Ophelia insistently assert their concepts of order (Desdemona asserts her love and loyalty; Ophelia dwells most on Hamlet's past perfections), Cordelia focuses on 'restoration' to cure all 'violent harms', and Lady Macbeth suppresses all contradictory feelings.

This is important, because tragedy reveals truths about life, and none of the heroines realises what those truths are. Ophelia discounts what Hamlet says because he is 'Blasted with ecstasy'; and Cordelia has only a fanciful, naïve idea of Lear's ordeal. All of the heroines, in one way or another, are closed away from the shocking, disturbing insights at the heart of the tragic experience. The heroines are on the margins, structurally and dramatically, therefore. Notice that we have found limitation in the heroines' feelings as well as in their intellect. Their speeches are based on a single state of emotion, as well as expounding a single state of mind. Shakespeare's creative method is therefore like that for the heroes, in that thought and feeling are simultaneous, indivisible. For example, Cordelia's emotions give her a powerful desire to soothe and nurse Lear; and at the same time her mind makes a distant fantasy of his actual sufferings, convincing her that 'restoration' is possible. We cannot say that her feelings come before her ideas, or vice versa: the two exist and develop together, making a convincing character whose words express dramatic energy.

Conclusions

1. The style of the heroines' speeches varies from formal control (Desdemona) to a much more volatile, metaphor-rich wildness (Lady Macbeth). However, the structure of the heroines' speeches relates to a single mental and emotional state, not the dynamic shifts and episodes found in the heroes' speeches.
2. Each heroine's language has a more limited range than that of the hero. The diction and imagery in these speeches tends to be predominantly of one or two kinds only. The difference is difficult to define, but we can say that Cordelia's language describes rather than experiences the destructive power of the storm, for example.
3. The heroines sense an attack on their concept of order, and are shocked by this. Their response is to grieve or attempt to soothe, but they remain divided from the truths revealed by tragic absurdity.
4. Gender issues are explored, and 'feminine' characteristics seem to be a helpless loyalty, love and pity, the desire to heal or nurse, and appreciation of beauty or nobility in men. However, these sexual

stereotypes are presented with irony: they typify the way the male and female characters think of themselves and each other, but irony indicates that Shakespeare does not share such stereotypes. For example, Lady Macbeth simplifies the male stereotype, thus denying the complex dynamics of the tragic situation. The irony is that the 'man' she imagines is inhuman, as impossible as the 'unsexed' woman she wishes to be.

Methods of Analysis

1. This chapter makes use of the same analytical techniques we have developed in previous chapters, examining rhythm and meter, the structure of the speech and the sentences, language, imagery and subject-matter.
2. Apply specific questions to the material. In this chapter we asked about issues of gender and sexual stereotyping, whether and how they are present in the speeches. We also deliberately compared the heroines' speeches to those of the male heroes. This enabled us to define the common features, and features present in the men's speeches that are absent from the women's.
3. Be aware of the danger of importing modern attitudes. This can lead to two errors: first, the fallacy of treating dramatic characters as if they were 'real' people (this can lead you to give them characteristics that are not deduced from the text); second, the temptation to speculate about what Shakespeare thought, instead of analysing the play.

Suggested Work

We have examined a speech from each 'heroine'. To develop your ideas, it is worth considering the depiction of femininity in a whole play, thus:

In *Othello* look at Emilia. To begin doing this you could study her speech at 4, ii, 138–46, which makes a revealing comparison with Desdemona's speech, analysed above. It is also instructive to study Desdemona's speeches from Act 1, as these will help you to understand her rebellion and broaden your grasp of gender stereotypes in relation to her and the play as a whole.

In *Hamlet* study Gertrude. The shock of madness Hamlet conveys to Ophelia has its counterpart in his effect on Gertrude. You could begin by analysing 3, iv, 88–124, from the famous 'closet scene' when Hamlet taxes his mother with her betrayal of his father.

In *King Lear* study 1, i, 54–106, when all three of the King's daughters answer his demand for love. You could then pursue your study to examine the characters of Goneril and Regan: they are aggressive and destructive, in contrast to Cordelia.

In *Macbeth* study other speeches of Lady Macbeth. You should begin by making a detailed study of her as she appears in the sleep-walking scene (5, i, 30–65); then look at her role in the banquet scene, Act 3, Scene iv.

5

Society in the Tragedies

In the first and second chapters we discussed something we called the 'world' of the play. The idea of a play's 'world' was useful because it helped us to understand conflicts between order and disorder, but it was an all-embracing idea. Characters, situation, dramatic effects, references to nature and the supernatural, all the elements of the play contribute to its 'world'. In this chapter our focus is narrower – on the social structures and social relationships found in the plays.

It is worth reminding ourselves of conclusions reached in the first two chapters. First, the imminent restoration of order, at the end of each play, poses a dilemma: tragedy raises disturbing truths; stability and order, on the other hand, bring half-truths and lies. Second, each of the plays conveys a strong, but distorted, social structure.

This chapter is based on close analysis of one extract from each play. Our conclusions therefore focus on how the social structure is presented to the audience by means of dramatic effects and features of the text, at one point in the drama. This may seem a limited approach, and does not allow us to go very far into political and social criticism. On the other hand, our approach does provide a very close, sharp view of the kind of society we meet when we see a performance. In addition to extract-analyses, a brief general discussion of each of the plays is included, commenting on the state of 'society' we found at the start (see Chapter 1), and developing some of the insights our analysis uncovers, with reference to other parts of the play. The concluding discussion at the end of this chapter helps to relate our study to some of the controversial issues about politics and society that are canvassed by critics.

*   *   *

In *Othello* each person manipulates or is manipulated in a dance of political exploitation. The extract we analysed in Chapter 1 was about Othello's patronage and the manipulation of political influence: Iago had employed three 'great ones of the city' to lobby on his behalf; both Othello and Brabantio rely on position and influence to obtain the Duke's support, and Iago manipulates Roderigo for his own ends. The following extract is a speech by Iago, from Act 2, Scene i:

Iago. Lay thy finger thus, and let thy soul be instructed: 220
    mark me, with what violence she first lov'd the Moor,
    but for bragging, and telling her fantastical lies; and
    will she love him still for prating? let not the discreet
    heart think so. Her eye must be fed, and what delight
    shall she have to look on the devil? When the blood 225
    is made dull with the act of sport, there should be
    again to inflame it, and give satiety a fresh appetite,
    loveliness in favour, sympathy in years, manners and
    beauties; all which the Moor is defective in: now, for
    want of these requir'd conveniences, her delicate 230
    tenderness will find itself abus'd, begin to heave the
    gorge, disrelish and abhor the Moor, very nature
    will instruct her to it, and compel her to some second
    choice. Now, sir, this granted (as it is a most pregnant
    and unforc'd position) who stands so eminently in 235
    the degree of this fortune as Cassio does? a knave
    very voluble, no farther conscionable than in putting
    on the mere form of civil and humane seeming, for
    the better compassing of his salt and hidden affec-
    tions: a subtle slippery knave, a finder out of occa- 240
    sions; that has an eye can stamp and counterfeit the
    true advantages never present themselves. Besides,

the knave is handsome, young, and hath all those
requisites in him that folly and green minds look
after; a pestilent complete knave, and the woman   245
has found him already.

(Othello, 2, i, 220–46)

Only Iago and Roderigo – the manipulator and his gull – are on
stage. We have just watched Othello's arrival at Cyprus, and before
that Iago's shocking cynicism was accepted, as entertainment, by
Desdemona and Cassio and other important people of Cyprus.
'Society', then, reacted to Iago with laughter, but was not disturbed
by his coarseness. The dramatic action of this part of the scene
shows Iago easily asserting his power, and making Roderigo do what
he wants him to do. Iago's subject is the rules that govern people's
behaviour, in his view.

Iago persuades Roderigo that an affair between Desdemona and
Cassio is likely. The language he uses, however, is much more
complex than the simple task of deceiving Roderigo would require:
there is strength and clashing variety in the diction. First, Iago's
insight into the world attracts these three phrases: his 'soul' is
'instructed', he admires the 'discreet heart', and his reasoning builds
an argument which is a 'most pregnant and unforc'd position'. These
phrases combine two different vocabularies: that of intellectual
debate ('discreet', 'instructed' and 'unforc'd position'), and words for
natural mysteries ('soul', 'heart' and 'pregnant'). The effect is that
Iago uses logic and intellect to reveal the core of life's meaning, its
'soul'.

Second, there is a strong contrast between outer appearance and
base reality in the way Iago describes people. Othello's attraction was
in 'bragging', 'telling her fantastical lies' and 'prating', language that
builds a progressively more insulting impression of empty, false
speech; and Cassio, the 'knave very voluble' (another deceptive
talker, then), puts on the '*mere form* of civil and humane seeming'.
He is 'subtle' and 'slippery', can 'stamp and counterfeit' good qualities, and his appearance ('handsome, young') will please 'folly and
green minds'.

Othello's base reality is expressed in the single word 'devil', while the reality of Cassio is his 'salt and hidden affections'. Together, the appearance and reality of Cassio make him outwardly smooth and whole ('complete') but truly diseased ('pestilent'), in the phrase 'a pestilent complete knave'. This phrase again combines different vocabularies, and 'pestilent' has the effect of emphasising the sarcasm of 'complete'. The language, then, puts two different vocabularies together to emphasise the hypocrisy of false appearances.

Images of eating and counterfeiting appear in this speech. Desdemona's eye must be 'fed' and satiety will crave a new 'appetite'. Othello's advances will make her 'begin to heave the gorge, disrelish and abhor the Moor', and she may taste Cassio's 'salt' affections. So, Desdemona's love is debased to the level of hunger and feeding; and the image suggests that her emotions are also decadent. She will manufacture a new appetite by desiring something more savoury than the plain fare of Othello. Iago's comparison of romantic and sexual relationships to feeding is part of a recurrent image in the play. We remember that Othello described how she would 'devour' his stories when they were courting.

Cassio's false façade is described as an ability to 'stamp' and 'counterfeit' true worth. The idea suggests a shallow impression. The false coin looks like something valuable, but is made of something base, not precious. The language and imagery together convey Iago's view that people are base and hidden, but if you understand them you can predict what they will do. For example, understanding that Cassio's fair exterior is not the truth, but is a cover for his 'salt and hidden affections', enables Iago to predict that he will seduce Desdemona. Iago's 'instructed . . . soul' understands and therefore predicts base nature.

Iago believes in a further natural law, however. In the middle of the speech he explains that Desdemona must want a suitable mate, one who is young, handsome, white and has sophisticated social manners, like herself: 'loveliness in favour, sympathy in years, manners and beauties' are needed to 'inflame' her 'blood'. In Iago's view her marriage to Othello went against nature: he is 'defective in' all the qualities she will naturally want, so once her blood is 'dull' and she reaches 'satiety' with the 'act of sport', she cannot take delight 'to look on the devil'. There are two suggestions here: first, that all appetites become 'dull' after they are satisfied, and second, that there is a natural order of attractions that Iago understands. The first of these is a cynical comment on people. All civilised structures, with their social ranks, sophisticated manners, customs and institutions, are discounted. They belong to the false 'appearance' that Iago ignores. The only truth about people is their basic instincts and appetites.

The second law Iago proposes seems different. He suggests that people will naturally mate with others in their own social class. So Desdemona must eventually turn to Cassio, because he is socially like her. Iago therefore suggests that social structures are all-powerful and determine people's behaviour according to class and background.

Iago's two 'laws' are not easily reconciled. We can put them together in a statement something like this: 'everybody follows instinctive, animal appetite; but they do it within their own social group'. It is easier to understand how these two ideas fit together when we realise that they have one vital element in common: they are both determinist ideas. In other words, Iago thinks that people never make up their own minds as individuals; their behaviour is always controlled by social or instinctive drives.

Iago speaks persuasively. He asks three rhetorical questions (questions which do not need to be answered because they imply the answer); then he hammers home his point by answering each question himself. He elaborates his reasons with lengthy descriptions – two of Cassio and one of Desdemona's sated appetite – which consist of phrases building towards a climax on a series of commas. So the rising tone which begins with 'abus'd' (l.231) leads up to the strongest word 'abhor' (l.232); then the elaboration continues, decreasing in tension during two further phrases. The speech, then, is structured in sections which have a controlled shape of crescendo and diminuendo, and their content combines several reasons into a single argument in support of Iago's conclusion. In addition, there are logical terms and a series of imperatives to emphasise that things can only be the way Iago says they are: 'this granted', 'must', 'will', 'nature will instruct' and 'compel her'.

The language, structure and imagery of this speech combine to convey a powerful effect: Iago is convinced that he understands human society, can predict it, and will therefore take advantage of his understanding to manipulate society's inevitable, natural laws. That is, his aim is to understand and control society.

Iago's argument has flaws, and the audience is ironically aware that his understanding is limited. For example, why did Desdemona marry Othello? In his account of their courtship (1, iii, 128–70) he says that she was attracted to him because he was *not* from her social group. Othello's social difference was all the 'witchcraft' that he used. Iago calls their marriage an unnatural aberration, yet the rest of his speech insists that it is impossible to go against the natural laws he believes in. So Iago's understanding, which he calls his 'instructed . . . soul', cannot account for everything that happens. Shakespeare, then, shows a character who is dedicated to understanding and manipulating the rules by which society operates, but also shows that society does not quite conform, cannot quite be predicted in this way.

Manipulation was the constant factor we found in the opening of the play, so we ask: can we discover more about society's power-structure as it is dramatised in *Othello*?

Brabantio calls for 'all my kindred' and 'my brother' when he pursues his case to the Duke. He will also enlist fellow-citizens to support him, saying 'I may command at most [houses]'. He is confident that the Duke and other senators will 'feel this wrong, as 'twere their own'. Brabantio is an important senior citizen, and relies on his position near to the top of Venice's traditional, hierarchical society. His power comes from belonging to the best rank of families, by birth.

Othello puts his faith in a different kind of power, and is equally confident: 'My services, which I have done the signiory, / Shall out-tongue his complaints' (all quotations are from Act 1, Scene ii). Othello's power is practical, then, because Venice needs him. He relies on his own abilities, not his birth, to influence the Duke; and this kind of power proves the stronger. What is Othello's relationship with Venice? He is foreign, a different colour, but he has to be accepted as a necessary warrior. Venice uses Othello's military strength to keep itself safe, and in return he uses their dependence on him to steal a white lord's daughter. The Duke's advice to Brabantio is doubly revealing. He first urges the practical point: Desdemona and Othello are already married, so why cry over spilt milk? 'He robs himself, that spends a bootless grief' (1, iii, 209). Later, the Duke tries to persuade Brabantio that Othello's personal qualities make him an honorary white man: 'Your son-in-law is far more fair than black' (1, iii, 290). In Act 1, then, there is a struggle between two kinds of power in society. We can call them old, inherited power and new, practical power. The society we are shown is in the process of changing, and there is an uneasy confusion about power as new political realities make inherited position less important.

These elements of the society shown in Act 1 are cynical. They contribute to the theme of Venetian decadence, and describe the relationship between a mercenary and his employing state. Iago's insights are also cynical: first, the edifice of society with its ideas of justice and morality is seen as sham, while the truth about people is that they are immoral, obeying base natural laws; second, you gain power if you realise how false the surface is. These two ideas also appear elsewhere in the play. For example, notice that Othello relies on his services in Act 1, not on a sense of justice or moral right. This supports Iago's belief that expediency and self-interest are more important than morality. Also, notice the beginning of Act 1, Scene iii, where the Duke and senators discuss a series of contradictory messages about the Turkish fleet: here, the council penetrates 'a pageant, to keep us in false gaze', and realises the truth – that the Turks are making for Cyprus. The First Senator reasons that the Turks would not neglect a chance of 'gain' and do something 'profitless' (1, iii, 29–30). In other words, he predicts what will happen by the same means Iago uses: he understands the basic natural law of self-interest. This understanding gives the Venetian council the power to predict and take steps against the Turkish attack.

*　　*　　*

We now turn to *Hamlet*. In Chapter 1 we noticed the atmosphere of fear and insecurity in Denmark. The men on the battlements were full of distrust and canvassed rumours about possible war. After seeing the Ghost, Hamlet remarks that 'the time is out of joint' (1, v, 196) and the play as a whole shows plentiful evidence that something is 'rotten' in the court and society of Elsinore. Our extract is from Act 5, Scene i, when Hamlet and Horatio discuss death following their conversation with the Grave-digger:

Ham.	Dost thou think Alexander looked o' this fashion i'th'earth?	
Hor.	E'en so.	
Ham.	And smelt so? Pah!	[*Puts down the skull*]
Hor.	E'en so, my lord.	195
Ham.	To what base uses we may return, Horatio! Why, may not imagination trace the noble dust of Alexander till a find it stopping a bung-hole?	
Hor.	'Twere to consider too curiously to consider so.	
Ham.	No, faith, not a jot, but to follow him thither with modesty enough, and likelihood to lead it. Alexander died, Alexander was buried, Alexander returneth to dust, the dust is earth, of earth we make loam, and why of that loam whereto he was converted might they not stop a beer-barrel?	200
		205
	Imperious Caesar, dead and turn'd to clay, Might stop a hole to keep the wind away. O that that earth which kept the world in awe Should patch a wall t'expel the winter's flaw. But soft, but soft awhile. Here comes the King, The Queen, the courtiers.	
		210

Enter [Bearers *with*] *a coffin, a* Priest, KING, QUEEN, LAERTES, Lords *Attendant.*

	Who is this they follow? And with such maimed rites? This doth betoken The corse they follow did with desp'rate hand Fordo it own life. 'Twas of some estate. Couch we awhile and mark.	215
Laer.	What ceremony else?	
Ham.	That is Laertes, a very noble youth. Mark.	

Laer. What ceremony else?

Priest. Her obsequies have been as far enlarg'd
As we have warranty. Her death was doubtful;   220
And but that great command o'ersways the order,
She should in ground unsanctified been lodg'd
Till the last trumpet: for charitable prayers
Shards, flints, and pebbles should be thrown on her.
Yet here she is allow'd her virgin crants,   225
Her maiden strewments, and the bringing home
Of bell and burial.

Laer. Must there no more be done?

Priest.   No more be done.
We should profane the service of the dead
To sing sage requiem and such rest to her   230
As to peace-parted souls.

(*Hamlet*, 5, i, 191–231)

This extract falls into two parts. First, Hamlet discusses the futility of fame with Horatio; then Laertes and the Priest discuss Ophelia's funeral. The extract takes place in a graveyard, and the audience has been watching ancient bones and a skull being dug out of an open grave. Hamlet and Horatio are on the stage, and are joined by a procession consisting of Ophelia's coffin and bearers, Laertes, the King and Queen, and other attendants. The heirarchy of Elsinore society is visually before us, then, but in a shocking new setting: the gruesome graveyard contrasts with the previous court scenes, set in banqueting halls, council chambers, or at the performance of a play. This scene suddenly places the Elsinore court in an incongruous, unexpected context, highlighting the artificiality of the King's authority and the court's ceremony, which suddenly appear trivial beside open graves.

Hamlet's language emphasises the contrast between glory in life and disgust in death. The phrases 'noble dust of Alexander', and 'Imperious Caesar' contrast with 'stopping a bung-hole' and 'clay', and the shocking change is reinforced by 'dust', 'earth', 'loam' and 'beer-barrel'. Notice that 'stopping a bung-hole' and 'beer-barrel' both have a faster, slightly ridiculous rhythm, unlike the stately 'noble dust of Alexander' or the monosyllables 'dust', 'earth' and 'loam'. The rhythm of 'stopping a bung-hole' comes out something like '*diddle-dee dum-dum*'. This makes the end of the process seem so contemptible and absurd that Hamlet is tempted to express it in derisory, bouncy language. In lines 206 to 209 Hamlet bursts into popular rhyme. We recognise this as another experience of the absurd. The absolute gulf between Alexander's magnificence in life on the one hand, and his eventual use as a plug on the other hand, is too ridiculous for Hamlet to accept – it is absurd and produces a comic urge, a comic effect expressed in the catchy rhyme.

In the second section of our extract, the Priest's language is academic and self-consciously formal: 'obsequies', 'warranty', 'unsanctified', 'charitable', 'strewments', all occur within his few lines. His constructions are also formal. He uses noun-phrases like 'the bringing home of', and inversions such as 'ground unsanctified'. His subject is the competing powers of religious and secular authority, where the King and the Church have been in conflict. They have compromised, the Church being forced to allow some grudging funeral ceremony. As Hamlet's sudden rhythm in 'stopping a bung-hole' creates a ridiculous effect, so the Priest's ponderous alliteration at the end of his speech, 'bell and burial', may satirise his pomposity.

The courtiers' entry as a procession, and the Priest's self-consciously pompous style, then, are both set within a context which emphasises how ridiculous they are. If Alexander's achievements were futile in the face of death, then Claudius is ridiculous, posturing in a graveyard. If dead bodies merely decompose, and old skulls are thrown out to make room for fresher bodies, how stupid do the Priest's words sound as he talks of people 'lodg'd' in their graves until 'the last trumpet'! What difference will 'Shards, flints, and pebbles' make when the body's destination is only to 'stop a hole', anyway?

In this extract from *Hamlet*, then, Shakespeare has put the facts of death on stage and into the language so that they undermine everything: there is no lasting distinction or value. Since everybody becomes a 'bung', everything is equally sordid. Society's ceremonial forms and inevitable moral compromises (Ophelia's grudging funeral is our example of this) are shown up for the false pretences they are.

We are encouraged to realise the futility and absurdity of 'society' in the play.

The insight dramatically presented here seems to have two elements which are present in the play as a whole. First, society operates by compromising between public and moral laws, and the brute facts of power, greed and lust. So, society is tainted, and can only produce a mixture of good and evil, or a pretence of good covering evil. This helps to explain the public distortions of truth, the plots, deceptions and cunning misunderstandings which abound in Claudius's court. Moral compromises are everywhere in *Hamlet*. Claudius, for example, tries to pray but is not willing to resign the kingdom and wife he has sinfully obtained, while Gertrude does not wish to think about her past adultery. In politics, Fortinbras is bought off by being offered safe passage to attack somebody else. Claudius sees Hamlet's mourning as excessive: he should grieve for a time, then forget it; and Gertrude tells her son that this is 'common'. Laertes is persuaded to pursue his revenge by means of poison and trickery. Hamlet expresses his distrust of society when he describes Rosencrantz and Guildenstern, 'whom I will trust as I will adders fang'd' (3, iv, 205).

Second, the complications of society, including people's attitudes, interpretations of each others' motives, subterfuges and so on, are repeatedly shown to be futile. They are irrelevant to the eventual outcome. For example, Claudius plots throughout the play, but none of his plots work. Hiding and eavesdropping produce, first, Hamlet's deliberate 'get thee to a nunnery' tirade, then the murder of Polonius. Spies (Rosencrantz and Guildenstern) are easily fooled and unable to understand the truth; and the plot to execute Hamlet brings about their deaths instead, announced in the final scene. Claudius's most intricate plot, the poisoned foil backed up by a poisoned drink, runs out of control and results in his own, Gertrude's and Laertes's deaths as well as Hamlet's. The plots against Claudius are equally ineffective: he is not beaten by the 'mousetrap', nor by any of Hamlet's resolutions about 'bloody' thoughts. It is Hamlet's passive attitude to Providence, expressed in 'the readiness is all' and 'there is a special Providence in the fall of a sparrow' (5, ii, 216–18), that finally destroys Claudius. In addition, in the first half of the play many characters explain and analyse society's complications at length: Polonius gives elaborate advice to Laertes, then Laertes and Polonius give lengthy advice to Ophelia; Polonius, Claudius and Gertrude discuss Hamlet, while Hamlet, Horatio and the sentries talk about rumours of war and national customs. Notice that none of this talk has an effect on the real events of the play. Polonius's and Ophelia's deaths make their long, anxious early speeches seem trivial and ridiculous. In *Hamlet*, then, society is seen as deceptive, fatally compromised and trivially complicated, and as irrelevant in the face of the real issues of life and death.

One further point interests us, because it relates the society of *Hamlet* to that of *Othello*. There is a contrast between the 'old' King, who is described as a chivalrous ideal, the champion of his country deciding battles in single combat, and with high morals, and the 'new' King, Claudius, a cynical politician who manipulates power. Like *Othello*, then, *Hamlet* shows a society in the process of changing from 'old' to 'new', and the source of power is uncertain during this change.

*   *   *

In Chapter 1 we noticed that artificial court manners play a part in the opening scene of *King Lear*. These manners contrast with Gloucester's unruly emotions, and show moral ambiguity (remember Edmund's insincerity in 'I shall study deserving'). The tragedy that develops in *King Lear* strips away layer after layer of society's artificial pretences. In Act 4, Scene vi, Lear meets blinded Gloucester in the country near Dover. Lear explains his new insights into society:

Lear.	What! Art mad? A man may see how this world
	goes with no eyes. Look with thine ears: see how
	yond justice rails upon yond simple thief. Hark, in 150
	thine ear: change places, and, handy-dandy, which
	is the justice, which is the thief? Thou hast seen a
	farmer's dog bark at a beggar?
Glou.	Ay, Sir.

Lear.   And the creature run from the cur? There thou
               might'st behold   155
            The great image of Authority:
            A dog's obeyed in office.
            Thou rascal beadle, hold thy bloody hand!
            Why dost thou lash that whore? Strip thine own back;
            Thou hotly lusts to use her in that kind   160
            For which thou whipp'st her. The usurer hangs the cozener.
            Thorough tatter'd clothes small vices do appear;
            Robes and furr'd gowns hide all. Plate sin with gold,
            And the strong lance of justice hurtless breaks;
            Arm it in rags, a pigmy's straw does pierce it.   165
            None does offend, none, I say, none; I'll able 'em:
            Take that of me, my friend, who have the power
            To seal th'accuser's lips. Get thee glass eyes;
            And, like a scurvy politician, seem
            To see the things thou dost not. Now, now, now, now;   170
            Pull off my boots; harder, harder; so.
                                    (*King Lear*, 4, vi, 148–71)

Lear speaks both prose (ll.148–53) and verse (ll.155–71) in this
extract. There is no obvious reason for his change as the subject-
matter of hypocrisy and injustice remains the same. The only change
which roughly coincides with the change from prose to verse is that
Lear begins to address 'Thou rascal beadle', and no longer talks to
Gloucester directly, in the fourth line of the main speech. The first
three lines of this speech are very irregular anyway, consisting of thirteen, nine and seven syllables respectively, so the poetry may be
taken to start when he addresses 'Thou rascal beadle'. It indicates
where he begins to speak in a more declamatory style.

    Lear's blank verse continues to be fairly irregular in the remainder
of the speech. Only five lines have iambic regularity (ll.158, 160,
162, 167 and 169), and the length of lines varies between thirteen
syllables (l.161) and nine syllables (l.171), while several others are
eleven syllables long. The length of phrases varies widely, also. They
come in half-lines (for example 'Thou rascal beadle, hold thy bloody
hand!') and some much longer (such as 'Thou hotly lusts to use her

in that kind / For which thou whipp'st her'); and in lines 166, 170 and 171 the speech breaks into short, disjointed starts full of repetition (see 'none' three times in line 166, 'now' four times in line 170 and 'harder' twice in line 171). The poetry creates a wild, varied pace and rhythm, then, and breaks into disturbed, repetitive fragments twice – when Lear declares 'None does offend', and at the end. The same fluctuation in speed and rhythm is found in Lear's preceding, prose, speech: very short phrases, including the ridicule-word 'handy-dandy', fill the sentence beginning 'Hark, in thine ear', while the final question of the speech is a single, much longer burst.

Lear uses a great deal of imagery. First, he introduces the idea of seeing 'with no eyes' and orders the blinded Gloucester to 'Look' with his 'ears' and 'Hark, in thine ear'. Then there are four images which show that values and authority in society are upside-down. First, Lear pictures judge and thief changing places; next, 'the creature run from the cur' shows a beast in authority over a human being; third, the image of a beadle whipping a whore for lusts he is guilty of himself brings the idea of changing places again in 'Strip thine own back'; and finally, 'The usurer hangs the cozener' conveys a world where all are equally sinful and authority is nonsense.

Lines 162–5 focus on outer appearances in the form of 'Robes and furr'd gowns' or a plating of 'gold' on the one hand, and 'tatter'd clothes' or 'rags' on the other. The former outer coverings, which only the rich can afford, are effective: they respectively 'hide all' and defend the wearer against the 'strong lance of justice'. The poor, on the other hand, cannot hide as their vices 'appear' through the holes in their clothing and even a 'pigmy's straw' can pierce them, they are so vulnerable. Finally, a 'politician' or trickster is imagined to be as blind as Gloucester but pretending to see with 'glass eyes'.

The subject-matter of this extract is clear from our look at the imagery: Lear describes an entirely sham appearance of order in society, and reveals that people are really all equally sinful. This view of society shares the *Othello* perception of falsely sophisticated appearances masking primitive humanity; and it shares the *Hamlet* view that all people are essentially the same: none of the distinctions of rank or social level are real. In this sense, society is cynically exposed as a sham in all three plays. In each case, however, there is a provoking force – an experience or energy which forces us to penetrate the false appearance of human society, so that we realise the cynical truth. In *Othello* there is a drive towards power and influence: characters desire an understanding of society in order to gain power and manipulate its workings. This applies to Iago, who desires power, and Othello himself, who obtains Desdemona by wielding his social power. In *Hamlet* confronting death is the experience which makes all social distinctions absurd. Realising that even the most glorious will end as a stopper in a 'bung-hole' deprives all social order of its meaning. What is the energy driving Lear's realisation in this extract?

Lear's language displays several insulting words – 'cur', 'dog', 'rascal', 'scurvy' – and his anger is also powerful in short words with 't' and 's' sounds: 'Strip', 'hotly lusts', 'whipp'st' and 'politician'. A different, ironic tone is full of heavy hatred and contempt: 'usurer' and 'cozener', 'Robes and furr'd gowns', 'Plate sin with gold' and 'glass eyes'. This tone typically has long vowels and softer or open consonants, suggesting the comfortable covering of the wealthy. The force of emotion driving Lear's speech, then, seems to be anger.

Another look at the imagery adds a further point. There are references to blindness, or seeing without eyes, throughout: the extract begins with 'A man may see . . . with no eyes', and at the end comes 'Get thee glass eyes'. Also, there are images of and a reference to removing clothes: the beadle must 'Strip thine own back', the poor show themselves through 'tatter'd clothes', and Lear ends with a frenzied demand to 'Pull off my boots; harder, harder; so'. These two ideas pose an interesting question: in the context of a false society, what do nakedness and blindness have in common? The answer is that both nullify false appearances. A naked man is the 'poor, bare, fork'd animal' Lear met as Poor Tom during the storm in Act 3. All 'naked creatures' are the same, not deceptively hidden inside 'Robes and furr'd gowns'. Similarly, a blind man is not dazzled by the appearance of sin plated 'with gold': in this sense, the blind see everybody as naked, so they can perceive the truth that judge and thief, beadle and whore, usurer and cozener, are interchangeable.

Society, then, is a cruel artificial appearance enabling the rich to persecute the poor. The energy of the play is directed against society: there is anger, and a desire to strip away all clothing, to show that people are equally natural and equally sinful. The urge to remove clothing surfaces at several points in Lear's own development, particularly in the storm scenes ('Off, off, you lendings. Come, unbutton here' [3, iv, 106–7]). Lear's abdication, the first drastic action of the play, may be unconsciously motivated by this same urge to remove his false layers of authority, and discover his natural self. The words 'unburthen'd' and 'divest' in Lear's abdication speech (1, i, 40 & 48) support this theory, as do many of the insights Lear reaches later, such as 'Take physic, Pomp; / Expose thyself to feel what wretches feel' (3, iv, 33–4).

At the same time, Lear's abdication begins a wide-ranging breakdown of social order. The bastard Edmund, Cornwall, Regan and Goneril all thrive while the characters who represent truth and honourable values either disguise themselves (Edgar, Kent), go mad or speak paradoxes (Lear, the Fool), or go into exile (Cordelia). Those remaining within reach of the evil unloosed when Lear relinquishes his authority are driven mad (Lear) and blinded (Gloucester). The picture of a society without moral values, where none can be judged, which Lear suggests in our extract when he says 'None does offend . . . I'll able 'em', reminds us of the cruelty and destruction released in the play when Lear removes 'authority' by abdicating the throne.

Therefore the play as a whole presents a paradox. There is a process of stripping away false layers of hypocrisy, injustice and unmerited authority, which reveals the naked truth. On the other hand, cruelty and unnatural destruction triumph when legitimate authority is removed. The social order is thus presented as both false and necessary: it is artificial, but its absence is devastating. This paradox reminds us of the irony we discussed when analysing the tragedies' endings. Then, we noticed a feeling of relief mingled with regret when order was about to be restored, and we concluded that the tragic experience reveals truth, while order relies on half-truths or distortion.

The three plays we have analysed so far present a broadly common view of society. In political terms they are all radical, even revolutionary critiques of corruption, injustice and exploitation. If we look at his exposure of false social structures and hypocritical public morality, we can conclude that Shakespeare was a radical and subversive dramatist who advocated the overthrow of rotten regimes. His other powerful and relevant idea complicates the picture, however. All three plays are cynical about human nature. The vast majority of people are not presented as decent: stripped of their pretences, they are no better than beasts following appetite. So, *if* a false, corrupt social order crumbles or is destroyed, *then* there will be chaos and anarchy, or the vicious tyranny of the strong over the weak. So our view of society in these three tragedies leaves us with a dilemma, not a solution.

This dilemma is connected to a change in the nature of power from old inherited supremacy to the new political power of force and manipulation. This change is dramatised in *King Lear* as well as *Othello* and *Hamlet*. Lear's age is repeatedly emphasised, and the authority he gives up at the start of the play is clearly the old, unquestioned and inherited kind of power. His social opponent in the play is Edmund, mouthpiece for a cynical 'natural' philosophy, social climber, plotter and manipulator. In all three plays, then, a profound and disturbing process of change is taking place, and all the structures and relationships of society are in process of being altered. In these unresolved circumstances we are given a radical political critique together with a strong sense of the futility of action.

* * *

We are now ready to look at *Macbeth*. Remember that we found bloodshed running amok in the opening scenes of the play. There was already a contrast between brutality in battle and the vague idealisms of Duncan. We concluded that the King's authority seemed frail when set against vivid images of butchery. In Act 4, Scene iii, Malcolm and Macduff discuss the English King with a Doctor, then Rosse enters and describes Scotland under Macbeth's rule:

Mal.	Comes the King forth, I pray you?	140
Doct.	Aye, Sir; there are a crew of wretched souls,	

	That stay his cure: their malady convinces	
	The great assay of art; but at his touch,	
	Such sanctity hath Heaven given his hand,	
	They presently amend.	
Mal.	I thank you, Doctor.	145
	[*Exit Doctor.*	
Macd.	What's the disease he means?	
Mal.	'Tis call'd the Evil:	
	A most miraculous work in this good King,	
	Which often, since my here-remain in England,	
	I have seen him do. How he solicits Heaven,	
	Himself best knows; but strangely-visited people,	150
	All swoln and ulcerous, pitiful to the eye,	
	The mere despair of surgery, he cures;	
	Hanging a golden stamp about their necks,	
	Put on with holy prayers: and 'tis spoken,	
	To the succeeding royalty he leaves	155
	This healing benediction. With this strange virtue,	
	He hath a heavenly gift of prophecy;	
	And sundry blessings hang about his throne,	
	That speak him full of grace.	
	Enter ROSSE.	
Macd.	See, who comes here.	
Mal.	My countryman; but yet I know him not.	160
Macd.	My ever-gentle cousin, welcome hither.	
Mal.	I know him now. Good God, betimes remove	
	The means that makes us strangers!	
Rosse.	Sir, amen.	
Macd.	Stands Scotland where it did?	
Rosse.	Alas, poor country!	
	Almost afraid to know itself. It cannot	165
	Be call'd our mother, but our grave; where nothing,	
	But who knows nothing, is once seen to smile;	
	Where sighs, and groans, and shrieks that rent the air	
	Are made, not mark'd; where violent sorrow seems	
	A modern ecstasy: the dead man's knell	170
	Is there scarce ask'd for who; and good men's lives	

Expire before the flowers in their caps,
Dying or ere they sicken.

(Macbeth, 4, iii, 140–73)

What is the dramatic context of this extract? The preceding scene ended with the brutal murder of Macduff's family. The final seconds of that scene are shocking, full of rapid movement as a messenger runs on and off, then a moment later the murderers arrive. A child is butchered on stage, and the characters chase each other out. The scene after our extract features the sleep-walking Lady Macbeth with her wild speech and bizarre actions. This scene is set in England, sandwiched between violent and grotesque dramas set in Scotland.

Apart from the brief appearance of a Doctor and the entry of Rosse, there is no violent movement in this scene: we watch two, and then three characters, who discuss their situation at length and peacefully. The dramatic contrast between Scotland and England is emphasised when Rosse tells Macduff of his family's murder. We saw how suddenly it happened. In contrast, Rosse reveals his news gradually, delaying the revelation for twelve lines and dropping hints until after Macduff says 'I guess at it'. Malcolm quickly urges Macduff to 'Dispute it like a man' and 'let grief convert to anger', taking the energy of Macduff's grief and harnessing it to help drive their military venture against Macbeth. In this scene, then, the dramatic atmosphere is so orderly that it can safely absorb and control a brutal shock. In the preceding scene, we took this same shock, dramatically speaking, straight between the eyes.

The extract we have selected to study contains two significant speeches – one by Malcolm and the other by Rosse. Malcolm describes the healing influence of the English King, while Rosse describes the evil influence of Macbeth's rule. The two speeches have contrasting subject-matter, then, and we can expect them to contrast in other ways as well. A quick look at rhythm confirms this: in Malcolm's speech only one line in fourteen is run-on, while Rosse's speech has five run-on lines out of ten. In addition, Malcolm begins and ends his speech in quite regular iambic meter (ll.147–8) and often uses a caesura to give stately pace to the poetry (ll.148–52). Rosse, on the other hand, speaks in broken or rushed phrasing.

Notice that he begins a phrase near the end of one line, which has to rush over the line-break before being stopped twice quickly in the next line: for example, 'It cannot / Be call'd our mother, but our grave; where nothing', and 'and shrieks that rent the air / Are made, not mark'd; where violent sorrow seems'.

Sentence-construction also helps to create the impression of stately order in Malcolm's speech and wild disturbance in Rosse's. Look at Malcolm's sentence between lines 149 and 156. It is in four parts, joined by two semi-colons and a colon. A summary makes the structure clear: 'I do not know how he does it, *but* he cures people, *by* hanging a holy object around their necks, *and* it is said his descendants will inherit this power.' The sentence also moves through time in an orderly manner, beginning with the origin of the King's power and ending with his descendants. Now look at Rosse's sentence which runs from line 165 to the end of his speech. The structure seems strong, leading to a list of examples of Scotland's pain, each one introduced by 'where'. But the grammar of each example is condensed and in a difficult order: look at the redundant verb 'made' in line 169, the awkwardness of contrasting 'violent sorrow' and 'modern ecstasy' where 'ecstasy' also contrasts with 'modern' (ll.169–70), the 'dead man's knell' as the subject in a passive construction leading to the preposition 'for' instead of the expected 'by' (ll.170–1), and the difficult reference of 'Dying [the lives] or ere they [the flowers] sicken' (l.173).

Malcolm's language is full of fine-sounding adjective/noun combinations: 'miraculous work', 'good King', 'golden stamp', 'holy prayers', 'succeeding royalty', 'healing benediction', 'strange virtue', 'heavenly gift' and 'sundry blessings'. The religious tone of the speech comes from 'miraculous', 'good', 'holy prayers', 'benediction', 'heavenly' and 'blessings' as well as 'Heaven' and 'full of grace'. Many of the words we have picked out end softly on a falling cadence (hear, for example, 'healing benediction') so the actor can intone these phrases like a prayer. Rosse's speech is in a different style, with plainer, shorter words, such as 'grave', 'knell', 'smile', 'shrieks' and 'rent' giving a harsher sound to the poetry. Notice also the insistent negatives in this speech: 'cannot', 'nothing' (twice), 'not mark'd' and 'scarce'.

The dominant ideas conveyed in this extract are the things described: the 'disease' cured by the English King, and the suffering state of people in Scotland. However, both are given added significance as metaphors as well as literal descriptions. First, the 'disease' Malcolm describes is called 'the Evil' and sufferers are 'strangely-visited'. Second, the physical 'golden stamp' hangs about the sufferers' necks, curing them, as metaphorical 'blessings hang about his throne' enabling the King to cure the body of his people. In Rosse's speech Macbeth's brutality is portrayed as an attack against nature itself in 'rent the air' and as human life expires more quickly than the bloom of flowers.

Our analysis of the style shows a very noticeable contrast between Malcolm's and Rosse's speeches, as we expected. But what is the precise difference between the 'good' and 'bad' societies described? When we ask this question, we realise that these pictures of Scotland and England have much in common. First, both of them have a destructive force, and this negative power is described in similar terms in both speeches. The phrase 'strangely-visited' suggests external evil spirits and therefore recalls the witches, and the disease-features 'swoln and ulcerous' are echoed in Rosse's 'sicken'. Destructive force is beyond understanding, also: Scotland is described as 'afraid to know itself', while the 'Evil' is beyond 'The great assay of art' and is 'The mere despair of surgery'. Both speeches, then, imply that knowledge is helpless against evil and evil itself is something 'strange' or supernatural. Only the 'miraculous' with 'sanctity' and 'grace' can cure the 'Evil'. Malcolm does not understand this power: 'How he solicits Heaven, / Himself best knows'. The impression is of prayer and faith curing that which knowledge cannot combat.

In this extract, then, society is portrayed as a battleground between two opposing supernatural forces, 'Evil' and 'Heaven'. The vital difference is in the person of the King. In Scotland, Macbeth is influenced by the 'evil' witches, while in England the King is 'full of grace'. The picture is of an entire society where the health and order of everything depends on the holiness or evil of the King. Where holiness rules, even the baffling power of evil cannot destroy the state, for society can be 'cured'. Where evil

rules, there is chaos, conveyed in terms of negatives and unnatural-
ness.

How, then, does a King become 'good' so that his influence will
preserve society from evil? The discussion which surrounds our
extract adds to our understanding. Malcolm lists Macbeth's evil
qualities – 'bloody, / Luxurious, avaricious, false, deceitful, / Sudden,
malicious, smacking of every sin . . . / That has a name' (4, iii,
57–60) – and 'the king-becoming graces' which are 'Justice, Verity,
Temp'rance, Stableness, / Bounty, Perseverance, Mercy, Lowliness, /
Devotion, Patience, Courage, Fortitude' (4, iii, 91–4). Notice also
that Malcolm's pretence of his own sinfulness, with Macduff's
answers, suggests that the King's sins and virtues can be weighed: not
only is society saved by a good King and ruined by a bad one, but it
will suffer or prosper exactly in proportion to the wickedness or
goodness of its King, being better if he is better and worse if he is
worse.

The theme of false appearances we analysed in the other three
plays gave rise to a paradoxical conclusion about society: that social
order is false but better than none. In *Macbeth* this paradox does not
appear, yet there is a theme of false appearances and underlying
reality. For example, earlier in Act 4, Scene iii, Malcolm declares that
he cannot rely on Macduff's friendly appearance:

> That which you are my thoughts cannot transpose:
> Angels are bright still, though the brightest fell:
> Though all things foul would wear the brows of grace,
> Yet grace must still look so.
>   (*Macbeth*, 4, iii, 21–4)

What is the difference between society as seen in *Macbeth*, and as
seen in the other three plays? Our extract from *Macbeth* reveals one
new element: the idea of supernatural forces. In *King Lear* destructive and chaotic forces are the basic foulness found in people. The
beadle 'hotly lusts', just as anybody else would. In *Hamlet* society is
seen from the perspective of death and decay, the universal and
natural destiny of all human life. The Ghost's influence promotes
the death-theme, but he does not exist as actively or solidly as

Macbeth's witches. Indeed, Hamlet has already guessed the Ghost's information ('O my prophetic soul!' [1, v, 41]), and he goes to elaborate lengths to find stronger proof of Claudius's guilt by means of the dumb-show. By contrast, in *Macbeth* we hear of a disease whose sufferers have been 'strangely-visited'; we hear the witches discuss their destructive magic, and see them influence Macbeth himself. On the other side is 'Heaven', a 'sanctity' and 'healing benediction' that is beyond our understanding. Individuals, and human society as a whole, are seen as victims, as a passive battleground between these two external forces.

Two consequences of this difference are, first, that *Macbeth* is the most religious of the four tragedies, and second, that the cynical Machiavellian philosophy of base 'nature' that is so powerfully expressed through Iago in *Othello*, Edmund in *King Lear*, and in many of Hamlet's own speeches, hardly makes an appearance in *Macbeth*.

Conclusions

1. In three of the tragedies, *Othello*, *Hamlet* and *King Lear*, the view of society presented in the plays has several common features:
   - Hierarchy, manners, vanity, fashion, rank and authority: the apparent 'order' of society is seen as a false and hypocritical structure, not real.
   - Basic human nature, including sexuality, avarice, brutality and (in *Hamlet*) futility in the face of death, is presented as an underlying truth about all people. The one exception to this conclusion could be Desdemona, whose purity is nonetheless powerless against Iago's successful manipulation of society.
   - Social order and good government are conveyed in literary, commercial and legal language, with even pace and phrasing, and fine words. Sometimes this style is exaggerated to satirise artificiality. Imagery attached to social order stresses appearance or surfaces.
   - Chaos and destruction attract jerky, broken rhythms, condensed syntax and short, harsh or repulsive-sounding words.

Imagery attached to chaos is often shocking and includes references to animal habits, natural disasters and sickness or mutilation of the human body.

2. There is a paradoxical relationship between order and chaos in society, similar to that which we found in the tragic heroes in Chapter 3. In particular, social order is seen as necessary but false; and the gulf between appearance and truth conveys the tragic sense of the 'absurd' in society as it does for the individual.

3. The artificial complexity of society always takes the form of cunning, exploitation, deception and compromise. Our analysis of *Hamlet* shows these in conflict with something absolute: death. In the other plays, we can think of the corrupt social order in conflict with other absolutes. For example, absolute romantic love, in *Othello*, and absolute honesty, in *King Lear*.

4. The presentation of society in *Macbeth* shares most of the features we find in the other tragedies; but *Macbeth* does present a different overall picture because it depicts an external, supernatural battle between absolute powers of good and evil. However, remember that in Chapter 2 we found that the ending of *Macbeth* conveyed the same ironic paradox as the other tragedies. We concluded that 'the restoration of order is a relief from tragic pain, but it also demands that we accept its half-truths and shallow calculations. As Rosse observes, we "must not" consider the infinite value of an individual, for if we do, sorrow that "hath no end" will be our lot. If, on the other hand, the kingdom is to be put back into order, such things have to be forgotten or ignored.' The idea of supernatural Good and Evil battling through humanity adds to our understanding of how the 'infinite value of an individual' is minimised, squeezed out between the clash of massive opposing forces, in this play.

5. We briefly discussed the political implications of Shakespeare's tragedies. Much of the social satire and criticism in the plays is clearly radical and subversive writing – for Shakespeare's or any other time. Pessimism and disgust at human nature complicate the picture, however. The plays seem to present a picture of social conflict and change, not any ideological message.

Methods of Analysis

1. In this chapter we have made use of the same analysis of rhythm, meter, diction, sentences and imagery as in previous chapters.
2. This time, however, we have looked at the results of analysis and asked a specific question. Ask the most obvious and straightforward question: what does this tell us about the way society is created in the play?
3. We regularly recalled insights from previous chapters. For example, we asked [a] does a conflict between order and chaos exist in the societies of these plays as in their 'worlds'? and [b] is society presented in the same way as the tragic hero? These questions are commonsense developments from previous study, and they proved very fruitful.

Suggested Work

1. In this chapter we have looked at how society itself is dramatised in the plays, but we have not discussed the hero's relationship with society. It will be useful for you to analyse another extract from the play you are studying, specifically focusing on this question. The following passages would reward study:

   In *Othello* look at 3, iii, 351–63, where Othello resigns his 'occupation', regretting his knowledge of the deceptiveness of society.

   In *Hamlet* look at 4, iv, 32–66, where Hamlet responds to seeing Fortinbras's army marching to war with a longing to undertake fine but empty actions with 'honour', as Fortinbras does.

   In *King Lear* look at 1, i, 121–38, when Lear describes the contradictory role he envisages for himself, and ends by absurdly offering 'this coronet [to] part between you' to Goneril and Regan.

   In *Macbeth* look at 1, vii, 1–28, where Macbeth reflects upon murdering Duncan in terms of actions and their consequences.
2. You may wish to study the plot of a whole play in order to further understand how society is seen to work. In that case it will be useful to have some questions which help you to organise

your notes, and make your thinking purposeful. Here are some suggestions:

- What is the social relationship between characters, and how far does it influence their relationship as a whole? (For example, in *Hamlet* it would be fruitful to analyse the relationship between Hamlet and Ophelia in this way.)
- Who is at the top of social order, and what is it about them that sustains their position?
- Is there a character who stands outside the social order of the play? Examine the reasons for this (in this context, the Fool and Edgar-as-Poor-Tom in *King Lear*, Horatio in *Hamlet*, Othello or Iago in *Othello*, and the murderers in *Macbeth* would make rewarding studies).

6

Humour in the Tragedies

There are comic episodes in all four plays. These are *Macbeth*'s Porter, *Hamlet*'s Grave-digger, *Lear*'s Fool, and Iago's witty exchanges with Desdemona, and Cassio's musicians, in *Othello*. Shakespeare has included these humorous scenes in plays whose overwhelming effect is to inspire the emotions of tragedy: pity, fear, horror, misery, despair, pain and so on. In this chapter, then, we will ask the obvious question: what is the relationship between tragedy on the one hand, and an episode of comedy on the other?

It will be helpful to bring our understanding of 'tragedy' up to date before we look at specific extracts. We have made several points about tragedy in earlier chapters, and these are beginning to form an 'idea' of Shakespearian tragedy. Now we want to explain this idea using the plainest possible words. We want to bring together the various ideas from earlier chapters, and arrive at a clear single definition, if possible.

First, tragedy is something that happens to the hero. We have described it as an event or an experience; and we have used more abstract terms for it, relating it to a 'conflict' or 'dislocation'. Also, we have described its effect on the hero's perceptions and his language; and we have found instances where the 'tragic experience' embraces other characters as well as the hero, or touches the play's society, 'world' or 'universe'. These insights are all refinements, however. All they show is that Shakespeare has created dramas where all the elements (individual, plot, society, nature, universe – as well as characterisation, poetry, dramatic form) are so integrated that they make a tragic 'whole'. Therefore, the events and experiences in the tragedy happen within every element of the play. These refinements should not make us lose sight of the basic fact, however: tragedy is something (an event or experience) that happens to the hero.

Second, tragedy disturbs reasoned order. We have described it as 'chaos' or 'disorder' in conflict with the order of the hero's mind, the order of the hero's society, the order of nature, or the religious or moral order of the play's universe. It has appeared as a rupture between appearance and reality, disrupting the hero's system of perception so truth cannot be known; and it is physically displayed as violent destruction of an established order (for example, Macbeth kills Duncan, Claudius kills the elder Hamlet, Lear abdicates, Othello loses command of himself and Cyprus). In fact, we have noticed numerous ways in which tragedy manifests itself as disrupting reason and order; but the common element is simply that it does.

Third, tragedy brings about what we have called 'gulfs', 'disproportion', 'contradictions' or 'dislocations' in the hero or his world. These gulfs have been found between appearance and reality, between what a man should be and what he is, between the order that should subsist in a world and the disorder that does, between what would be right and what is possible, between chaos and reason, between Hamlet's thoughts and his emotions, between Othello's love and his suspicions, and so on. These gulfs, or dislocations, tend to break apart the hero's heart and mind: they are extreme and painful, and they are so wide that they are beyond measure, so nothing makes sense. We have described this 'does not make sense' quality of tragedy as 'absurd'. So, tragedy brings about the 'absurd'.

Let us put these points as briefly and clearly as possible, then: tragedy is something that happens to the hero which disrupts order so nothing makes sense, thus bringing absurdity. Two other points are joined to our understanding, and are worth remembering at this stage.

First, part of the tragedy is concerned with the relationship between absolutes on the one hand, and the compromises, half-truths and other relative balances of ordinary life on the other. For example, in *Hamlet* the ideas of death and absolute right and wrong fill Hamlet's mind, and are in destructive conflict with his world which is dominated by hypocrisy, negotiations, deals between appetite and conscience or between grief and time, and other compromises. In *Othello* the hero feels that his love is absolute: he senses that his happiness with Desdemona is so 'absolute' that nothing can rival it, so 'If it were now to die, / 'Twere now to be most happy' (2, i, 189–90). Part of the bitterness of tragedy has to do with these 'absolutes': in themselves, they provoke our admiration; but they are in conflict with the complexity of ordinary life, and the conflict is destructive.

Second, the question of values is relevant. In all four plays tragedy severs the connection between order and value. So, the highest is not morally the best. For example, in *King Lear* we know that the two worst daughters hold power and the best is cast off; and we have found that Lear conveys a society where there is no connection between people's positions (such as a Justice or a thief, a Beadle or a whore – see Chapter 5) and their value. These two points are part of our understanding of what happens to the hero, and how absurdity arises.

Now, there are various responses to tragedy. When the world does not make sense, one response is to go mad (Lear), another is to consider suicide (Hamlet) and yet another is to destroy the perceived cause of the experience (Othello and, to an extent, Macbeth). All these responses inspire the emotions we expect from tragedy: despair, misery, fury, fear, are inspired when reality is too painfully nonsensical – too 'absurd' – to bear. These responses bring tragedy to an end, also; so violent death, suicide and madness are 'limits' of the tragic experience. 'Absurd' also means 'ridiculous', however: absurdity is the raw material of comedy. We have often heard people say 'I didn't know whether to laugh or cry!'. We will look at the comic scenes from this standpoint, asking: does the humorous material in the play share common features with the tragic material? Is laughter an alternative response, or another 'limit', to tragedy?

* * *

Our first extract in this chapter comes from *Macbeth*:

Porter.   Here's a knocking, indeed! If a man were Porter
of Hell Gate, he should have old turning the key.
[*Knocking.*] Knock, knock, knock. Who's there,
i'th'name of Belzebub?—Here's a farmer, that
hang'd himself on th' expectation of plenty: come in,   5
time-pleaser; have napkins enow about you; here
you'll sweat for't. [*Knocking.*] Knock, knock. Who's
there, i'th'other devil's name?—Faith, here's an
equivocator, that could swear in both the scales
against either scale; who committed treason enough   10
for God's sake, yet could not equivocate to heaven:
O! come in, equivocator. [*Knocking.*] Knock, knock,
knock. Who's there?—Faith, here's an English tailor
come hither for stealing out of a French hose: come
in, tailor; here you may roast your goose. [*Knocking.*]   15
Knock, knock. Never at quiet! What are you?—But
this place is too cold for Hell. I'll devil-porter it no
further: I had thought to have let in some of all
professions, that go the primrose way to th'everlasting bonfire. [*Knocking.*] Anon, anon: I pray you,   20
remember the Porter.   [*Opens the gate.*
(*Macbeth*, 2, iii, 1–21)

This interlude occurs at an extraordinarily tense moment in the
developing tragedy. We have seen the gory Macbeths after the
murder of Duncan, and bloodshed has proved a cataclysmic experience for Macbeth himself. The 'multitudinous seas' will turn red
before his hands are clean, and he says 'To know my deed, 'twere
best not know myself'. The knocking at the castle gate has begun
before the end of Scene ii; and the Macbeths hurriedly scurry away
so that they can arrive as if from bed, Macbeth calling with desperate
regret: 'Wake Duncan with thy knocking: I would thou couldst!'.
After our extract, Lenox describes the horrors of a night full of evil
portents, and in line 64 Macduff rushes on from Duncan's chamber,
shouting 'O horror! horror! horror!', having discovered the bodies.
The Porter, then, has the stage for a very short time, sandwiched

between .horrors and blood. The dramatic effect of a comic old cynic, rambling with deliberate slowness at this crucial moment in the drama, is extraordinary. The Porter's excruciating slowness teases the audience; and his character, which causes the gate to be opened so tardily, ironically helps Macbeth to avoid discovery.

Dramatically, then, this comic interlude demonstrates Shakespeare's daring and confidence. Why, then, does he take the enormous risk of introducing laughter at such a moment? To answer this question we will look at the Porter's speech in detail.

The Porter speaks prose. The previous scene was full of powerful metaphors ('Glamis hath murther'd Sleep' or 'What hands are here? Ha! they pluck out mine eyes.' [2, ii, 41 & 58]) and the most intense, impressive language ('all great Neptune's ocean' or 'the multitudinous seas incarnadine' [2, ii, 59 & 61]), so the Porter's homely diction is a complete contrast. He uses colloquial terms such as 'farmer', 'time-pleaser', 'napkins', 'tailor', 'French hose', 'roast your goose'. His command of metaphor is also colloquial – he uses the common figures of speech of everyday people, such as 'old turning the key', 'you'll sweat for't', and 'that go the primrose way to th'everlasting bonfire'. Even his references to the supernatural are in common language. He uses 'Hell Gate' rather than 'the Gate of Hell', and his devils are 'Belzebub' (a foolish-sounding word) and 'th'other devil' whose name he does not bother to remember. The effect of this sudden contrast in language is a marked drop in tension, or bathos.

The Porter's phrases are varied in length. Some are mere exclamations ('Here's a knocking, indeed!') while the 'equivocator' is described in three longer and more structured clauses. The whole is punctuated by knockings on the gate and the Porter's own repetitive echo of 'Knock, knock, knock'. What is the structure of the whole speech, then? The Porter begins by imagining himself 'Porter of Hell Gate', and starts to list the people knocking for admittance. The most striking thing at this stage is that his list is potentially endless as there are endless different kinds of sinners. Having listed three kinds of sinner, he breaks off, and points out how long he could have continued ('I had thought to have let in some of all professions'). This structure establishes a kind of comic conflict between the Porter's rambling list of sinners which could go on forever, and the urgent, repeated knocking. Thus, the tension between urgent suspense and delay, that the audience feels, is conveyed within the speech. Comically, it is the cold rather than any urgency that resolves the conflict and forces him to open the gate.

The content of the speech is ironically suited to the main tragedy. The idea of Macbeth's castle as 'Hell' reminds us of Lady Macbeth's line about 'the fatal entrance of Duncan / Under my battlements' (1, v, 39-40); and the Porter's cynicism portrays a world of greed, deceit and, later in conversation with Macduff, lechery and drunkenness. This cynicism is expressed through dense allusions full of ambiguous or double meanings. For example, 'goose' is a smoothing iron a tailor may use, but is also a swelling caused by venereal disease, and the secondary meaning is enhanced by connection to 'sweat' and 'roast'; meanwhile, 'goose' also brings to mind killing the goose that laid the golden egg – something the tailor may have done by trying to get rich too quickly, and, by parallel, the same thing Macbeth has done by murdering Duncan just as he received such honours from the King. These complex, multiple allusions and puns convey a world so ambiguous, and language so questionable, that reality is a multi-layered seethe of innuendo. The words have become a game which plays around cynical ideas merely for the fun of it, with no intention of communicating anything important. The final form of such language is a riddle, such as the insoluble phrase about the 'equivocator': 'could swear in both the scales against either scale'.

How does the content of this speech relate to the main play? There is no explicit connection: the Porter merely has his own ideas, so any connection appears to be accidental. However, the large issues discussed here are sin, damnation and Hell; and these are the same as Macbeth confronts in, for example, his speech 'If it were done, when 'tis done . . .' (1, vii, 1). We can describe the connection between the comedy and the main tragedy in more detail than this. Several accidents within the speech remind us of the main action. We already noticed the allusion in 'roast your goose'; there is also 'committed treason enough for God's sake [as did Macbeth], yet could not equivocate to heaven'. We have heard Macbeth attempt to reason away the consequences of the murder; and the scene just finished expressed his horror because he could no longer 'equivocate to heaven'. Notice also that the farmer, the equivocator and the tailor make nonsense out of their situations and trap themselves in disaster. The Porter's commentary on them is thus a further exploration, from a comic standpoint, of the nonsense Macbeth has made of loyalty and morality, and the trap in which his action has caught him. The characteristics of the Porter's comic speech, then, are rough, colloquial language used punningly, dense with double meanings and riddling, presenting a vision of multiple sins and trickery in the world, and focusing derisively on issues which are central to the main tragedy.

The audience, then, is invited to laugh at the tragedy of the main action. The horror of damnation, frighteningly expressed by Macbeth in Scene ii, is the subject of laughter in Scene iii. This shows extraordinary confidence on Shakespeare's part, as we have remarked, but the final effect suggests two further points. First, the invitation to laugh at the central issues of Macbeth's tragedy means that the play calls for two responses from us, in reaction to the same theme. Thus, it puts the audience in an ironic position in relation to the tragedy itself: we experience the hero's terror, and realise the stupidity of his sufferings at the same time. Second, the comic scene highlights riddles, complex nonsense – the ridiculous or 'absurd' face of the tragic issues referred to. The comic 'ridiculous' is very close to the tragic 'absurd'.

*   *   *

Our second comic extract comes from *Othello*, and on the surface it appears very different from Macbeth's Porter. While anxiously waiting for Othello's ship to arrive at Cyprus, Desdemona and Iago pass the time in a 'witty' conversation. Desdemona playfully asks Iago to praise a 'deserving woman indeed', and he replies:

Iago.   She that was ever fair, and never proud,
        Had tongue at will, and yet was never loud,
        Never lack'd gold, and yet went never gay,   150
        Fled from her wish, and yet said 'Now I may;'

> She that, being anger'd, her revenge being nigh,
> Bade her wrong stay, and her displeasure fly;
> She that in wisdom never was so frail
> To change the cod's head for the salmon's tail;   155
> She that could think, and ne'er disclose her mind,
> See suitors following, and not look behind;
> She was a wight, if ever such wight were—
> Des.   To do what?
> Iago.   To suckle fools, and chronicle small beer.   160
> Des.   O most lame and impotent conclusion: do not learn
>   of him, Emilia, though he be thy husband; how say
>   you, Cassio, is he not a most profane and liberal
>   counsellor?
>
>   (*Othello*, 2, i, 148–64)

The beginning of the scene described a storm, with images which suggest a return to chaos (the sea 'Seems to cast water on the burning bear, / And quench the guards of the ever-fixed pole' [2, i, 14–15]). Two ships have arrived safely, one carrying Cassio and the other Desdemona, Iago, Emilia and Roderigo; all these characters are on stage together with Montano, three gentlemen and a Messenger. While they wait, worrying whether Othello's ship has survived the storm, Iago entertains them with scandalous witticisms. Desdemona is 'not merry, but I do beguile / The thing I am, by seeming otherwise' (2, i, 122–3). Immediately after the extract, Cassio indulges in 'courteous' behaviour with Desdemona and Iago confides his foul suspicions and plans to the audience. Then Othello arrives. This interlude, then, is similar to the Porter's scene in *Macbeth*: the audience and characters wait anxiously between a wild event (the storm) and discovery of its consequences. It is a dramatic pause, but – as in *Macbeth* – there hardly seems room for wit and laughter at this moment.

Iago speaks in couplets, with strong and largely regular caesurae (in all of the lines except 154–5 which are a couplet without a pause). The opening feet of eight lines are reversed ('*She* that was *ever fair*'), otherwise the iambic meter is unbroken. The sing-song regularity of these couplets is emphasised even more when

Desdemona interrupts, after which Iago speaks the final bathetic line as if she had not spoken. The regular rhythm and rhyme Iago uses have a doggerel effect, giving a tone of foolishness or childishness. Iago's words are also plain, describing widely accepted qualities in simple terms: 'fair', 'proud', 'loud', 'gay', 'frail'. The style, then, is like that of a nursery rhyme or a riddle. However, the most striking feature of this style is that it is written to be delivered with comic timing. For example, listen to line 151 – 'Fled from her wish, and yet said "Now I may;"' – in the mouth of a good comedian; or notice the skill of Desdemona's interruption which makes us wait a moment longer for the comic anti-climax of Iago's final line. We will analyse this episode in detail, looking for its relationship to the main tragedy; but we must not forget that it is funny: it makes us laugh.

The subject of the speech is a 'deserving' or virtuous woman, but Iago manages to make his list of female virtues negative. What he gives us is a list of the faults of women, while describing 'she that' does not have these faults. In addition, his final line is an anti-climax, since in his view any good woman is a trivial fool. Iago implies that all women have the faults listed: they are proud, nagging, vain, overdressed, either frigid or lustful, revengeful, stupid, unable to keep confidences, and always ogling the men. The content of this humour is cynical, then: it portrays a world where lust, vanity and stupidity are universal. Notice also that Iago's jokes are about virtue and vice among women – a central issue in Othello's tragedy. Iago's final bathos has an additional implication, because he asserts that good people are ineffectual (i.e. they only 'suckle fools' and 'chronicle small beer'). This echoes his opinion of Othello's goodness. We remember his view that Othello has a 'free and open nature' which will 'as tenderly be led by the nose . . . as asses are' (1, iii, 397–400). Therefore the idea that goodness and weakness go together connects this comic extract with Othello's tragedy.

Several ironic lines show that Shakespeare ties this humorous excursion into the main concerns of the tragedy in a more detailed way as well. For example, Desdemona advises Emilia: 'do not learn of him, Emilia, though he be thy husband'. We know that Desdemona's utter obedience to Othello is a crucial element in the tragedy, and her absolute loyalty is the subject of her conversation with Emilia in Act 4, Scene iii. It is therefore ironic that Desdemona should counsel disobedience. The dramatic irony of Iago's honesty is also strong in this episode. The other characters call Iago 'honest' with insistent repetition throughout the play. The audience, knowing his villainy, winces each time the epithet is applied. Yet, when we examine the play more closely, Iago tells surprisingly few lies, and speaks with surprising openness, both to Roderigo and Othello, about the suspiciousness of his own nature and the baseness of his opinions. In a technical sense, Iago is surprisingly 'honest'. This intensifies the audience's fear and tension: we long for Othello to realise Iago's true character, yet even when the villain tells the truth, Othello fails to recognise his danger. Here, Iago puts forward a cynical analysis of women, supposedly as a joke to shock and entertain Desdemona. In fact, these are his real views. Earlier, for example, he told Roderigo: 'It cannot be that Desdemona should long continue her love unto the Moor . . . When she is sated with his body . . . she must have change, she must' (1, iii, 342–53). We know Iago's misogyny, and his belief that female promiscuity is a universal law of nature. At the start of this banter with Desdemona, Iago warned: 'O gentle lady, do not put me to't, for I am nothing, if not critical'. Here again, then, Iago is honest; and the audience winces when Desdemona fails to take him seriously. She lightly remarks to Cassio: 'is he not a most profane and liberal counsellor?'.

There is only one example of ambiguity in this speech, but the density of meanings it suggests reminds us of Macbeth's Porter. The phrase 'To change the cod's head for the salmon's tail' either means to give away the best of a bad thing for the worst of a better, or to give away something useful for something useless, or to go to a coarse taste from a delicacy. With the bawdy double meanings of 'cod' and 'tail', however, it also suggests a stupid woman who gives up a potent man and goes instead to a weak, effeminate one. Each of these meanings, and their multiple complexity, is ridiculous enough to suggest the 'absurd'.

As with Macbeth's Porter, the audience is invited to laugh at a serious issue of the tragedy: the supposed faults and lusts of women. Again, the audience is put into a newly ironic situation in relation to the main tragedy. In effect, we have been tricked; and we may feel ashamed of ourselves. We have laughed at nobility and virtue, derided the romantic ideal because of a dirty joke, and been tricked into laughing with Iago, whose villainy we know. The episode may also enhance our emotional identity with the innocent victim, since Desdemona is tricked with us.

* * *

Now let us look at comedy in *Hamlet*. Act 5 opens '*Enter two Clowns* (*—the* Grave-digger *and* Another)':

Grave. Is she to be buried in Christian burial, when she wilfully seeks her own salvation?
Other. I tell thee she is, therefore make her grave straight. The crowner hath sat on her and finds it Christian burial.
Grave. How can that be, unless she drowned herself in her own defence?
Other. Why, 'tis found so.
Grave. It must be *se offendendo*, it cannot be else. For here lies the point: if I drown myself wittingly, it argues an act, and an act hath three branches—it is to act, to do, to perform; argal, she drowned herself wittingly.
Other. Nay, but hear you, Goodman Delver—
Grave. Give me leave. Here lies the water—good. Here stands the man—good. If the man go to this water and drown himself, it is, will he nill he, he goes, mark you that. But if the water come to him and drown him, he drowns not himself. Argal, he that is not guilty of his own death shortens not his own life.
Other. But is this law?
Grave. Ay, marry is't, crowner's quest law.
Other. Will you ha' the truth an't? If this had not been a gentlewoman, she should have been buried out o' Christian burial.
Grave. Why, there thou say'st. And the more pity that

great folk should have countenance in this world to
drown or hang themselves more than their even-
Christen. Come, my spade. there is no ancient
gentlemen but gardeners, ditchers, and grave-   30
makers—they hold up Adam's profession.   [*He digs.*]

(*Hamlet*, 5, i, 1–31)

The preceding scene ends with Gertrude's moving description of the
drowned Ophelia, and Laertes's valedictory words 'Too much of
water hast thou, poor Ophelia' (4, vii, 184), the play creating a
strong mood of melancholy lamentation. Following this extract,
Hamlet and Horatio enter. They stand aloof and philosophise on the
subject of death and burials, then Hamlet enters a punning conversation with the Grave-digger, and turns away to reminisce over
Yorick's skull, before he is interrupted by the arrival of the court
characters for Ophelia's funeral. The 'clowns', then, come between a
moving account of a death and Hamlet's meditations on death. The
comic nonsense in the Grave-digger's first line, making fun of
Ophelia's death in 'wilfully seeks her own salvation', is entirely unexpected: again, Shakespeare chooses the most unlikely moment to
introduce laughter.

The Grave-digger and his companion converse in prose, as befits
'vulgar' characters. The language they use, however, is remarkable for
chopped logic, absurd arguments, malapropisms and frequent puns.
The Grave-digger himself combines contradictory elements so as to
reverse the normal implications of a phrase. For example, to 'wilfully' seek 'salvation' cannot be a sin, surely – yet since 'seek her own
salvation' is a euphemism for 'take her own life' the meaning is
reversed. This attacks the absurdity of religious law which would
punish poor Ophelia, even after her death. Similarly 'drowned
herself in her own defence' (ll.6–7) makes nonsense of 'in her own
defence', with the echoing idea that suicide is a 'defence' against life's
suffering. His latin tag '*se offendendo*' (a mistake for its opposite, '*se
defendendo*') is a further play on this paradox, and he quickly introduces further legalistic terms in an absurd context, such as 'wittingly', 'argal' (for *ergo*, 'therefore'), 'branches', and his own bathetic

'will he nill he'. Notice that this style repeatedly promises and then denies meaning. For example, the confident statement 'an act hath three branches' is followed by three words for an act, and no further meaning at all. Meaning is progressively removed from the words until the Grave-digger's finale: first, he suggests the hilarious absurdity 'if the water come to him and drown him', then he gives his legal conclusion, which is a masterpiece of self-evident nothingness: 'he that is not guilty of his own death shortens not his own life'. The comedy of this style arises out of the contrast between a highly patterned logical structure and total absence of sense. Thus, the line 'if the water come to him' makes us laugh because we predict it: it is the inevitable converse after 'If the man go to this water'. In addition, the extract is studded with puns. Thus, 'Straight' (l.2) means both 'straightaway' and 'narrow', with a further suggestion of 'virtuous' as the antithesis of 'crooked'; and 'The crowner hath sat on her' (l.4) conjures a gross image but also means that the court has considered her case.

How does this style relate to the main tragedy? First, we have noticed a contrast between patterned, logical features and nonsensical content. This reminds us of the gulf between appearance and reality found elsewhere in the play. The Grave-digger's pretentious language ('argal', 'wittingly', 'crowner's quest law', '*se offendendo*' and so on) bears no relation to sense. In the same way, we remember from Chapter 3 that Hamlet berates himself for lack of proper feeling ('it cannot be but I am pigeon-liver'd') because he 'Must like a whore unpack my heart with words'; and in the presence of an elaborate appearance of emotion from the Player ('all his visage wann'd; / Tears in his eyes, distraction in his aspect, / A broken voice') Hamlet points out that it signifies nothing inside: 'What's Hecuba to him, or he to her . . .?'. So, the Grave-digger's comic style is a further contribution to devaluing language, so creating absurdity, in the play.

Second, we are invited to laugh at the themes of the main tragedy. In *Macbeth* and *Othello* the Porter's and Iago's choice of subjects (Hell and female faults respectively) seem to relate to the main issues of the play by chance. In *Hamlet* the comic scene is more integrated with the main action, since the grave-diggers are preparing Ophelia's grave and discuss her death. Their subject is the morality of suicide, and they try to make sense of religious law. In addition, the second Grave-digger reveals the true state of affairs: he points out the corrupt compromise society has reached between a principle (that suicides should not be buried in consecrated ground) and the brute facts of power (the Church is forced to do as the King says). He expresses this in terms of class: 'If this had not been a gentlewoman . . .'. The Grave-digger comments: 'And the more pity that great folk should have countenance in this world . . . more than their even-Christen' (ll.26–9). The content of this comic scene, then, is directly related to the themes of suicide, death and God's laws which lie at the heart of the tragedy in *Hamlet*, and contributes to an analysis of corrupt injustice in society. What exactly makes us laugh, then? We laugh at absurdity: all the legal mumbo-jumbo is hopeless nonsense, and that is funny. But the particular mumbo-jumbo in this scene is religious law about suicide. Remember that Hamlet's first soliloquy began: 'O . . . that the Everlasting had not fix'd / His canon 'gainst self-slaughter' (1, ii, 131–2). In Act 3, Scene i he longs to kill himself: death is 'a consummation / Devoutly to be wish'd', and he imagines making his 'quietus . . . / With a bare bodkin' were it not for 'the dread of something after death' (3, i, 63–78). The horror of eternal punishment is a powerful element in *Hamlet*: the Ghost died carrying only his 'crimes . . . of nature', yet this is how he describes his punishment:

> But that I am forbid
> To tell the secrets of my prison-house,
> I could a tale unfold whose lightest word
> Would harrow up thy soul, freeze thy young blood,
> Make thy two eyes like stars start from their spheres . . .
> (1, v, 13–17)

Hamlet, then, has struggled to come to terms with God's law against suicide; and the audience has witnessed his terror and agony in the dilemma caused by his suffering and his consequent desire for death. Once we laugh at the Grave-digger's nonsense, we acknowledge that this problem is not only insoluble and in conflict with human sympathies, as Hamlet has painfully found it to be: it is also utterly ridiculous. 'What is the point of punishing a dead body after the soul has sinned?', we ask, laughing. Suddenly, we are in a new relationship to Hamlet's agony, a complicated relationship where we react with laughter and tears – two emotions at the same time, and so it is ironic. Comedy in *Hamlet*, then, is clearly another response to absurdity: laughter is the other 'limit' in a tragic world.

* * *

Now we can move on to our final comic extract, from *King Lear*. It comes from Act 1, Scene iv:

Fool.   Dost thou know the difference, my boy, between a
       bitter Fool and a sweet one?   135
Lear. No, lad; teach me.
Fool.   That lord that counsell'd thee
             To give away thy land,
          Come place him here by me,
             Do thou for him stand: 140
          The sweet and bitter fool
             Will presently appear;
          The one in motley here,
             The other found out there.
Lear. Dost thou call me fool, boy?   145
Fool.   All thy other titles thou hast given away; that thou
       wast born with.
Kent. This is not altogether Fool, my lord.
Fool.   No, faith, lords and great men will not let me; if I
       had a monopoly out, they would have part on't: 150
       and ladies too, they will not let me have all the fool
       to myself; they'll be snatching. Nuncle, give me an
       egg, and I'll give thee two crowns.
Lear. What two crowns shall they be?
Fool.   Why, after I have cut the egg i'th'middle and eat   155
       up the meat, the two crowns of the egg. When thou
       clovest thy crown i'th'middle, and gav'st away

both parts, thou bor'st thine ass on thy back o'er
the dirt: thou hadst little wit in thy bald crown
when thou gav'st thy golden one away. If I speak   160
like myself in this let him be whipp'd that first finds
it so.

>   *Fools had ne'er less grace in a year;*
>   *For wise men are grown foppish,*
>   *And know not how their wits to wear,*   165
>   *Their manners are so apish.*

Lear.   When were you wont to be so full of songs, sirrah?

Fool.   I have used it, Nuncle, e'er since thou mad'st thy
daughters like thy mothers; for when thou gav'st them
the rod and putt'st down thine own breeches,   170

>   *Then they for sudden joy did weep,*
>   *And I for sorrow sung,*
>   *That such a king should play bo-peep,*
>   *And go the fools among.*

    Prithee, Nuncle, keep a schoolmaster that can   175
teach thy Fool to lie: I would fain learn to lie.

Lear.   And you lie, sirrah, we'll have you whipp'd.

Fool.   I marvel what kin thou and thy daughters are:
they'll have me whipp'd for speaking true, thou'lt
have me whipp'd for lying; and sometimes I am   180
whipp'd for holding my peace. I had rather be any
kind o'thing than a fool; and yet I would not be
thee, Nuncle; thou hast pared thy wit o'both sides,
and left nothing i'th'middle: here comes one o'the
parings.   185

        Enter GONERIL.

              (*King Lear*, 1, iv, 134–85)

At the beginning of this scene Kent and Lear attack Goneril's
steward, Oswald; but the main events preceding this scene are Lear's
opening actions, dividing his kingdom, throwing off Cordelia and
banishing Kent. The audience knows how volatile the old King is,
and anxiously awaits the outcome of his foolishness. Our foreboding
is increased by Gloucester's speech, 'These late eclipses in the sun

and moon . . . ' etc. (1, ii, 100–14), and Goneril's plots against Lear, which convey a sense of imminent doom. After this extract, Goneril and Lear have a violent quarrel. As in the other plays, then, comedy delays tragic developments at a time when the audience waits anxiously.

This conversation is in prose, with three short songs by the Fool. In the songs there is simple rhyme and rhythm except the rhyme of 'foppish' and 'apish' in lines 164 and 166, where the badness of the rhyme emphasises the silliness of the sounds and of the word 'apish'. The songs are in a childish style, so their effect reminds us of Iago's couplets. The first one (ll.137–44) is in the form of a riddle, but the answer is obvious. The 'sweet' fool is the Fool. Standing next to him is the 'bitter fool', Lear, standing for any lord who gave him such idiotic advice.

The Fool speaks a simple English, using words of one syllable most of the time and only common two-syllable or longer words (e.g. 'mothers', 'daughters', 'presently', 'breeches'). The two exceptions are 'monopoly' (l.150) and 'schoolmaster' (l.175). The very length of these words highlights absurdity in contrast with single-syllable bathos: he talks of a monopoly of *fools* and a schoolmaster to teach *lies*. Some of the Fool's phrases give a childishly affectionate or comically pathetic tone suitable to the nursery. For example, he cheekily calls Lear 'my boy' in line 134, boyishly offers a joke in lines 152–3 ('Nuncle, give me an egg, and I'll give thee two crowns') and begs for a tutor in 'Prithee, Nuncle' and 'I would fain learn to lie'. This simple, childish style is in contradiction to the structure of the scene, because the Fool leads the conversation and is intellectually in charge. Lear's role is that of the stooge in a comedy double-act, his lines merely feeding the Fool's predictably prepared jokes. In this way authority and order are both reversed (the Fool teaches Lear) and ironically sustained (the Fool speaks mock-childishly and calls Lear 'Nuncle').

The structure of the Fool's sentences is also noticeable. They are neatly constructed and some have elements of symmetry. For example, the sentence at lines 178–81 begins with a proposition, then after a colon gives three clauses to justify the statement; and there is neat antithesis in 'thou hadst little wit in thy bald crown when thou gav'st thy golden one away' (ll.159–60). This reminds us of the Grave-digger from *Hamlet*, whose elaborately logical structures expose utter inanity of content. The Fool is slightly different. His surface logic highlights the absurdities of what Lear has done, but his own ideas are not inane.

The Fool's imagery echoes recurrent themes of the play: the breaking of a shell to reveal inner emptiness, and a reversal of roles between parents and children. For example, the Fool refers to 'two crowns of the egg', which leads to the further comparison of an empty eggshell with Lear's 'bald crown' with 'little wit' in it, and is reinforced later by 'thou hast pared thy wit o' both sides, and left nothing i' th' middle'. Here the Fool's image reminds us of Lear's and Cordelia's exchange about 'nothing' and 'nothing will come of nothing' (1, i, 86–9), Lear's unconscious irony in 'this coronet part between you' (1, i, 138), and a number of other contributory figurative ideas (but see Chapter 7 for a fuller discussion of how these images work in the whole play). Also, the Fool points out Lear's childishness both by speaking the language of the nursery himself, and explicitly when he says 'when thou gav'st them the rod and putt'st down thine own breeches'. This reminds us of Lear's expressed wish to become Cordelia's child: 'I lov'd her most, and thought to set my rest / On her kind nursery' (1, i, 122–3).

This extract is the only one of the four we have looked at whose subject-matter is entirely integrated with the main tragedy, because the hero himself participates. Shakespeare underlines the relevance of the scene insistently: Lear asks 'Dost thou call me fool, boy?' in line 145, in case we did not realise the point of the riddle; Kent helpfully points out 'This is not altogether Fool, my Lord', in case we did not notice his intelligence; the Fool pedantically explains his image of the egg: 'When thou clovest thy crown i'th'middle, and gav'st away both parts . . . ' etc.; and the Fool's final speech is about Lear, his daughters and being a Fool.

There is a second level of more subtle references to the main tragedy. For example, when the Fool says 'I marvel what kin thou and thy daughters are', the idea connects with Lear's 'my sometime daughter' (1, i, 119) and 'Are you our daughter' (1, iv, 216) when he is crossed by Cordelia and Goneril respectively. These in turn relate to a rich field of images in which the relationship between parents and children is described as unnatural, or they are termed 'monstrous', 'kite', 'sharper than a serpent's tooth', and other horrid and bestial epithets. Second, the Fool imagines 'That lord that counsell'd thee / To give away thy land' when the only advice Lear had was the opposite of this, from Kent; and Kent is with them on stage. The irony is that the only lord who still stands with Lear and the Fool is he who gave the opposite advice.

Our relationship to Lear is complicated by the comedy. Think about the dramatic impact of the Fool castigating and teasing Lear's mistakes so devastatingly. In the first scene of the play we saw Cordelia's and Kent's attempts to speak reason to the King, who reacted with violent wrath. In this scene Lear is a ridiculous old man who has made a mistake of comically obvious stupidity; and he tamely feeds 'stooge' lines for the Fool's jokes. The ensuing scenes will introduce us to Lear's temper again, and his vast self-pity in moving lines like 'You see me here, you Gods, a poor old man, / As full of grief as age; wretched in both!' (2, iv, 270–1). The question, which individuals must decide for themselves, is how far we sympathise with Lear. Self-pity and intemperate anger are unappealing emotions, yet they are expressed with such poetic power that they may overwhelm us. In the play, Shakespeare maintains a constant tension between our sympathy for Lear and his unattractive or stupid qualities. Comedy, which exposes his absurdity to ridicule yet in an affectionate tone (see the gentleness of 'yet I would not be thee, Nuncle', in the extract), stretches this tension further, maintaining, at a critical level, the stress upon our relationship with the tragic hero.

We can pursue this point a stage further. One subject of the play is a distinction between logic and emotion. We are repeatedly reminded that reason will not solve human problems; only something unexplainable but felt – the heart – can lead us to mercy and grace. For example, Lear cries 'O! reason not the need; our basest beggars / Are in the poorest thing superfluous' (2, iv, 262–3) and Gloucester later claims that he can 'see . . . feelingly' (4, vi, 147). The comedy in this scene strains our sympathy, as we have noticed. The Fool's logic is so devastating, Lear so ridiculous, that our emotional sympathy with him is clearly against our reason. So the comedy creates a crucial effect, the dramatic realisation of a vital theme of the play. This humour goes beyond an 'exploration' of the absurd; it helps to establish the absurd as central to a human understanding of the world. Human beings will always have their ridiculous side: they will always be absurd and irrational. So, humanity will never be redeemed by reason. Something else is needed, then, something which has to do with common experience and sympathetic understanding. The humour in the play is a key to realising this. This is part of what Lear means when he says: 'Take physic, Pomp; / Expose thyself to feel what wretches feel' (3, iv, 33–4).

Conclusions

1. In each of the four extracts, humour ridicules an aspect of the tragedy. In *Macbeth* the subject was Hell and damnation; in *Othello* Iago's butt was virtuous women, but more generally virtuous fools (like Othello himself); in *Hamlet* the hypocritical mess of religious law, society and suicide is parodied; and in *King Lear* Lear's own irrational actions are held up to laughter. Humour in the tragedies, then, serves a satirical purpose: it uses mock-logic to expose corruption, hypocrisy and stupidity, and to highlight the ridiculous.

2. The Porter, Iago, the Grave-digger and the Fool all use a dense, 'witty' style. We have noticed some common features of this style. There are many puns and phrases of multiple or ambiguous meaning. There is a highly patterned or mock-rational surface texture, either in a potentially endless list (*Macbeth*), recurrent bathos (*Othello*), the use of quasi-legal terms (*Hamlet*), or a neat, patterned sentence-structure (*King Lear*). This mock-logical style devalues language by making senseless sense.

3. Comedy in these plays always relates to the main tragic action and themes. The content of the comic scenes refers to the main issues in detail, and on different levels of subtlety. In two cases (*Macbeth* and *Othello*) the connection is implicit: the comic subject reminds us of the main action as if by chance. In *Hamlet*

the explicit subject of comedy is Ophelia's death, and in *King Lear* it is Lear's own foolishness. The introduction of humour places these tragic issues under a new angle of scrutiny, bringing out the ridiculous, or the comic-absurd. Thus, humour contributes to the multiple-focus structure of the plays: the fullness or 'thickness' of their dramatic effect.

4. We have considered humour as one 'limit' of tragic experience. We mean by this that the disturbing 'gulfs' and absurdities experienced by the hero are potentially both painful and ridiculous. So, despair and laughter are possible responses to tragedy. The comic scenes dramatically create this complex reaction in the audience, so that we become simultaneously aware of pain and the ridiculous. This intensifies our feeling of the close relationship between laughter and tears. It also complicates, adding irony to, the relationship between audience and tragedy.

5. The comic scenes represent extraordinary dramatic daring: we are invited to laugh at the heart of the hero's pain. The audience's feelings are manipulated, then, and the effect seems to be that we are provoked to explore both 'limits' of the tragic experience ourselves.

Methods of Analysis

1. In this chapter we have made use of the same analysis as in previous chapters, including close focus on rhythm and meter where the text is in verse, and detailed description of the diction, sentences and imagery.

2. This time, however, we have looked at the results of analysis and asked specific questions.

   • First, we carefully defined the subject-matter we are invited to laugh at. For example, in *Othello* the butt of Iago's jokes is the virtues and faults of women; but his final line expresses contempt for all good people, whom he regards as ineffectual. Reaching a thorough definition of the subject helped us to relate the comedy to Othello's own gullibility as well as the more obvious question of Desdemona's virtue.

- Second, we thought about the whole play, looking for similar or related themes in the main tragedy. It was easy to find a general relationship between comic and tragic subjects. For example, in *Macbeth* the general subjects of Hell and damnation are obviously present in both. We described and defined the subjects in detail again, however. So we noticed that the Porter's farmer, equivocator and tailor all had several points in common with Macbeth.
- Finally, we asked: how is our relationship to the main tragedy affected by the related comic passage? In this question we examined our feelings in response to the tragic hero's experience, and in response to the comedy.

3. Notice that we have been able to examine how comic scenes relate to the tragedies, by constructing thorough, careful definitions of the subject-matter in both places. We can call this method **analysis by summary-definitions**. It is invaluable when you want to compare more than single speeches or single images from different aspects of the play. The method works by reducing two large amounts of material to condensed statements (summary-definitions), then considering the two statements together, defining how they compare with each other. Here is an example, set out in methodical order. The example is drawn from our analysis of comedy in *Hamlet* in this chapter:

- *What is the subject-matter of the Grave-digger extract?*
  Summary-definition: The grave-diggers discuss religious laws about suicide and the burial of suicides, and the hypocrisy of the compromise in Ophelia's burial.
- *What does this relate to in the whole play?*
  Summary-definition: Hamlet struggles with his desire for suicidal death as a relief from suffering, and his fear and horror at God's punishment of both suicides and naturally sinful humanity.
- *How do these two summaries help us understand the effect of the comic scene?*
  We react to Hamlet's painful dilemma with an ironic combination of laughter (the religious laws are ridiculous) and sympathy. Hence his suffering becomes both pitiable and senseless

to us. Or, the religious laws are both senseless and cruel, in their effect upon Hamlet.

We have made use of analysis by summary-definitions throughout this chapter. The method helps you to think clearly about complicated elements of the text and is particularly useful for organising your understanding of irony.

Suggested Work

In order to expand upon the understanding of humour in the tragedies that we have reached in this chapter, it is worthwhile to pursue two avenues of enquiry. First, look at other comic scenes and passages in the play you are studying. This will add detail by providing further evidence of close relations between the subject-matter of comedy and that of the main tragic action. Second, notice the features of comic style we have found in this chapter, and look for them elsewhere in the play. Comic style is characterised by dense punning and double-meanings, and an overtly rational or patterned diction and linguistic structure. In the play, where else do you find these features?

In *Macbeth* the only other comic material is the remainder of the Porter's scene, so you can make a detailed study of 2, iii, 22–41. On the other hand, we find patterned rhyming with bizarre words and content in the scenes involving the three witches. You may wish to study these, therefore, and seek to draw conclusions relating comedy and horror, from analysing the common features of style. The relevant passages are: 1, i, entire; 1, iii, 1–37; 4, i, 1–47; but you may also consider elements of the remainder of the scene as well.

In *Othello* the other comic episodes you can study are: just before our extract, 2, i, 100–47; and 3, i, 1–29, when Cassio employs a Clown and musicians to play music for Desdemona. Many of the features of comic style also appear in Iago's conversation with Roderigo in 1, iii, 301–80, and would repay close study.

In *Hamlet* there are a number of comic passages. It is worthwhile to analyse the dialogue between Hamlet and the Grave-digger which follows our extract: look at 5, i, 32–205. You may also look at

Hamlet teasing Polonius (2, ii, 171–220). In addition, the play is full of riddles, which are most plentiful during Hamlet's 'antic disposition'. Most of Hamlet's conversations at this stage of the play – whether with Rosencrantz and Guildenstern, Polonius or Ophelia – display many of the features of comic style that we have noticed. You can develop your sense of the function of this style in the play by analysing 3, iv, 334–78, where Hamlet proposes riddles first to Rosencrantz and Guildenstern, then to Polonius.

In *King Lear* you may carry out a detailed analysis of further comedy from both Edgar and the Fool, in 3, vi, 6–83, when Lear and his companions hold a mock-trial of Goneril and Regan. The features of style found in the Fool and in Edgar's speeches as 'Poor Tom' are also evident in some of Lear's speeches. We analysed one of these in Chapter 5. Look also at 4, vi, 83–137. You may draw conclusions about comedy and madness from a close examination of these speeches.

Thinking about the relationship between comedy and tragedy leads us to complex ironies at the core of Shakespeare's tragic creations. You should feel confident to pursue your realisations and insights as far as you can, always building upon detailed study. In doing so you will make frequent use of the method I call 'analysis by summary-definitions' until it becomes second-nature to you, to draw effective comparisons between different aspects of the play, and to realise echoes and other ironic connections between parts of the whole tragedy.

7

Imagery and the Tragic Universe

We have met various aspects of a 'tragic world' in different chapters. We have looked at the first and last moments of these plays; and we have explored how the tragedy is dramatised through the portrayal of the protagonist, women, society, and by means of humour. Each of our chapters so far has been based on short extracts, one from each of the tragedies; and we have built our developing analysis of the plays carefully, exploiting detailed analysis of short extracts to the full and making sparing use of references to the rest of the play in each case.

Despite our extract-based approach, we have found a number of insights which seem to be central to Shakespearian tragedy because they appear again and again; and our understanding of these central ideas has developed progressively. We have added further deductions to previous conclusions in each chapter. So, we know that the conflict between order and chaos appears in a number of forms. We know that the gulf between these two forms of truth often becomes so wide that reason cannot bridge it, so life becomes 'absurd', and that the effect of this 'absurdity' destabilises the individual and is destructive in the play's world.

These insights have appeared, no matter which aspect of the play we have used as a way in. So, order, chaos and the absurd are relevant to all the different elements we have looked at: individual characters, society, the opening and closing dramatic worlds, and so on.

Now we want to discover more about how Shakespeare created each play as a dramatic whole. Instead of focusing on short extracts in isolation, we now want to understand how the many elements of the plays are made to hold together. We can do this by looking at imagery.

Our method is to choose one image we have met in a previous chapter, from each of the plays; then we study that image and others that are closely related to it in the play concerned. Our aim is to describe how the imagery works: what is its dramatic and poetic effect, and what does it contribute to the whole Shakespearian tragedy?

But first, we should ask: what is an image? It is a comparison between two things – one literal and one figurative; and it is expressed in the form of a simile or a metaphor. However, we want to discuss the *effect* of an image, and find an image's *contribution to the play*. So we are looking for definitions of two things about the image: first, what it adds to the text, and second, what the image does to us, as audience or reader, when we receive that part of the text. A brief example will help to make this clear, and serve as an introduction to the discussion of imagery.

In Act 1 of *Othello* the Moor describes Desdemona: she would 'with a greedy ear / Devour up my discourse' (1, iii, 149–50). First, let us define the metaphor. Othello compares Desdemona's ears listening to his story to a greedy creature 'devouring' his story. Now, what effect does this figurative idea have upon the audience, and what does it contribute to the play?

First, the image conjures an unexpected idea in our minds. Othello tells of his adventures and Desdemona listens, yet 'greedy' and 'devour' convey her as active and him as passive. The audience, then, is prompted to imagine their courtship with the impetus and energy coming from Desdemona rather than Othello. This 'image-idea' which has been momentarily introduced into our minds suits the end of Othello's story, where Desdemona takes the initiative, and virtually proposes to him as a 'hint' which encourages him to speak. The image, then, helps us to understand her double-talk when she hints at her love to him: 'if I had a friend that lov'd her, / I should but teach him how to tell my story, / And that would woo her' (1, iii, 164–6).

The image also contributes to a complex portrayal, highlighting ironies in Othello's account. For example, this image attributes all appetite, the force of attraction, to Desdemona; but Othello deliberately manipulates her feelings, taking the initiative himself: 'I . . . took once a pliant hour, and found good means / To draw from her a prayer' (1, iii, 150–2). Why does Othello try to give the impression that Desdemona took the initiative in their courtship? One answer is that this suits his purpose: he has been accused of using magic to entrap her, so he makes a counter-claim. It was the other way around, and she courted him. Another suggestion is that he feels uncomfortable trying to express his own passions: Othello finds it difficult to admit to being vulnerable. So he emphasises Desdemona's passion in this speech. This idea is supported by his patronising remarks about marriage in the previous scene, when he seems to marry her ('confine' his 'unhoused free condition' [1, ii, 26–7]) grudgingly, only as a favour to Desdemona. So, the image expressed in 'greedy' and 'devour' is dramatically true as part of Othello's defence against Brabantio; and it is part of the subtle revelation of Othello's own character.

The word 'devour' has a further effect on the audience: it is normally associated with wild animals, so we receive a momentary impression from this image, which portrays Desdemona's appetite for Othello as a bestial or primitive appetite. This has a most disturbing effect because we already have a number of repulsive bestial images in our minds: Iago used vivid animal imagery a few minutes ago, to portray Othello's and Desdemona's love-making, and 'devour' recalls his degrading picture of their love. The idea of animals also provokes our sense of the universal 'order' of the world, our cultural sense that animals are at the lower, primitive end of the scale, opposed to purity, ideals and other civilised virtues. So Othello's word 'devour', applied to Desdemona, is like a small electric shock which momentarily jolts her down to the vulgar end of creation.

'Devour' seems unnecessarily strong as part of Othello's justification to the Duke. In terms of character, it hints that Othello may be over-eager to attribute all the passion to his wife, which in turn suggests that he denies his own passions. The image, then, acts as a sort of signal, warning us that Othello is not entirely frank, or at ease, in this speech.

Analysing one image has revealed several connections between the image itself and its immediate context. We have also described what happens within our minds, assuming that we constantly receive impressions as we listen to the play. The idea is that our impressions are added to and modified as the play goes on, so words and images join others from earlier in the play, as we hear them and take them in. Also, the audience is not just a passive empty vessel, being steadily filled up with the play. First, our minds contain certain universal ideas, and words or images can trigger our responses by touching these. For example, our background and culture have given us conventional ideas about high and low, civilised and vulgar forms of feeling and behaviour. Here, the hint of animal behaviour provokes our conditioned reaction of disgust or social disapproval. Second, our minds are active, sorting and making connections in the mass of material we take in as we watch a play. So, in the case of the image of Desdemona 'devouring' Othello's words, our minds link this hint of bestiality with other bestiality we have taken in: for example, Iago's 'your daughter, and the Moor, are now making the beast with two backs' (1, i, 116). The text of the play is thus a single continuous stuff made up of words, images, emotions and all the rest of our sense-impressions as we sit in the audience. When we analyse images, we will repeatedly refer to these processes that are set off in our minds.

*   *   *

In *Othello*, Act 3, Scene iii, Othello says:

> If she be false, O, then heaven mocks itself,
> I'll not believe it.
> > (*Othello*, 3, iii, 282–3)

We met this in Chapter 3. Our comment at that stage was that the phrase 'heaven mocks itself' is insoluble: it makes no sense. Our starting-point here is the image Othello uses: he compares

Desdemona to heaven. What effect does this have upon the audience? First, 'heaven' is far greater than any individual human being, so we receive an impression of Desdemona as far greater and more significant than she literally is. This expresses the way Othello perceives her, so the hyperbolic image helps us to understand his subjective feelings: the overwhelming importance of Desdemona to him. Second, the mention of 'heaven' calls forth a series of conditioned associations: it is a religious word and stands for a place of salvation, our aim throughout life, the final place of goodness; and it is a place of absolute beauty and peace. Third, 'heaven' is not part of the natural world: it is supernatural, too pure to be physical. All of this simply describes the various ideas that are called to our minds when we hear the word 'heaven'. In our minds, then, Desdemona seems to be of supreme importance to the whole world. Without her (or 'heaven'), the order of everything else would have no apex, and would collapse completely. Finally, 'heaven' is above the level of physical existence, so there is a suggestion that Othello thinks of Desdemona as a bodiless ideal rather than a physical woman.

Now we can begin to look for similar images elsewhere in the play, so we want to have a clear idea of the features of this image, which will help us to identify them elsewhere. This is a comparison between a human being and something vast, of universal significance. Also, the image-idea is an ultimate or absolute idea (there is nothing higher than 'heaven'), and it is a religious concept. So we look for other images in the play which have these features. About five minutes earlier, Othello said:

> . . . I do love thee, and when I love thee not,
> Chaos is come again.
>
> (*Othello*, 3, iii, 92–3)

Othello compares the feeling of not loving Desdemona to 'Chaos', the state of universal disorder that existed before God created the world, as described in Genesis, at the beginning of the Bible. So this image also compares something on a human scale to something of cosmic significance; the image-idea ('chaos') is an absolute; and it is a religious idea. The Book of Genesis was well known to

Shakespeare's audience, probably better known than it is today, when many people assume that God 'created' the world in six days. In fact, what God 'created' was 'without form and void; and darkness was upon the face of the deep'. In other words, it was chaos. The six further acts of creation are: the division of light from darkness; the division of waters below from those above; the division of the land from the sea; the division of the day from the night; the making of birds for the air and fish for the sea; and the making of animals and man for the land. Most of Genesis, then, is not about creation at all. It tells of God imposing order onto chaos by dividing things from each other and putting everything into its right place. When Othello mentions 'Chaos', then, he imagines the undoing of Genesis – something so fundamentally against the will of God, and so destructive of the entire universe, that we could not exaggerate the cosmic size of the idea.

First, this image provokes a conventional response from the audience: the reference to chaos touches the audience's cultural conditioning, and we feel fear and horror at the idea of universal destruction. Second, Othello clearly feels the same way we do about chaos, so the image expresses a fundamental horror in his feelings, something so utterly destabilising that he compares it to 'Chaos'. So, the image helps us to understand Othello's feelings.

Also, Othello compares something entirely within himself – his love or lack of love for Desdemona – to something which embraces the whole universe. So this image connects different aspects of the play. Tragic experience within the hero is analogous to disturbance of the play's universe. The image, then, is part of the texture of the play, binding it together into a single whole, like a thread tying together the individual human being and the vastness around him. We can call this connecting effect of the image a 'vertical' connection, between the smaller, human aspects of the drama and the vaster and more abstract concepts of the idea-system.

Now look at these two images together. The idea that Desdemona is 'heaven' makes her crucial: if she is false, then 'heaven' is not real, but a mockery, and the whole order of the universe consequently collapses. The image that Othello not loving her brings 'Chaos' is another part of the same idea, therefore. If his love for her is absent, then the whole order of the universe inside him collapses. In this case, the two images from different times in the play contribute to a single, progressive revelation of Desdemona's significance to Othello: they are like two phrases from one poem, despite the fact that they are uttered in different dramatic contexts and that several minutes of complicated plot (Iago makes known his suspicions of her and Cassio) separate them. In the audience's mind, these two ideas connect with each other, and both contribute to a 'whole' understanding of Othello's tragic experience which is built up through a wide variety of scenes, actions and times. It can be useful to think of such connecting, growing and modifying images as a kind of poem, which you can analyse as a distinct 'horizontal' thread which passes behind the particulars of changing scenes in the plot of the play.

We have looked at two images from *Othello*, and found that they work as both 'vertical' and 'horizontal' threads weaving the play into a single entity. We used a description of the features of our first image to help us find the second. This method can be repeated, and you will find further examples which are part of the same connecting thread throughout the play. Some share all the same features as the image we first noticed; others may only share one feature. It is very rewarding to follow up all the connections you can find. The following are examples of further images in *Othello* which connect with the two we have analysed.

Later in the same scene, Othello compares the idea that Iago is slandering Desdemona to 'deeds to make heaven weep' because 'nothing canst thou to damnation add / Greater than that' (3, iii, 377–9). This reinforces the religious ideas with 'heaven' and 'damnation', suggesting that her falsity, and the false accusation of her, are equally horrific ideas. Then Othello compares himself to a vast and powerful natural force, 'the Pontic sea' (3, iii, 460), again magnifying his emotions. On the other hand, his image of 'yond marble heaven' (3, iii, 467) denotes a modification within him: heaven is no longer love and Desdemona, but is cold, hard and unchangeable, hence 'marble'. This change in the image-idea of heaven tells us a great deal about the change in Othello as he re-builds his shattered personality, and prepares to murder Desdemona. When Othello accuses Desdemona of adultery, he describes her supposed sin: 'Heaven stops the nose at it, and the moon winks' (4, ii, 79). By this time, Desdemona has been completely separated from 'heaven'. The 'marble heaven' Othello took as his mentor now disgustedly rejects Desdemona. So, a thread of 'heaven' images tells the story of Othello's developing, self-modifying personality.

On arriving in Cyprus, Othello sees his love as more vital than his life (2, i, 189–93) and imagines their meeting has the power to render natural chaos insignificant:

> If after every tempest come such calmness,
> May the winds blow, till they have waken'd death,
> And let the labouring bark climb hills of seas,
> Olympus-high, and duck again as low
> As hell's from heaven.
>
> > (*Othello*, 2, i, 185–9)

Notice that 'waken'd death', seas 'Olympus-high', and the reference to heaven and hell as absolute extremes all contribute to the same vision of Genesis being undone that we found in our second image. At the beginning of Act 2 the Second Gentleman introduced the idea that God's division of waters, land and sky is unmade by the chaotic storm: 'The chiding billow seems to pelt the clouds . . . / Seems to cast water on the burning bear, / And quench the guards of the ever-fixed pole' (2, i, 12–15). Thus, potential 'chaos' exists in the natural world of the play as well as within Othello, and in the play's cosmos. The 'vertical' connection of imagery which spans from private, individual emotion to encompass the play's universe, is powerful again in a further picture of catastrophic chaos, after Othello has killed Desdemona:

> Methinks it should be now a huge eclipse
> Of sun and moon, and that the affrighted globe
> Should yawn at alteration.
>
> > (*Othello*, 5, ii, 100–2)

These are only a few of the images which can be found that are clearly connected to the one we originally noticed ('then heaven mocks itself'). They show how richly woven the image-ideas of the play are; and they reinforce the points we found from our analysis. Images work to bind different aspects of the play into a single whole, both 'vertically' through layers of drama and meaning, and 'horizontally' behind the plot as the play is performed. The 'horizontal' thread shows images which, like phrases from a poem, can be cumulatively revealing if we analyse them together. Also, changes in the use of an image-idea can tell a story of their own which supplements and explains the natural story of the drama itself.

*   *   *

We now turn to *Hamlet*. In Chapter 3 we analysed the speech in which Hamlet decides to probe his uncle's guilt. He says:

> I'll tent him to the quick.
>   (*Hamlet*, 2, ii, 593)

Hamlet compares his uncle's sinful guilt to an open wound. His plot, to arrange that the players play 'something like the murder of my father' so that he can watch his uncle's reaction, is compared to searching and cleansing, or 'tenting', the wound. We can imagine the 'quick' to be Claudius's heart, the centre of life in his body. This image, then, is about probing beneath a skin and finding that the body is infected inside. The idea conveys a feeling of repulsion, associated with ideas of disease and gory foulness. This may help us to understand Hamlet's own feelings: he is repelled by sexuality (see his disgust at his own sexuality, expressed to Ophelia in Act 3, Scene i), and his own feeling of horror and disgust at probing the foulness of Claudius's sins is aptly conveyed by this image. In addition, the idea of looking beneath a 'fair' surface and finding corruption there connects with contradictions between appearances and reality in the play as a whole.

What are the features of this image, then? There is a military element in the idea of searching a wound, and the idea that there is infection beneath the surface has the structure of fair appearance hiding foul reality. Now we can look for other images which share these features. In the next scene both Polonius and the King use images in which a fair appearance covers corruption. Polonius says that 'with devotion's visage / And pious action we do sugar o'er / The devil himself' (3, i, 47–9), then Claudius describes 'The harlot's cheek, beautied with plast'ring art' and compares this to his 'deed' and his 'painted word' (3, i, 51–3). Polonius's image applies to religious hypocrisy in general, while the King applies the same moral to himself. So, these two image-ideas have a 'vertical' effect, linking the individual hypocrite to the hypocrisy which is rife in society. They are also both ironic. Polonius gives his opinion while advising Ophelia to give a false show of devotion; and Claudius remains a hypocrite, still speaking 'painted' words to the world. The King's image has the effect of confirming Hamlet's, which we heard only three pages before: if Hamlet 'tents' Claudius, he will find infection. So, these two images connect 'horizontally' and the image-ideas advance the story by first guessing and then revealing the existence of corruption beneath the surface.

The military suggestion in Hamlet's image is echoed by a further image of digging down beneath the surface. When Hamlet decides to out-plot his uncle he imagines doing so in these terms:

> For 'tis the sport to have the enginer
> Hoist with his own petard, and 't shall go hard
> But I will delve one yard below their mines
> And blow them at the moon.
> (*Hamlet*, 3, iv, 208–11)

Hamlet expresses some glee at the prospect of beating Claudius's strategies, calling it 'the sport'. Here, the underground workings are not infection but a potentially explosive danger; but Hamlet's intention to 'delve' more deeply reminds us of his decision to probe Claudius 'to the quick'. Both images, then, contribute to a recurrent idea of penetrating beneath the surface. Whether in relation to infection or deceit, this deep digging and searching is part of Hamlet's duty and mission throughout the play.

The image-idea of dirt or infection representing lust and sin also repeatedly occurs in the play. In the closet scene, for example, Hamlet promises to show Gertrude 'the inmost part' of herself. He imagines his mother and uncle 'honeying and making love / Over the nasty sty' (3, iv, 93–4) and calls her sin an act which 'takes off the rose / From the fair forehead of an innocent love / And sets a blister there' (3, iv, 42–4). Following the filthy 'sty' and diseased 'blister', Hamlet uses a metaphor identical to the first one we analysed:

> Mother, for love of grace,
> Lay not that flattering unction to your soul
> . . .
> It will but skin and film the ulcerous place,
> Whiles rank corruption, mining all within,
> Infects unseen.
> (*Hamlet*, 3, iv, 146–51)

The echo of probing Claudius's wound is unmistakable, and the audience associates these two ideas; also, the word 'mining' recalls the military again, yet the effect is ironic. The connection of these two images highlights the fact that Hamlet is not probing his uncle's sin, as he determined to do, but is 'tenting' his mother 'to the quick' instead. So, the story of this image reveals how Hamlet's actions have been diverted from what he originally intended.

Inside the individual – within the King and Queen – is a disease of corruption which must be probed and exposed, not covered over ('skin and film the ulcerous place') with new skin. Image-connections bind this personal level of analysis to society, as we noticed in Polonius's idea of 'devotion's visage'. In Hamlet's speeches, similar images expand the idea of infection to embrace the whole of the heavens, and the world. The firmament is 'but a foul and pestilent congregation of vapours' despite its fine appearance as 'this majestical roof fretted with golden fire' (2, ii, 300–3); and the world is possessed by 'things rank and gross in nature' (1, ii, 136). These ideas recur so regularly, indeed, that we can notice a further effect. The word 'rank', meaning foul-smelling and rotting, occurs frequently throughout the play: each time the word is uttered, it reminds us of infection-imagery and expresses Hamlet's anger and disgust. So the repeated use of 'rank' has a subsidiary effect like a trigger, supporting the images of corruption we have found, making the 'horizontal' thread of these images more continuous and substantial as a motif throughout the play.

*   *   *

In Chapter 1 we analysed the opening minutes of *Macbeth*, when the captain begins a speech:

> As whence the sun 'gins his reflection,
> Shipwracking storms and direful thunders break , . . .
>   (*Macbeth*, 1, ii, 25–6)

This image compares their victory over the rebels succeeded by a new attack from Norway, to storms following sunshine. The idea of huge forces of nature is added to our minds, and the immediate effect is to vividly convey the wildness and turbulence of the battle. However, there are two other elements in the audience's reaction to this image. First, the word 'Shipwracking' brings to mind natural forces causing disaster on the human scale. So, not only is the battle a turbulence as great as a natural storm, but we are reminded that human endeavours are puny in the face of overwhelming natural power. Second, the subject is a moment which seems to be lucky, a moment of victory, which turns out to be deceitful because suddenly there is a new threat. The image-idea reminds us that nature is unpredictable, and appearances (we remember proverbs about 'out of a clear sky') are deceptive.

This image brings a strong 'vertical' connection: the affairs of human beings are magnified, being likened to forces of nature; and we will find that this effect is common in *Macbeth*, a play in which forces both natural (for example, Birnam Wood coming to Dunsinane) and supernatural (the witches) play a prominent role in the affairs of humanity. The mention of storm and thunder here is particularly significant. In Scene i the witches met by thunder and lightning; and in Scene iii, following this extract, the setting is a heath with thunder. So, the recurrent, 'horizontally' connected metaphor, comparing human 'storms' to storms in external nature, is strongly underlined.

The Captain's comparison of battle and weather, then, is integrated into the drama in several ways. Now we want to find other images which display similar features. First, this image likens human broils to forces of nature, referring upwards in scale. Second, it suggests both helpless humanity ('Shipwracking') and a deceptive, fickle fate.

The unpredictable, quick-changing weather in the Captain's image is acted out in the play in the form of actual changes. For example, notice that Duncan describes the sweet air of Macbeth's castle when he arrives: 'This castle hath a pleasant seat; the air / Nimbly and sweetly recommends itself' (1, vi, 1–2); but in the morning Lenox reports a wild and omen-filled night: 'The night has been unruly . . . chimneys were blown down . . . lamentings heard i'th'air . . . the obscure bird clamour'd the livelong night' (2, iii, 53–9). So the Captain's image stands in the second scene of the play like a prophecy. It conveys a sense of insecurity to the audience, which prepares us for the Macbeths' hypocrisy about the murder. It also presages later shocks and changes, such as Malcolm's pretended confession of vice to Macduff, and the revelations in Act 5 which show how Macbeth was misled by the fiend 'that lies like truth' (5, v, 44). It is therefore part of a thread that begins with the apparent contradiction 'Fair is foul' (1, i, 11).

In Act 3, Scene iv Macbeth contrasts Banquo's Ghost to the strongest of wild beasts: 'Approach thou like the rugged Russian bear, / The arm'd rhinoceros, or th'Hyrcan tiger; / Take any shape but that . . .' (99–101). This idea refers us to wild nature again, so we are reminded of the actual and figurative storms of Act 1; but in this case the image-idea of natural force is less terrifying than its referent. The ideas build a hierarchy of scale, therefore. We can say that these images lead us up to the horrors of supernatural things via nature's power, which exceeds Man's power but which is itself exceeded by the supernatural. This point is further underlined in Act 4, Scene i, when Macbeth lists a series of natural disasters culminating in worldwide destruction, which are less important than the witches' prophetic knowledge:

Though you untie the winds, and let them fight

> Against the Churches; though the yesty waves
> Confound and swallow navigation up;
> Though bladed corn be lodg'd, and trees blown down;
> Though castles topple on their warders' heads;
> Though palaces, and pyramids, do slope
> Their heads to their foundations; though the treasure
> Of Nature's germens tumble all together,
> Even till destruction sicken, answer me . . .
>
> (*Macbeth*, 4, i, 52–60)

These disasters are like those the Captain referred to, the destruction of all human endeavours ('castles', 'palaces', 'pyramids') by a force of nature – the wind. Macbeth's picture of disasters reaches absolute proportions, however, in the waste of all procreation 'Even till destruction sicken'. This idea would bring biblical images to the audience's mind, reminding them of destruction at the end of the world, the Apocalypse; and the lines 'though the yesty waves / Confound and swallow navigation up' have overtones of chaos, the original confusion and darkness Othello found so terrifying. So, in this version of the image, Macbeth goes further. The terror of Banquo's Ghost eclipsed wild beasts; but the witches' foreknowledge is depicted as transcending the whole universe, including hints of the beginning and end of the world. We are lifted to the supernatural, using nature's power as a stage of comparison on the way. At the same time, the image conveys the evil and madness of Macbeth's distorted state of mind. These ideas create a clear 'vertical' connection in the form of a hierarchy of terror and power. This works both as a ladder by which the audience can ascend to the intensity of Macbeth's fears, and as a measure to reveal the extent of his evil madness.

This vertical thread in the imagery of *Macbeth* is frequent and persistent. We have found images where the comparison leads us upwards in scale, from human to worldwide to supernatural levels of reference. There are also important ideas which the imagery reduces to human scale. When meditating the murder of Duncan, Macbeth personifies Justice, 'this even-handed Justice / Commends th'ingredience of our poison'd chalice / To our own lips' (1, vii, 10–12) and imagines 'Pity, like a naked new-born babe' (1, vii, 21); and in Act

2, Scene ii he cries '"Macbeth does murder sleep",—the innocent Sleep' (2, ii, 35). So the imagery simultaneously turns abstract ideas into immediate and concrete things, and connects human events with the all-embracing range of the supernatural. The vertical thread of images, unifying vast and small in the play, works in both directions.

*   *   *

We now move on to *King Lear*. In Chapter 6 we met these lines from the Fool:

> Nuncle, give me an egg, and I'll give thee two crowns . . . Why, after I have cut the egg i'th'middle and eat up the meat, the two crowns of the egg.
>
> (*King Lear*, 1, iv, 152–6)

The Fool compares Lear's division of his kingdom and abdication of power to cutting an egg and eating the inside, so that only two halves of the shell are left. The pun on 'crown' (symbol of royalty and half-shell) explains the relevance of the image-idea to Lear's actions. Later in the speech 'crown' gains a third meaning: 'thou hadst little wit in thy bald crown . . .' (l.159). This image has a prominent 'vertical' function, the great being compared to the little: the catastrophic division of the kingdom which brings chaos and horrors during the play, and the loss of power which causes Lear's personal crisis, are compared to a childish trick with a small, everyday thing – an egg. The immediate effect is bathos, pointing out the comedy in that such a powerful man should be so foolish. The idea connects with Kent's objections in Act 1, Scene i, and Goneril's and Regan's comments on their father's behaviour; it adds a derisory example to our store of brief, pithy criticisms of Lear's error. So this image-idea joins an already-established dramatic thread. The interesting point is that this thread of criticisms is compiled both by Lear's friends (Kent and the Fool) and his enemies (Goneril and Regan).

The Fool's image has many more connections than these,

however. The next stage of analysing this image has already been done, in Chapter 6. We found several related images, including: 'thou hast pared thy wit o'both sides, and left nothing i'th'middle' (1, iv, 183–4), which is another image from the Fool of food being peeled and left empty; Lear's ironic 'part this coronet between you', which unconsciously highlights the uselessness of half a crown (it will fall off the side of your head!); and Lear's and Cordelia's exchange about 'nothing' when she first defies him. Notice that we arrived at these connections using our standard method. The Fool's image is of something with an outer covering being split and emptied (so it connects with 'pared thy wit'); the pun on 'crown' relates it to Lear's division of his kingdom (so it connects with 'part this coronet'); and it is an image of emptiness (so it connects with 'nothing'). There are many similar images. For example: in the same scene the Fool finds a third kind of food that leaves an empty shell after eating, when he points at Lear and says 'That's a shealed peascod' (1, iv, 197); at lines 126–32 the Fool and Lear have an exchange about 'nothing'; and at 1, v, 25–30 the Fool riddles about oysters and snails in their shells. In this last case, the shell stands for Lear's kingly power which he gave 'away to his daughters' leaving 'his horns without a case'. These threads of imagery are relatively easy to trace through the play, and they work to highlight its unity. They indicate to us how different elements of the drama are all relevant to the whole.

Something else also happens to this image-idea, however. Let us find the most abstract description of the idea, as this will give us the widest possible reference to related effects. The Fool imagines a shell broken, with emptiness, lack of substance inside, an empty or witless head. By association, then, it is possibly a broken head, emptied of what it once held. Let us pursue the idea of something splitting or broken.

Gloucester begins the idea by referring to 'the bond crack'd 'twixt son and father' in his speech about the disorder of the times (1, ii, 105). Before going out into the storm, Lear says:

> . . . but this heart
> Shall break into a hundred thousand flaws

> Or ere I'll weep. O Fool! I shall go mad.
> (*King Lear*, 2, iv, 282–4)

The material from which Lear's heart is made is not specified, but it must be hard and brittle to shatter into 'a hundred thousand flaws', and we may well associate this with the eggshell in the Fool's original joke. So, the audience receives a connection which makes the original idea grow: splitting a kingdom and being empty of power is analogous to breaking or shattering Lear, who will then be empty of 'wit' or mad. Simultaneously, the idea of shattering next to the idea of madness reminds us of the Fool's 'thou hadst little wit in thy bald crown', which in turn refers our minds to the Fool's suggestion that Lear should wear his 'coxcomb', a hat to signify the foolishness or emptiness of his head (see 1, iv, 99–107).

The idea of a person breaking or collapsing is also not new to us. Lear's line is the first to harness the brittleness of a shell and the shattering of heart and reason; but the Fool has already riddled that 'one's nose stands i'th'middle on's face' in order to 'keep one's eyes of either side's nose' (see 1, iv, 19–22), suggesting comically that if it were not for the nose, the rest of the head would collapse inwards.

Now look at Lear's speech to the storm, at the start of Act 3, Scene ii:

> Blow, winds, and crack your cheeks! rage! blow!
> You cataracts and hurricanoes, spout
> Till you have drench'd our steeples, drown'd the cocks!
> You sulph'rous and thought-executing fires,
> Vaunt-couriers of oak-cleaving thunderbolts,
> Singe my white head! And thou, all-shaking thunder,
> Strike flat the thick rotundity o'th'world!
> Crack Nature's moulds, all germens spill at once
> That makes ingrateful man!
> (*King Lear*, 3, ii, 1–9)

I have quoted this speech in full because there is a wealth of metaphors which illustrate the connections we are pursuing. We will begin with the idea of breaking or splitting. This occurs in 'crack your cheeks', 'oak-cleaving thunderbolts' and 'Crack Nature's moulds'. These three separate metaphors set up an echo in the audience's mind which includes Lear's 'heart shall break', the Fool's eggshell, and Gloucester's 'crack'd' filial bond. However, these breakages are not all the same: 'crack your cheeks' is force breaking out under extreme stress; 'oak-cleaving' is a symbol of strength (the oak) being split by elemental force; and 'Crack Nature's moulds' is a vision of destruction which refers, with other parts of the speech, to the Apocalypse or a return of chaos. In the first case, wild destructive winds escape; then the hard and strong oak is shattered; finally, all creative life spills out, wasted, leaving 'Nature's moulds' empty like the Fool's eaten egg. Notice, then, that we are subjected to a bewildering variety of versions of cracking or breaking. Negative destruction (the winds) and all positive things of value ('all germens') escape when the shell is broken; the 'shell' is variously something protecting Lear (eggshell, rind of a fruit, peascod, the oysters' and snails' shells, Lear's head) and Lear himself (his glass 'heart', the oak); and the power Lear gave away, leaving himself defenceless, is variously the empty middle (of the egg, fruit, peascod, Nature's moulds) and the protective shell (of oyster or snail, or the 'house' the Fool punningly likens to intelligence and a helmet at 3, ii, 25, moments after Lear's speech to the storm). This variety of actions in the imagery reflects the dramatic situation: there is a real storm, which Lear understands as an attack upon him but which he also willingly embraces, urging it to destroy the world as well. Therefore, Lear is both the victim and the origin of the storm's energy. The images in this speech complicate each other and set up reverberations in the audience's mind that make the play a poetic whole. However, their significance constantly changes, turns around and grows multiple branches until the echo they create for us is as sonorous and complex as possible.

We have looked at ideas of 'breaking', but there are two other forms of destruction in this speech: water and floods are denoted by 'spout', 'drench'd' and 'drown'd', and 'Singe' suggests destruction by fire. The speech as a whole reminds us of biblical stories of destruction, such as the Flood, so its effect is comparable to that of Othello's and Macbeth's versions of universal catastrophe. How does this develop the Fool's joke about an eggshell? First, the 'vertical' effect is enhanced because the image works on tiny and vast scales:

an eggshell can be the emblem of a person, a kingdom and the world. Second, the 'horizontal' effect brings together several strands of ideas about destruction. Here, Shakespeare has made a kind of 'crossroads' or 'crux' of metaphors by triggering a number of associations and echoes that have been established during the play so far, and bringing them together. In terms of the 'horizontal' connections in the play, then, this speech feels like an acceleration. Since the audience's mind is prompted to travel to numerous earlier moments in a very short time (in other words, our associative thoughts are unusually active during this speech), the speech gives an impression of heightened experience. It is as if an extent of time is compressed into a moment. A useful way to think of this dramatic event is to call it 'inclusive', since it includes so much of the play's time up to that point, includes the greatest and the least, the highest and lowest, comedy and tragedy, suffering and wrath, breaking, flood and fire, and so on.

Finally, we should notice that the convex shape of eggshell, rind, peascod, snail-and-oyster-shell and Lear's own 'bald crown' has been used to marry individual and universal destruction, by appearing in successive lines. Lear sees the elemental fury of the storm as an attack. It is simultaneously an attack on himself and on the world, and these are connected by the similar shapes we envisage in 'Singe my white head!' and 'Strike flat the thick rotundity o'th'world!' (ll.6–7).

Our analysis of imagery in *King Lear* has introduced further complexity to our understanding of the network of images which texture a Shakespearian tragedy. Image-ideas are reversed or modified during the play, creating references which compare in both directions. Also, image-ideas from one established thread borrow a single attribute from another thread, as 'rotundity' suddenly connects the thread of empty shells and heads with that of universal, apocalyptic destruction. When we want to pursue the development of metaphors to this level of detail, we begin by framing a description of the image-idea that is as wide and abstract as possible. In this case, we reduced the Fool's complex idea about an egg to the simple idea of 'breaking' or 'splitting'; and in our final point we made use of the idea of 'roundness'. The more we think in these generalised, abstract terms, using concepts of shape or the structure of metaphors, the more our analysis will lead us to appreciate imagery as a subtle and volatile dramatic story in its own right – part of the poetic fabric of the play.

*   *   *

It is worth recording two general thoughts which have arisen out of this chapter's studies. First, we have found similar images in different dictions. For example, we find that the comic riddling of the Fool from *King Lear* produces the image of an egg, essentially expressing the same image-idea as Lear in his most forceful speeches (see 'crack Nature's moulds'). The unifying effect of imagery thus works between different styles, as well as having the 'horizontal' effect of connecting ideas that we have discussed.

Second, we cannot help noticing that this investigation of imagery has led us to three powerful expressions of a fear of chaos, in three of the four tragedies; that we have also become involved in contrasts between appearances and reality in discussion of all four of the plays; and that many of the images we have found are comparisons of different scales, or highlight the irrational (see 'heaven mocks itself' from *Othello* or the Fool's egg from *King Lear*). So imagery is related to the central tragic themes we summarised at the start of this chapter.

Conclusions

1. The 'image-idea' is an idea added to the literal action of the play. Images work to produce an immediate dramatic effect, such as conveying the character's emotions vividly to the audience.
2. Images recur within the play, and occur within a context of other imagery often closely comparable or structurally related. There is a whole 'shape' or structure of imagery, therefore, which cuts across boundaries in the play's plot such as different characters or scenes.
3. Images often recur in a modified form, or develop new attributes

by appearing in ironic and unexpected contexts. The 'image-idea' is not static, therefore: it can have a developing 'story' of its own. The effect produced by this linear or 'horizontal' development of images is to set up and then recurrently play upon reactions and associations in our minds as we sit in the audience. Our responses are provoked, modified and enlarged as the thread of a particular 'image-idea' is developed in the play.

4. The play as a whole has a unifying structure in the dramatic and poetic identity of the individual and the universe. Imagery connects events on the human scale with the vast or 'cosmic' scale, making a 'vertical' tie which is a prominent part of the play's unifying structure.

5. Many images suggest that the character externalises personal qualities, and attributes them to God or the Gods. In this sense imagery in the tragedies often seems to imply that Man creates God out of his own needs. The imagery helps us to see the universe as an enlargement of personal experience. This often takes the form of natural and divine powers either invoked by Man in his aid, or imagined as adversaries.

6. The tragic 'universe' is one limit of space into which the tragic experience reaches. The pervasive conflicts we have repeatedly noticed are those between order and chaos, appearance and reality, destruction and creation. The imagery carries these into different contexts, showing them to be present in the cosmos, as in the natural world, as within Man.

Methods of Analysis

We chose one image from each play, from extracts we had already analysed. Then we followed these steps:

1. Define the comparison by saying what is being compared to what.

2. Describe the immediate dramatic purpose and effect of the image. To do this, think about how the image-idea helps our understanding of the character's experience, or expresses some

part of a theme. Ask what the added 'image-idea' does to us, in the audience.

3. Describe the features of the image. Do this by ignoring the complex direct relationship between the 'image-idea' and what it is compared to, and by finding general or abstract terms to describe it. For example, we ignored the details of Claudius's guilt, and Hamlet's plot to probe by using a play to provoke his uncle's reaction. We focused on the general idea of 'infection' instead.

4. Find other images which have the same features, or one of the same features, as the one you first chose. When you have found further examples in this way, describe how they affect the audience. Think about how the audience is reminded of the previous image, and the differences between the contexts; and ask whether the new example adds to or modifies the audience's feelings.

5. Expect to find that the kind of image you are studying becomes connected with other threads of imagery in the play, perhaps because one feature of an image occurs in common with a different idea.

6. Describe the effect of the imagery you have studied, as part of the whole play's texture. In doing this, think of how the image works 'vertically' and 'horizontally' to link together different elements and different times in the play.

While studying imagery in this way, you will find yourself revealing new insights into characters, themes, irony and the structure of ideas in the play.

Suggested Work

You may pick any other image which occurs in a passage you are studying, and research it throughout the play using the method suggested above. The method is just as rewarding if you pick a word which is of importance in the play you are studying, and select a number of occasions when that word is used. Here are some suggestions which come from passages we have studied in this book:

In *Othello* you could start with the metaphor of Desdemona as a half-wild hawk (3, iii, 264–7; see Chapter 3) and look at other images concerning birds and animals. If you wish to study a prominent word in the play, try 'honest', the word so often and ironically used to describe Iago, and begin at 'This fellow's of exceeding *honesty*' (3, iii, 262) which we also discussed in Chapter 3.

In *Hamlet* you could begin with Hamlet's 'like a whore' (2, ii, 581; see Chapter 3) and look at images elsewhere in the play which refer to whores, prostitution and bawds. If you wish to study a prominent word in the play, try 'dreaded' (1, i, 28; see Chapter 1), and look for 'dread', 'fear', and derivatives such as 'fearful', 'frighted' and so on, which occur frequently in the play.

In *Macbeth* you could begin with 'Put rancours in the vessel of my peace' (3, i, 66; see Chapter 3) and look at other images which refer to poisons in drink and food, or cups and other vessels. If you wish to study prominent words in the play, try 'water', 'rain' and 'sea', beginning with 'rain' at 1, i, 2, and tracing these words through the rest of the play.

In *King Lear* you could begin with 'Robes and furr'd gowns hide all' (4, vi, 163; see Chapter 5) and seek further images referring to clothing. If you wish to study a prominent word in the play, try 'nature' (which occurs twice in 2, iv, 264; see Chapter 3) and trace 'nature', 'natural', 'unnatural' and other derivatives through other parts of the play.

General Conclusions to Part I

1. There is an experience which, for convenience, we have called 'the tragic experience'. It is dramatically conveyed as an area defined by what it surpasses, or a gulf between two sides of a conflict. It is expressed by largely inadequate reactions to it, or attempts to convey it which dislocate sense and language. Typically it attacks sanity, order and civilisation.

2. The 'tragic world' or 'tragic cosmos' has characteristics and a structure common to all the plays. In particular, an ascendancy of a chaos – whether moral, emotional, brutal or sexual – which shatters order and sense.

3. The protagonist struggles in an intellectual and emotional relationship with these forces, which are portrayed as within the hero: the hero is a microcosm of the tragic 'cosmos'.

4. The audience's experience is dramatically formed to mirror that of the protagonist. Even where 'empathy' is problematic (for example, in *Othello* and *Macbeth*) the drama subjects us to the same structure and involves us in exploring the realisations that the main character encounters.

5. Studying the four tragedies leaves us with a rich understanding of unresolved conflicts, and dilemmas on human, social and political, and philosophical levels. It does not reveal 'Shakespeare's solution' to any of these problems. A search for 'Shakespeare's solution' would be in vain.

6. Dynamic rather than static ideas and approaches to these plays bring rewards.

PART 2

THE CONTEXT AND THE CRITICS

8

The Tragedies in Shakespeare's Works

How many tragedies did Shakespeare write, and why have we chosen to study only four of them? Shakespeare's plays were published together for the first time seven years after his death, in the First Folio of 1623. Twelve plays are included as 'Tragedies' in the First Folio. *Troilus and Cressida* was withdrawn and then re-inserted during printing, and is now more commonly grouped with 'problem plays'. *Cymbeline* is clearly not a tragedy. It belongs with the late 'romance' plays or tragi-comedies. *Julius Caesar*, *Titus Andronicus*, *Coriolanus* and *Antony and Cleopatra* are chronicles of Roman history, but they could all make a claim to be 'tragic' plays. *Romeo and Juliet* and *Timon of Athens* are arguably tragedies, although *Romeo and Juliet* was written in the early 1590s, ten years before the earliest of the others, and is a different kind of play, being a double love-tragedy. The remaining four, *Hamlet*, *Othello*, *Macbeth* and *King Lear* are the subject of this volume.

There is no theoretical reason why we chose to treat the four 'Great Tragedies' and ignore *Timon of Athens* in this book. It was done for practical reasons, to keep the size down. Each of the chapters in Part I analyses an extract from each play, and it would be over-complicated and unwieldy to include a fifth play. The book would have become cumbersome, longer and heavier; and *Timon* has no claim to inclusion that would outweigh this disadvantage. *Timon* is more rarely set and studied on English literature courses, and is much less frequently performed in the theatre, than the other four plays. Many editors believe that the text is either another dramatist's revision of Shakespeare, Shakespeare's revision of another dramatist, or a rough draft or 'unfinished sketch', in any case.

Classifying Shakespeare's plays brings up a number of controversies and uncertainties, so much so that there is a group of plays now commonly called 'problem plays' largely because they are difficult to place in any of the other categories. A 'tragedy' is almost equally difficult to define. By the time we have read Aristotle's *Poetics*, definitions from Shakespeare's contemporaries, and a number of modern critics (see Chapters 9 and 10 for some discussion of this point), we find there is so little agreement on the issue that we are almost back to where we began: a tragedy is a play that ends in disaster or death.

'Classifying' the plays is only a means to an end, however. We want to understand how Shakespeare's works developed during his writing life, because it is useful to have a grasp of where the four tragedies we are studying fit in. It is best to begin with a chronological list of the plays, as far as the literary historians and editors have been able to work out their dates of composition:

1589	Henry 6 Part 1	History
1590	Henry 6 Part 2	History
1591	Henry 6 Part 3	History
1592	Richard 3	History
1593	The Comedy of Errors	Comedy
1593	Titus Andronicus	Roman Chronicle
1594	The Taming of the Shrew	Comedy
1594	Love's Labours Lost	Comedy
1595	The Two Gentlemen of Verona	Comedy
1595	Romeo and Juliet	Tragedy
1595	Richard 2	History
1596	A Midsummer Night's Dream	Comedy
1596	King John	History
1597	The Merchant of Venice	Comedy
1597	Henry 4 Part 1	History
1598	Much Ado About Nothing	Comedy
1598	Henry 5	History

1598	Henry 4 Part 2	History
1599	Julius Caesar	Roman Tragedy
1599	As You Like It	Comedy
1599	The Merry Wives of Windsor	Comedy
1600	Twelfth Night	Comedy
1601	**Hamlet**	Tragedy
1602	Troilus and Cressida	Problem Play
1602	All's Well That Ends Well	Problem Play
1603	Measure for Measure	Problem Play
1604	**Othello**	Tragedy
1604	Timon of Athens	Tragedy
1605	**King Lear**	Tragedy
1606	**Macbeth**	Tragedy
1607	Antony and Cleopatra	Roman Tragedy
1608	Coriolanus	Roman Chronicle
1609	Pericles, Prince of Tyre	Tragi-comedy
1609	Cymbeline	Tragi-comedy
1610	The Winter's Tale	Tragi-comedy
1611	The Tempest	Tragi-comedy
1612	Henry 8	History

A forest of scraps of evidence and historical controversies lies behind this list of the supposed dates of composition of Shakespeare's plays. Experts use internal evidence (references to current events in the text of the play; analysis of Shakespeare's verse-development; references, in the text, to other publications whose dates we know) and external evidence (records or accounts of performances; entries in the *Stationers' Register*; dates on Quarto title-pages in the case of the few plays that were separately published) when they date the plays. For most of the plays, there is evidence that places them within a slot of two or three years, but nothing concrete to help us be more precise than that. The 'classification' given in the right-hand column is also a controversial matter, although the majority of Shakespeare's plays do belong clearly within one of the classifications or another. The above table will be good enough to serve us, however. We only want to draw general conclusions from it, so many of the detailed arguments between scholars need not worry us.

Certain points are obvious. Of the first eighteen plays, the only tragedy is *Romeo and Juliet*, which sits alone at that time, surrounded by comedies and histories. The final six plays are not tragedies: from 1607 until his death, Shakespeare wrote tragi-comedy and history. There is comedy almost everywhere, but no comedy between 1601 (when we think *Hamlet* was written) and 1606 (when *Macbeth* was written). Those five years are filled with the four 'Great Tragedies' we are studying in this book, together with an unfinished or 'sketched' tragedy (*Timon of Athens*) and the three darkest problem plays. In other words, the writing from those five years is filled with unremitting trouble and seriousness. In this chapter we want to understand, if we can, why a man who regularly wrote delightful comedies up to the turn of the century (when we suppose *Twelfth Night* was composed) should be overtaken by the critical and disillusioned preoccupations about every aspect of life and eternity that fill the plays of 1601–06?

We know hardly anything about Shakespeare's life. Each minor incident that has come down to us, through either documents or rumour, has given rise to frenzied and far-fetched speculations. For example, the story of a young Shakespeare's brush with the law for deer-stealing at Stratford rests on an anecdote from Nicholas Rowe's *Life*, dated 1709, which is corroborated by others who must have obtained the story from local gossip. This story has not only been used to explain Shakespeare leaving Stratford to join a London company of players (but there is no evidence that his move was as simple or sudden as this: we know nothing of his life between 1584 and about 1592); it has also been said to have inspired the characterisation and action in several scenes in several plays where local 'Justices' are satirised. It is much more likely, of course, that Shakespeare had a healthily sceptical attitude towards the law and had met or heard about quite a number of ignorant 'Justices'. Any perceptive person will laugh at self-important, pompous ignorance. Meanwhile, the story about deer-stealing itself is like most of the other information we have: it says hardly anything about Shakespeare the individual. It could have happened to anyone. What we know from the records of his life also has this 'anonymous' quality. Shakespeare lived nearly fifty-two years. He had a wife and three children. He was probably not always faithful to his wife. He made quite a good living as a playwright and actor, and acquired a reasonable amount of property which he left in a will at his death. Most contemporary reports suggest that he was a pleasant-looking man, and his manner was probably charming. In the five years leading to the 'tragic' period in his writing, Shakespeare's son Hamnet died (1596) and his father died (1601), although John Shakespeare's death was in September, probably after the composition of *Hamlet*. We do not know how these deaths affected the playwright's outlook on life, however. This summary could be the biography of many thousands of the men of that time. The only unusual fact is that he worked in the theatre, but we knew that already.

So we will not find the answer to our question about the 'tragic' five years by studying Shakespeare's life. What we know of his life was ordinary, and everything about him that was extraordinary we know from his writings. If we are to find out why he wrote with such a clouded outlook during those five years, we have to turn to his writings themselves for a hint. We will not find a biographical answer, of course, because what we are doing is circular: we are looking in his writing to explain something in his writing. We only aim to construct some understanding of movement or development in his writing, so that we have a fuller grasp of where the tragedies stand within his whole life's work.

The structure of a play can be thought of as in three parts: exposition, complication and resolution. Exposition introduces the characters and circumstances. Complication, the main middle part of the plot, consists of machinations by a villain, misunderstandings, secrets, quarrels, civil wars and all the other elements which prevent the characters from reaching a solution to their problems. Resolution is the final part of the play. It solves the problems of 'complication' either happily or disastrously. In a comedy, the solution is happy and typically brings about marriages between the characters. The dramatic effect – the entertainment of comedy – relies on the audience sharing the characters' happiness at the end, not troubled by ambiguous thoughts and feelings. It follows that the 'complications' of the plot should be 'comic', or light-hearted, themselves. For example, in *A Midsummer Night's Dream*, the complications arise out of a quarrel between Oberon and Titania, and the mischievous use of a magic love-charm. The quarrel is only a temporary threat, for they can be reconciled: the love-charm is easily removed by the same magic that laid it on. So, resolution of all the characters' difficulties is always possible, and there is no villain in the play. In *Much Ado About Nothing*, another comedy, there is a villain, Sir John the Bastard, but his badness is never allowed to disturb the fun of the play. In Act 1 he declares his character: 'though I cannot be said to be a flattering honest man, it must not be denied but I am a plain-dealing villain' (1, iii, 23–5). His dominant characteristics are discontent and envy, throughout the play; and at the end we hear that he has run away as his villainy has been discovered. Benedick ends the play with the assertion that Don John's villainy cannot distract us from our pleasure in the marriages of two couples: 'Think not on him till tomorrow. I'll devise thee brave punishments for him. Strike up, pipers!' (5, iv, 122–4). Notice that even punishing the evildoer will be fun: the punishments will be 'brave' and we feel no compunction at all for Don John. These two plays are typical of the comedies, and underline the point that the resolution at the end of a comedy cannot afford to be troubled by disturbing complexity or moral dilemmas.

In 1597 Shakespeare wrote *The Merchant of Venice*. The villain in this comedy is Shylock the Jew. At first glance his wicked plot, to kill Antonio by forcing the law to award him a pound of flesh, makes him a heartless villain. We should feel no regret when he is outsmarted and punished at the end, and the happy ending brings two weddings and sets Antonio free. It should be an unclouded pleasure for the audience. In short, this should be a delightful comedy; but it is not. Shylock's persecution at the hands of Venice's Christians, and his eloquence when he pleads his common humanity, are too powerful to be forgotten at the end of the play. Shylock is not a simple, two-dimensional villain like Don John from *Much Ado*. Here is a sample of his complaint:

> Hath not a Jew eyes? Hath not a Jew hands, organs, dimensions, senses, affections, passions?—fed with the same food, hurt with the

same weapons, subject to the same diseases, healed by the same means, warmed and cooled by the same winter and summer as a Christian is? If you prick us, do we not bleed? If you tickle us, do we not laugh? If you poison us, do we not die? And if you wrong us, shall we not revenge? If we are like you in the rest, we will resemble you in that. If a Jew wrong a Christian, what is his humility? Revenge! If a Christian wrong a Jew, what should his sufferance be by Christian example? Why revenge!

(3, i, 52–60)

Shylock's justification rests upon persuasive logic. His assertion of human equality rests upon undeniable truths: Jews and Christians are equally subject to wounding, death, the seasons, and so on. Shylock uses the word 'humility' with a withering weight of irony. This attack upon Christian hypocrisy has a tone of outraged, exasperated passion beyond anything Don John said or could say.

The Christians punish Shylock in the end, by depriving him of his money. They force him to give half to his daughter, who has robbed him and run away with a Christian, the other half to Antonio, and they force him to become a Christian. He leaves the stage saying 'I pray you give me leave to go from hence. / I am not well' (4, i, 390–1). The audience does not feel 'well' either, because we find the issues of persecution and revenge, and the justice meted out by a Christian court, morally unsettling. It is reasonable to deduce that Shylock's character has become too serious a 'complication' for pure comedy: he has become too complex and affecting, and his point of view is too eloquently dramatised. On the other hand, the 'resolution' has not been adjusted: it is a simple 'comic' resolution where the villain is merely damned and punished.

Twelfth Night was apparently written in 1600, the year before *Hamlet*. In this comedy a similar problem arises in the character of Malvolio, who is tricked and made the butt of a cruel practical joke, although much of the trickery makes us laugh and Malvolio does not possess the power to move us accorded to Shylock. The 'resolution' at the end of *Twelfth Night*, however, does take account of the problem: the simplicity of the earlier comedies would not be sufficient to satisfy the audience, and in the middle of their happiness, speeding to their weddings, the two dominant figures pause to solve the unfinished difficulty of Malvolio. Olivia gives a sympathetic judgement of him, saying 'He hath been most notoriously abused'; and the Duke raises the prospect of a future reconciliation: 'Pursue him, and entreat him to a peace' (5, i, 365 & 366).

This discussion of four comedies suggests that Shakespeare was reaching the limitations of comic form. This happened particularly in *The Merchant of Venice*, where serious and insoluble issues arise from the persecution of Shylock. I do not suggest that Shakespeare's comedies were 'out of control': after all, the date we have for *Much Ado* is 1598. We have noticed, however, that there is a kind of subject-matter, and a fluent passion in its expression, which seem to disturb a comedy. We could say that Shylock is a potentially tragic character, living in a world he perceives as unjust, suffering deep emotional pain, and reacting to this with the destructive motive of revenge. This is a brief, simplified discussion. A more thorough study of Shakespeare's development would also look at his dramatic style (for example, to show that Shylock's fluency conveys waves of passion, and the writing is in a free form in contrast to the patterned, formal verse we find in most of, say, *Love's Labours Lost*), and would examine other elements of other comedies, showing that there are potentially tragic elements in most of the comedies (for example, in *Much Ado About Nothing* we would examine Claudio, whose cruel self-righteousness in accusing the girl he supposedly loves is shocking). We could say that Shakespeare explored the limits of comedy, in a variety of different ways.

The early history plays turn on the characters of the King and his nobles. For example, in *Richard 3* the audience is fascinated by the King's cruelty: it is a psychologically convincing and emotionally disturbing spectacle, but it is a one-man spectacle where Richard himself holds our attention throughout the play. Such history plays bring a certain view of 'history' to life on stage: that the health of the country depends on the characters of kings and those in power. Richmond puts this view clearly in his description of England in the Wars of the Roses:

> England hath long been mad, and scarr'd herself:
> The brother blindly shed the brother's blood;

The father rashly slaughter'd his own son;
The son, compell'd, been butcher to the sire.
All this divided York and Lancaster—
Divided, in their dire division.

(5, v, 23–8)

The sense of this is: when two noble families fight, their battle has direct and disastrous consequences for the whole of the country. So, in this simple view, famous people make history happen.

In about 1597, the same year that apparently produced *The Merchant of Venice*, Shakespeare wrote the first part of *Henry 4*. In this play the reigning King does not have the dominant part. His son Hal, a cynical Prince of Wales, has drinking, whoring and thieving companions. They occupy quite a large amount of the play's time. In particular, there is Sir John Falstaff, a clever but gluttonous drunkard who expresses cynical views about politics and war. To show how much Shakespeare's view of history in this play differs from that dramatised in *Richard 3*, we only have to look at the scene where Falstaff recruits soldiers for the King's army. The King has given Falstaff a licence to recruit. Falstaff abuses this, corruptly accepting bribes from those who can afford to pay him, and filling the army with beggars, cripples, the mad and homeless wanderers instead. When challenged for having recruited such pitiful specimens, Falstaff replies: 'food for powder, food for powder, they'll fill a pit as well as better' (4, ii, 63–4). This remark – and many others from Falstaff – shows that the simple view of history has been exploded. He implies that a soldier's only purpose is to be killed; and his actions make a mockery of the King's supposed power. In this play, then, history becomes more complicated, involving ordinary people, and the play enters into a debate which questions the reality of honour, politics or power.

The themes raised in *Henry 4* put a debate on stage about the nature of society, and about the complicated processes that make 'historic' or 'political' events happen. It is reasonable to see this growth of new themes leading to the tragedies out of the history plays, with their structural dependance on a central figure. All four of the Great Tragedies can be read as challenging dramatisations of the nature of power, developing Falstaff's themes on a larger scale. So, in both comedies and histories, we can find strain or a potential conflict between new, disturbing subject-matter and the conventional dramatic form. The proper vehicle for this subject-matter was tragedy. It seems reasonable to suppose that Shakespeare's ideas and feelings, as they developed, made a period of tragic writing increasingly likely throughout the second half of the 1590s.

We must still beware of inventing a biography for Shakespeare: we do not know why these thoughts and emotions came to him. However, we can discern that they did; and we can see that they demanded a new vehicle – tragedy – outside his favourite dramatic forms of comedy and history.

9

The Context of the Tragedies

This chapter discusses Shakespeare's tragedies as they relate to the social and historical moment when they were written. Our discussion is deliberately brief, since the main purpose of this book is Part I, where we analyse the texts. If, after reading this chapter, you want to explore the historical context in more detail, look up the specialised books mentioned in 'Further Reading'. The points discussed in this chapter are general observations.

The Tragedies and their Audience

First, it seems that Elizabethan and Jacobean plays were political events in a way that does not happen today. A large popular audience saw Shakespeare's plays; the educated class in the capital discussed them; and they were likely to be performed at court in the presence of the King and other nobles (*Othello* and *King Lear* were certainly performed at the court of King James). In fact, a play could reach every sector of society from the greatest to the least; and this made the theatre an influential medium. Only television occupies a comparable position in the modern world. Shakespeare's company was called the Lord Chamberlain's Men, and re-named the King's Men only days after James came to the throne. They were a prominent company, and their plays attracted a great deal of public and royal attention. This point about the political importance of plays is demonstrated by the performance of *Richard 2* on 7 February 1601, the day before Essex's failed rebellion against Queen Elizabeth. This performance was specially ordered and paid for by Essex's faction, in the hope that the sight of a King being deposed on stage would drum up support for the rebellion: they planned to depose Elizabeth the following day. The acting company suffered some displeasure from the Queen as a result of performing 'for' the rebels. The records show that everyone concerned, including Queen Elizabeth, saw this performance of *Richard 2* as a significant political act.

Plays were also expected to teach lessons. In the present day, we are brought up to appreciate 'art for art's sake' or 'culture for culture's sake'; but in Shakespeare's time people thought about a play as having a moral, and discussed the lessons that could be learned from it. For example, Sir Philip Sidney thought that tragedies 'maketh Kings fear to be tyrants, and tyrants manifest their tyrannical humours'; and he saw that tragedy 'teacheth the uncertainty of this world, and upon how weak foundations gilden roofs are builded'. The point is that the people of Shakespeare's time thought of a play as an event in history, an action with a purpose and a lesson for its audience.

With this in mind, we can consider the four tragedies to see where they carried messages for Shakespeare's own time, and for his royal audience in particular. We will begin with *Hamlet*, since it was written in the same year as the *Richard 2* débâcle already mentioned. It is likely that Hamlet's idea of using a play for a political purpose reflects the Essex faction's attempt to use *Richard 2*. Also, the discussions of theatrical fashion, and the political persecution of the players, which has led them to leave their city home and wander the roads to Elsinore in *Hamlet*, were suggested by the Lord Chamberlain's Men's recent brush with political authority. These connections between the play and contemporary events are likely; but they only support a more general point, that political meddling in the theatre, and censorship of plays, were commonplace during the period. For example, in 1589 the premier company in London, the Queen's Men, got into trouble by becoming involved with anti-ecclesiastical tracts written under the name 'Martin Marprelate'. A smaller company also involved in the controversy was broken up; the Queen's Men were punished by being sent out of London for a time, banished to the provinces. Another two companies, Admiral's and Strange's, fell foul of the same trouble in November, and in dispute with an angry Lord Mayor some of Strange's men found themselves in prison. In June 1599, only a year or so before Shakespeare wrote *Hamlet*, the Archbishop of Canterbury and the Bishop of London jointly issued an edict prohibiting the publication of satires, and ordered a great burning of numbers of books they declared offensive. One result of a ban on published satire was that more satire was acted on the stage. So Shakespeare may have been thinking of the 1601 *Richard 2* when he wrote the players' scenes in *Hamlet*; but he would also have had a lifetime's experience of political interference and pressure in his mind.

When we try to relate something from a play to an event in the history of the time, we almost always come up with this same answer: yes, the writer may have been inspired by such-and-such particular incident. On the other hand, he must have known about several other similar incidents! So the single facts of history give way to a general understanding of what people did, thought about and discussed at the time.

In relation to the monarchy, *Hamlet*, *Macbeth* and *King Lear* all have a theme which was a matter of political argument throughout the Tudor and Stuart periods: the question of kingship. Students frequently hear of something called the 'Divine Right' of a monarch; but the argument was more complicated than this simple idea suggests. For example, there was the theory of the 'King's two bodies', which proposed that the King had a 'Body Politic' and a 'Body Natural'. The King's 'Body Natural' was supposed to be 'mortal, subject to all Infirmities', but his 'Body Politic . . . cannot be seen or handled' and was 'void of Infancy, and Old Age, and other natural Defects'.[1] This distinction seems to suggest that private faults of character proceeded from the King's 'nature', but in his government of the nation (or 'Body Politic') the King was always without fault. This sounds like a clever way of excusing immoral monarchs; but here is James the First's opinion: 'Kings are justly called Gods for that

---

[1] From Plowden, *Reports*, 1779, p. 213, and quoted in Michael Mangan, *A Preface to Shakespeare's Tragedies*, New York, 1991.

they exercise a manner or resemblance of divine power upon earth' (from a speech to Parliament, 1610). In addition to these ideas, there was debate about the practical question: what is a 'good' King?

The argument over this issue can be identified with two opposed ways of looking at society and the world: the cynical or practical, and the moral or idealistic. The first view emphasises the advantage of a strong King with good political skills; the second looks for virtue and conscience in a King: he should be a 'good' or 'saintly' man. Finally, the King's responsibility to and for the country was much in people's minds. The monarch should not neglect the government, and had a direct effect on the well-being of the nation as a whole.

All three royal tragedies are initiated because something has ruptured the relationship between the monarch and his nation. In *Hamlet* the King has obtained the throne criminally: Claudius has no 'right' to rule Denmark, and the Queen is an adulterer. It is clear that part of Hamlet's responsibility to set things right stems from his right to the throne. He owes it to Denmark to kill the usurper, as the Ghost insists: 'Let not the royal bed of Denmark be / A couch for luxury and damned incest' (1, v, 82–3). *Hamlet* relates to the questions of kingship in other, subtler ways as well, however. We are told much about Old Hamlet's character and reign, and we are shown how Claudius rules. These two portraits are like the old and new ideas of a King. The old emphasis on honour, military heroism, strength and virtue (Old Hamlet) gives way to the new idea of political skill, manipulation, clever use of posturing and threats (Claudius). The conflict between these two kinds of government is not merely black and white in the play: Claudius deals adroitly and successfully with the threat from Norway and Fortinbras; and he has a good, co-operative relationship with his counsellors (represented by Polonius). Hamlet himself engages in a duel of political plotting against his uncle. We should think about the true nature of royal power, after seeing *Hamlet*.

In *King Lear* Lear himself ruptures the proper position of a King by abdicating. He seeks the respect and rights of a King, but wants to rid himself of the duties. He is not clear about whether or not he wishes to retain a King's power, as his abdication speech gives away the monarch's 'sway' but some later speeches threaten to take it back. Lear's ill-advised action causes obvious disruption, and mention of 'eclipses'. (1, ii, 100) implies that his abdication throws the whole cosmos out of kilter. However, the play also provides numerous more immediate lessons about government. Edgar, who will eventually ascend the throne, transforms himself into a mad beggar during the play. In symbolic and metaphoric terms, his flexibility is praised: in evil times he bends with the wind rather than standing up to be blown down. Socially, he is a noble who has taken 'physic' by exposing himself 'to feel what wretches feel' (3, iv, 33–4). The play seems to recommend an experience of common humanity and sympathy between ruler and citizen, and Edgar's progress is presented as an education for a 'good' King.

In *Macbeth* the violent murder of the King sets off the main action, and heavenly portents again show that the universe is shaken by the enormity of this crime. Several of Macbeth's speeches, and the development of the plot, show the axiom that evil spawns evil. The 'assassination' cannot 'trammel up the consequence' and crimes only 'teach bloody instructions' which 'return to plague th'inventor' (1, vii, 2–10). The multiplying bloodshed of the second, third and fourth acts are the 'consequence' of vice in the ruler.

Macbeth, like *Hamlet* and *King Lear*, has more detailed lessons about the nature of kingship and the character of a 'good' King. The discussion between Macduff and Malcolm concerning Malcolm's supposed vices and actual virtues, in Act 4, Scene iii, and the description of the saintly English King in the same scene, are contributions to a lesson in governance that is clearly intended.

During the first years of James the First's reign, the King was eager to unify his two realms, making England and Scotland one. This became a contentious political issue. *King Lear*, acted at court in the King's presence in December 1606, was relevant to the question of the Union. The theme of the play – the partition of Lear's kingdom and the chaos that ensues – would hold obvious resonances for the court audience; Albany and Cornwall were the titles held by James's two sons; and the character of the Fool has often been thought to be modelled on that of Archie Armstrong, James's jester who enjoyed much licence because of the King's fondness for him. On a more moral note, James was widely accused of extravagance in his household and of financial mismanagement, and Lear's hundred knights may represent implicit criticism of this side of James's character. The play, however, does not take sides in the Union debate; and if Lear's knights are a reference to over-spending, the criticism is gentle, as Lear's attachment to his followers is presented with sympathetic understanding. As Lear says, 'O! reason not the need' (2, iv, 262). It is also possible to see Lear's misunderstanding of the role and duties of a King, and particularly his treatment of the country, Cordelia and others as if they were merely his possessions, as an oblique lesson for James.

Macbeth also contains specific references that would have been recognised when it was performed. The Porter's comment on 'equivocators' is thought to be an allusion to the 'equivocation' of the Gunpowder Plot conspirators (1605), and in Act 4, Scene i James's accession to the throne is alluded to in the vision of the future afforded by the witches. Macbeth sees some 'That two-fold balls and treble sceptres carry', these being the insignia used in the English and Scottish coronations. The play therefore explicitly traces James's ancestry to the good man Banquo. This may also explain why Shakespeare changed Banquo's character from Holinshed, where he appears as Macbeth's co-conspirator. King James was fascinated by witchcraft and magic, and had been 'touching' people to cure them of 'King's evil' in 1604, much as the saintly English King is said to do in the play (see 4, iii, 146, etc.).

There is much circumstantial information about the tragedies in relation to contemporary events, then. However, in each case the play explores a larger and more subtle collection of issues which were relevant to the court audience. We cannot draw firm conclusions about Shakespeare's intention or the reception of his plays by Elizabeth; but it seems that the plays performed for James amount to little less than a lesson for the King, teaching him the importance of virtue in a ruler. The interdependent relationship between King and country is emphasised in the plots of these plays and underlined in their language; and each one can be construed as a warning of the inevitable consequences of error or vice in the person of a King.

The Renaissance and Far-reaching Changes

The following brief discussion introduces some vast changes which occurred over centuries. Our generalisations should therefore be treated with great caution. However, the social, economic and ideological conflicts mentioned here were very much alive in Shakespeare's time. So we should not doubt that they affected Shakespeare and his audiences, although historians disagree about when and how quickly these developments took place.

The Reformation is a word which describes the relative breaking up of the Catholic Church, and the formation of numerous Protestant and Puritan Protestant Churches and sects until there came to be, broadly, two kinds of Christianity in Western Europe. In England, Henry the Eighth passed the Act of Supremacy in 1534, setting up the Protestant Church of England and incorporating the monarch as head of the Church as well as the state. The new Church had to fight to establish itself, throughout Shakespeare's life. It had two enemies, the traditionalist Catholics and the new Puritan sects; and religious matters were very unsettled, in a state of multiplying struggles, throughout.

Broadly, the Catholic Church had relied on a strict hierarchical structure with the Pope at its apex. The Catholic Church was thus a vast institution and its function was to instruct people in what to believe and how to worship. The Catholic emphasis was on obedience, and your place in the hierarchy was regarded as fixed: you had no direct relationship with God because your religious instruction came to you from the Church via your priest. Protestant religions, on the other hand, tended to emphasise individual faith and believed that each person could pray to God and receive illumination from God in private.[2]

Catholic thought therefore emphasised the idea of 'authority'. Truth could be discovered by listening to 'authority', which was there to decide right ideas and then hand them down to those of

---

[2] One of the most readable accounts of this essential difference between Catholic and Protestant outlooks is in George Bernard Shaw's play *Saint Joan*, London, 1924, in Scene iv, pp. 86–100 of the Penguin edition (1946).

inferior 'authority'. As the Protestant Churches became stronger and more established, however, a new pattern of thought began to appear. We recognise this new way of thinking as similar to the 'scientific' ideas that have dominated much of the twentieth century. This pattern of thought began at the opposite end from 'authority': it started with observation of nature and derived its principles from analysing what it could see, hear, taste, smell and touch – from the senses. Francis Bacon's treatises *The Advancement of Learning* (1605) and *Novum Organum* (1620) advocated this new way to study the world, saying that 'the true way' of 'searching into and discovering truth' is a method that 'derives axioms from the senses and particulars, rising by a gradual and unbroken ascent, so that it arrives at the most general axioms last of all'.[3]

During the same centuries that saw the Reformation, a massive change in the organisation of society also took place, and the economies of European countries were transformed. Briefly, in the 'medieval' era the majority of people lived in small towns and villages; and their livelihood depended on agriculture. Social organisation was predominantly 'feudal'. That is, society consisted of a hierarchy (comparable to that in the Catholic Church) headed by the King and the nobles. Every individual was born into a specific place in this hierarchy, and there was little movement up or down. However, international trade and financial sophistication grew, cities became much larger in the process called 'urbanisation', and the economies of Western Europe gradually came to devote the lion's share of their economic activity to commerce rather than agriculture and the land. As these economic changes took place, the structure of society also had to alter. There was a growing number of people who lived in a city and gained their livelihood from trade or commerce, and who therefore had no set place within the old 'feudal' hierarchy. This new class has been given the name 'bourgeoisie'. It grew in numbers, wealth and influence throughout the Renaissance. In modern England, of course, only a small minority of the population is employed in agriculture.

---

[3] From *Novum Organum*, translated from Latin by Ellis and Spedding, in *Works of Francis Bacon*, Vol. IV, 1843, p. 50.

We have mentioned religious, economic and social changes; and we have tentatively described a change in the way people thought. These changes were occurring, therefore, in every aspect of life, and it is important to imagine this. Whatever you did, whichever way you turned your eyes, whatever branch of knowledge you studied, whichever social group you belonged to, you would meet some off-shoot of these vast, centuries-long conflicts. On the one hand was the pressure of 'authority' – whether religious or secular – and a pre-existing hierarchical structure like a huge pyramid, unmoving and fixed, in which your place was set. On the other hand was a different pressure to find your individual place, make up your own mind, and live according to your own conscience in a world where you could make your own life by using your own qualities and efforts. All of these factors are clearly reflected in Shakespeare's dramatic presentation of order and disorder in the plays.

We should never be tempted to think of any part of these vast processes as passive, or static. The conflicts I have mentioned were a vital, continuous battle; and there is much evidence that the authorities in Queen Elizabeth's time fought using propaganda, attempting to re-invent an only half-real social heirarchy by persuading people that 'order' was necessary. The political censorship of plays, mentioned earlier in this chapter, can be seen as part of a larger struggle to suppress or set limits on individual freedoms of thought, expression and action. The battle, however, was not 'won' or 'lost', nor was it a single battle. In contrast to 'static', we can use the word 'dynamic' to describe the situation. This means that it consisted of energies or forces, the directions in which they moved, and their action or pressure on each other.

It is important to accept that the conflicts Shakespeare dramatised in his tragedies are 'dynamic'. A brief example will make this clear. In *Othello*, the 'new' man who works out his own view of the world, deducing his opinions from experience and observation of life, is Iago. His speech in Act 1, Scene iii is an assertion of the 'new' way of thinking:

> . . . 'tis in ourselves, that we are thus, or thus: our bodies are gardens, to the which our wills are gardeners, so that if we will plant nettles, or

sow lettuce, set hyssop, and weed up thyme; supply it with one gender
of herbs, or distract it with many; either to have it sterile with idle-
ness, or manur'd with industry, why, the power, and corrigible
authority of this, lies in our wills.

(1, iii, 319–26)

Othello, on the other hand, often conjures the magnificence of a traditional, military order and medieval ideals, such as honour. His love
for Desdemona has strong overtones of medieval courtly love where
the woman's purity is worshipped and she is idolised. Othello's
speech bidding goodbye to his 'occupation' contains:

> O farewell,
> Farewell the neighing steed, and the shrill trump,
> The spirit-stirring drum, the ear-piercing fife;
> The royal banner, and all quality,
> Pride, pomp and circumstance of glorious war!
>
> (3, iii, 356–60)

The conflict between these two opposed ideas of the truth about life
is obvious; but the important point for us to remember is that they
are dramatised dynamically, not statically. Iago is intellectually supe-
rior: he is much cleverer than Othello. Also, the play shows that his
analysis of life is largely correct, in practical terms. When he predicts
people's behaviour, and carries out experiments to test his theory, the
theory works. Yet, Iago frightens and repels us, and is destructive.
Othello is not clever. We long to tell him some practical home-
truths to prevent him from foolishly blundering into Iago's trap.
Furthermore, the glories Othello praises, the 'royal banner, and all
quality', may only exist in his imagination. Shakespeare does not
present war as glorious in *Macbeth*, for example. Yet Othello is
attractive and his language magnificent.

So the conflict between these two views of the world cannot be
resolved. We in the audience can neither deny the evidence of our
minds, nor refuse the wonder of Othello's glory and honour. Instead
we witness a dynamic struggle in which each side transforms itself
constantly, and no resolution can remain fixed. Remember that our
analysis of the end of the play, in Chapter 2, described an uneasy

balance of tensions, between the restoration of order and truths revealed during the tragedy. Even at the end of the play, then, there is tension: there is a dynamic situation.

The Malcontent or 'Machiavel'

Iago's cynical and practical philosophy, quoted in the last section, raises another issue that was current for Shakespeare's time. Niccolò Machiavelli (1469–1527) was an Italian writer whose handbook for politicians, *The Prince*, became notorious. In *The Prince* Machiavelli recommends ruthlessness, murder, betrayal, manipulation, deceit, lying and the use of false propaganda as the best means to obtain and keep power. Machiavelli himself was apparently a disillusioned democrat, who wrote this shocking work in a spirit of bitter irony. In most European countries he was thought of as a kind of devil, however: his book presented such a cynical, self-interested view of how politics really works that the authorities fought its ideas, and branded him as a figure of popular fear and outrage. At the same time (we must never forget that history is complex and dynamic) *The Prince* was an enormously influential book. So Machiavelli's name and public character came to be associated with the cold logic of a 'new' way of thinking, and a cynical way of looking at the world. The 'Machiavel', a character who showed these characteristics, and put forward cynical and heartless arguments, became a developing figure on stage, and participated in the dynamic conflicts we discussed in the previous section, as a character in the drama.

In English drama, the 'Machiavel' was also typically a dissatisfied man, often one engaged in revenge, or destructively getting his own back on society. It appeared (logically) that a man who would always and only pursue his own interests – whether greedy for money, a woman, or power – would also always be dissatisfied. So the character of the 'malcontent' developed from a variety of traditions including ideas about melancholy and the shock of Machiavelli's analysis of power. In the 1590s, before the Church edict of 1599 already mentioned, there was much satirical writing. John Marston created *The Malcontent*, one of the first characters of the kind; but there are many other examples in Elizabethan and Jacobean drama. Some memorable versions of the Machiavel or Malcontent are Bosola from Webster's *The Duchess of Malfi*, Barabas from Marlowe's *The Jew of Malta*, and Deflores from Middleton's *The Changeling*.

In Shakespeare's tragedies, the same character-type is recognisable in Iago from *Othello*, Edmund from *King Lear*, Macbeth himself, in some ways, from *Macbeth*, and both Hamlet and Claudius from *Hamlet*. However, Shakespeare seems to have been responsible for developing the type, turning a traditionally villainous, negative cipher into credible dramatic figures, and producing tragic dilemmas from their existence and actions.

There is no space in this chapter for a full essay on these character-types as they appear in the four Great Tragedies. Also, many examples of 'Machiavellian' attitudes will occur to you from your knowledge of the plays, or have already cropped up among the extracts we analysed in Part I. However, one further point is worth noting. In Shakespeare, a cynical approach to life is closely associated with ideas of 'nature' and what is 'natural'. So, Edmund declares 'Thou, Nature, art my goddess; to thy law / My services are bound' (*King Lear*, 1, ii, 1–2); and Lear expresses his romantic contempt for a merely practical, 'natural' view of life in: 'Allow not nature more than nature needs, / Man's life is cheap as beast's' (2, iv, 264–5). In Shakespeare's tragedies this opposition becomes a serious debate. Like the conflicts discussed in the previous section, it remains a dilemma, an unresolved dynamic conflict: for truths can be found on both sides.

Shakespeare and Tragedy

The four plays we study in this book are 'tragedies'. What do we mean by that? As I remarked in the preceding chapter, 'tragedy' is notoriously difficult to define, and a tour through the different theories leaves us back where we started: a tragedy is a story that ends in disaster. So we cannot expect to find a pleasing, neat definition of 'tragedy', as there is no such thing.

On the other hand, the different definitions and theories contain ideas that can be helpful when we think about the plays. So it is useful to look at the theories and compare them to what actually happens in Shakespeare's tragedies: if nothing else, they will stimulate thought. They may help us to distinguish between our reactions of sadness, horror, sympathy, grief and satisfaction when we see a play, and to question what actually happens in a play that inspires us to use the word 'tragic'. We will begin with the ancient Greek critic Aristotle, because his influence has been so widely misunderstood that we should clarify what he wrote, and whether it was relevant, at the start. Aristotle wrote an analytical treatise called *The Poetics*, which tried to define the 'tragic' in classical Greek plays.

In the late seventeenth and eighteenth centuries many writers and critics took Aristotle's ideas as a prescription. They believed that a tragedy *ought* to follow Aristotle's 'rules', and that a play that did not fit this description was not a proper tragedy. This showed a misunderstanding of Aristotle. *The Poetics* was a critical book, analysing Greek tragedies Aristotle had read and seen, but it was used as a textbook of 'rules' instead. In addition, many of the ideas taken from *The Poetics* were added to, exaggerated, distorted or misinterpreted. Eventually, therefore, the learned critics of the English neo-classical age had an elaborate set of rules in their minds; and they were convinced that those rules must be adhered to in the writing of plays.

One particular idea of Aristotle's was notoriously misused. In *The Poetics* there is a section about 'unity' which suggests that the action in a tragedy 'must be a complete unit, and the events of which it is made up must be so plotted that if any of these elements is moved or removed the whole is altered and upset'. This idea became exaggerated and turned into a rule for plays: tragedy should observe the Three Unities of Time (the action should span less than a day), Place (there should be a single setting throughout) and Action (there should be one main character, and one development of plot towards one main event, the catastrophe). Of course Shakespeare's tragedies break all such rules again and again. They have comic scenes and sub-plots; they dart back and forth from Dunsinane to England to Dover to Gloucester to Venice to Cyprus; and they span weeks, months or even years of time. If we re-read what Aristotle actually wrote, however, we have an entirely different impression. Our analysis of comedy in Chapter 6, for example, shows that Shakespeare wrote comic scenes using the same subject-matter as the central themes of the tragedy. Every aspect of a Shakespearian tragedy contributes to a whole effect, and that is a more sensible interpretation of what Aristotle meant when he described 'unity'.

The neo-classical writers used their 'rules' to adapt Shakespeare's plays. An example of this is John Dryden's version of *Antony and Cleopatra*, which he called *All for Love* (1678). Dryden's version concentrates on the final plot, when Caesar and Antony's wife Octavia are trying to separate Antony from Cleopatra. The version ends tragically with the deaths of Antony and Cleopatra, but the action is simplified, being condensed into a single day, in a single place. Shakespeare's play was not performed at all for about a hundred years: Dryden's 'improved' version was preferred. In 1681 Nahum Tate re-wrote *King Lear*, leaving out the Fool and giving the play a happy ending with Cordelia alive and Lear restored to his kingdom. Tate's adaptation was performed for about 160 years until, in 1838, Shakespeare's original *King Lear* was revived.

In his Preface to *All for Love* Dryden wrote that it was 'almost a miracle' that Shakespeare 'should by the force of his imagination perform so much', since he was 'untaught by any, and, as Ben Jonson tells us, without learning'. These remarks display the patronising attitude of Dryden's time. Shakespeare was seen as a brilliant but uneducated playwright, and they were convinced that their 'learning' gave them the right to improve his plays. Similarly, Nahum Tate thought he had to 'rectify' the 'Regularity and Probability of the Tale' in *King Lear*. The adaptations of this time had a common tendency to cut anything shocking or startling, and to cut comedy and sub-plots, so simplifying the central story.

What did Aristotle really say? Here is a brief summary of his ideas. He suggested that a tragedy is a story that inspires pity and fear. In it, a person in a high position falls 'from good fortune to misfortune'. The main character must not be perfect or vicious, but 'the man in between these extremes', because 'pity is induced by undeserved misfortune, and fear by the misfortunes of normal people'. So the cause of the fall 'must not be vice, but a great error'. The effect of a tragedy occurs because it is 'by means of pity and fear effecting its purgation of these emotions', which Aristotle calls 'the particular tragic pleasure'. 'Irony and Disclosure' are prominent elements in tragedies. Irony is 'a reversal in the course of events' which undermines the audience's expectations, and disclosure is a change from ignorance to knowledge which 'produces its finest effect when it is connected with Irony'.[4]

There is no evidence that Shakespeare was influenced by these ideas, if he knew of them at all. On the other hand, some points are worth considering. First, it is noticeable that Hamlet, Othello, Lear and Macbeth all fall from high positions, and are all partly brought down by 'a great error' in their own character. We can agree with Aristotle that we identify with these characters easily because they are not perfect or utterly villainous: their flawed humanity appeals to us and enables us to pity them, and feel their fear. Macbeth is more like an out-and-out villain than the others, but even he commands our pity after his wife's death (5, v, 17–28), and we are not honest if we deny having felt the temptations and fears he wrestles with in his great speech 'If it were done . . . ' etc. (1, vii, 1–28).

Second, the 'great error' in the tragic hero repays some thought. It has been traditional to think Lear senile or wrathful, Hamlet indecisive, Macbeth ambitious and Othello jealous. A very little thought takes us beyond these simplicities. In Shakespeare's tragedies there is something in each hero's character that precipitates his disaster – something the hero cannot control, so that the steps towards tragedy seem inevitable in his character. This tragic 'error' or 'flaw' is very complicated in Shakespeare, however. For example, Othello's susceptibility to suggestion is a tragic weakness. He is credulous and, as Iago remarks, 'easily led by the nose'. Yet we cannot say 'Othello was too credulous, that was his error', and leave it at that. Othello's credulousness is also a quality of trust in other people, and inseparable from his ideals. In short, Othello's most attractive quality is, at the same time, his weakness. In this way the 'great error' in the hero's character, in Shakespearian tragedy, always leads us into further questions and tragic irony, which brings us to a third comment.

---

[4] The quotations in this paragraph are drawn from *Aristotle on the Art of Fiction: An English Translation of Aristotle's Poetics*, tr. L.J.Potts, Cambridge, 1962, pp. 24–35.

Shakespeare's tragedies are full of what Aristotle calls irony and disclosure. For example, the disclosure of Edgar, and Edmund's confession, at the end of *King Lear*, Laertes's confession at the end of *Hamlet*, the various ingenious ways in which the witches' prophecies prove misleading at the end of *Macbeth*, and the revelations of Iago's villainy at the end of *Othello*, all show irony and disclosure to be at the heart of Shakespeare's tragic method. So, although Aristotle did not influence Shakespeare, his ideas can help us to think about how Shakespeare's tragedies work.

Now we can look at ideas of tragedy from Shakespeare's own time. Here are two attempts to describe tragedy from 1595 and 1610 respectively. The earlier one comes from Sir Philip Sidney's *An Apology for Poetry*:

> . . . the high and excellent Tragedy, that openeth the greatest wounds, and showeth forth the ulcers that are covered with tissue; that maketh Kings fear to be tyrants, and tyrants manifest their tyrannical humours; that, with stirring the affects of admiration and commiseration, teacheth the uncertainty of this world, and upon how weak foundations gilden roofs are builded.

Each phrase of this definition reminds us of some important feature in Shakespeare's tragedies. We may guess that the Bard had Sidney in mind when we hear Hamlet beg his mother not to 'skin and film the ulcerous place'. Descriptions of Scotland under Macbeth's reign 'maketh Kings fear to be tyrants', and Lear is full of 'tyrannical humours' in the first two acts. 'The uncertainty of this world' is a clear lesson of all four plays, and there is much in all of them to show the 'weak foundations' of pomp, high rank and splendour. The definition as a whole, however, suggests that tragedies are didactic: they teach us lessons. If we are kings, we learn the duties and virtues a King must have. If we are ordinary people, we can still learn the wisdom that human pride is based on weak foundations. So, Sidney's Elizabethan view describes tragedy as having a purpose, to teach the audience.

The later definition is drawn from Fulke Greville's *Life of Sidney*. He put forward a different view of tragedy, distinguishing between 'ancient tragedy' which was concerned:

> . . . to exemplify the disastrous miseries of man's life . . . and so out of that melancholic vision, stir horror, or murmur against Divine Providence

and 'Modern tragedy', which showed

> God's revenging aspect upon every particular sin, to the despair, or confusion of mortality.[5]

Greville's implication is that the tragedies of his own time (which include Shakespeare's) are predominantly submissive and conservative. The emphasis on tragedy teaching us has gone, but the tragic attitude of 'despair, or confusion of mortality' at 'God's revenging aspect' implies passive submission and avoidance of 'sin'. In Chapter 2 we considered the ending of each play, and found a complex, ambivalent attitude to the restoration of authority and political order in each case. On the other hand, the plays do suggest that order must be restored, that somebody must be in authority; and deviations from the norm (such as Hamlet's excessive mourning, or Lear's partial abdication *and* Cordelia's unpolitical sincerity) are cruelly punished. Equally, however, Shakespearian tragedy is full of the elements Greville finds in the ancients. Hamlet's 'To be or not to be' soliloquy, for example, exactly fits Greville's phrase 'out of that melancholic vision, stir horror, or murmur against Divine Providence'.

If we look at the history of English tragedy before Shakespeare, we are taken back to early morality plays and chronicle plays. These two traditions are clearly present in the kind of tragedy Shakespeare synthesised. The chronicle plays narrated a heroic form of history, and, as we know, Shakespeare wrote several histories in the early part of his career. The discussion of Falstaff in Chapter 8, and our discussion of kingship in the tragedies earlier in this chapter, show that the

---

[5] Both Sidney and Greville are quoted in Michael Mangan, *A Preface to Shakespeare's Tragedies*, New York, 1991.

'chronicle' element developed into a complex theme which is integrated into the tragedy. The morality plays, with their explicit
teaching function, are also recognisable antecedents. Some theatrical
elements of the morality plays contributed to these tragedies. First,
the morality plays dramatised supernatural beings, and Shakespeare
used ghosts and the witches in this tradition. Second, some of
Shakespeare's characters are drawn in such a way as to represent a
specific opinion or temptation, as in the morality plays. For
example, the witches in *Macbeth* appeal directly to one side of the
hero's nature in order to draw him into error. Also, Edmund's self-
confession at the start of Act 1, Scene ii of *King Lear*, Iago's declaration of hatred in Act 1, Scene i of *Othello*, and even characters such
as the foppish lord Osric in *Hamlet*, show the remnants of self-con-
fessing allegorical figures that are found in the morality play tradition. Essentially, the Machiavel or Malcontent figure mentioned
earlier in this chapter is of the same kind: a theatrical figure easily
recognised by the contemporary audience as a meaningful type.

During Shakespeare's youth there was a fashion for tragedies in
which a bitter character would cause widespread destruction with
the motive of revenge. Kyd's *Spanish Tragedy* (1594) is a good
example of this kind, but by no means the only one. The prevalence
of revenge as a tragic motive, however, may have suggested
Shakespeare's choice of revenge for his most ambitious philosophical
essay in motive, the play *Hamlet*. Also, we must remember the conclusions we have drawn from discussion of Elizabethan times and
the larger conflicts of social and economic change. The subversive
ideas of the political and social opposition, those radically different
ways of thinking that Tudor propaganda sought to suppress, found
expression in a multitude of verse satires during the 1590s, as we
have said. After the Church edict of 1599, however, much of the
same shocking and subversive material, banned from published
verse, transferred itself to the stage. We can see the social criticism,
comic satire and shockingly negative Machiavels of the tragedies as
inheritors of this tradition also.

Having briefly discussed Aristotle, contemporary definitions of
tragedy, and the English tradition, it is clear that we can trace many
elements of Shakespearian tragedy to antecedents, and that theories

about the nature of tragedy can help us to crystallise our own ideas. On the other hand, our discussion has continually returned to the same truth: Shakespeare's tragedies are more, greater than and different from anything else. The advantage of discussing the context of the plays is that it enhances our wonder at what Shakespeare made out of his own genius coupled with all the threads of tradition available to him.

Our analysis of the plays in Part I suggests that Shakespearian tragedy has distinctive features. We have emphasised two particular points: that the tragedy works on a number of levels at once (from within an individual character to throughout the imagined universe); and that the central content consists of insoluble dilemmas (such as appearance/reality and order/disorder) which convey an effect of senselessness or the 'absurd'. The historical discussion in this chapter can be considered in conjunction with Chapter 10, which gives examples of some traditional and some modern critics' attempts to define Shakespearian tragedy.

10

Sample of Critical Views

Thousands of books and articles have been written about Shakespeare's tragedies by academic critics. Several hundred are published each year. They are often written in a confusing, over-complicated or pretentious style: academics are just as fond of showing off as anybody else! It is important to remember, then, that since you have read the tragedy, your ideas are just as valid as theirs. Always be sceptical about their ideas: you are not under an obligation to agree with them. On the other hand, your mind can be stimulated by discussing your text with your teacher, or in a class. Treat the critics in the same way: it can be stimulating to debate the text, challenging your ideas and theirs. This is the spirit in which you should read 'the critics'.

Four critical views of Shakespeare's tragedies are presented in this chapter. They differ considerably. Each extract discusses the critic's approach to the tragedies; and all four attempt to define the essence of Shakespearian tragedy. Naturally, this chapter cannot represent the many different schools of criticism that exist, or the vast range of approaches to Shakespearian tragedy that have been tried. Our aim is to provide a sample: there are different ways of looking at the plays, all of which can be enlightening, and these extracts should provoke you into thinking about them. If you are interested in exploring more critical views, find a good library and begin by using the suggestions in 'Further Reading' at the end of this book.

*   *   *

Our first critic is A. C. Bradley, and we look at part of his *Shakespearean Tragedy*, which was published in 1904 and has had an enormous influence on all subsequent work in the field. Whether to agree or disagree, whether to build on his work or diverge from it – all the critics discuss Bradley's view. It could be called the starting-point for twentieth-century criticism of the tragedies. The part of Bradley's argument we focus upon comes from the first lecture, 'The Substance of Shakespearean Tragedy', and develops his views on the general question of what Shakespearian tragedy is.

Bradley begins by stating that a Shakespearian tragedy contains 'exceptional calamity' that leads to the death of a man 'in high estate'. But it is also obviously much more than this. However much calamity came in the form of lightning-bolts from nature or chance, it would not be tragic. Also, a calamity like that suffered by Job in the Old Testament is not tragic. It was well nigh more than Job could bear, but it was produced by the action of a supernatural power. Bradley's point is that the calamities of tragedy do not simply happen, nor are they sent down from above: they mainly proceed from actions, 'the actions of men'.

We watch a group of people in their particular situation; and we watch their actions which result from the 'co-operation of their characters' in their situation. Each action leads to another, and this leads to a further action, and so on until the connected series of actions leads to a catastrophe which appears to be 'inevitable'. In our imaginations this creates the impression that the people concerned have both caused and suffered from the events and the catastrophe at the end. This is particularly true of the main characters and especially true of the hero, who 'always contributes in some measure to the disaster in which he perishes'. The fact that men are presented first and foremost as agents responsible for making their own sufferings, modifies the emotions of pity and fear we feel, accordingly.

The story or 'action' of a Shakespearian tragedy has more elements than human actions alone, of course; but the deeds are the 'predominant' element. What is more, these deeds are not half-conscious or causeless actions, but 'characteristic' deeds in the sense that they proceed from the character of the doer. So Bradley believes that the core of the tragedy lies in 'action issuing from character'. Shakespeare's main interest was in this, but we must not confuse it with a psychological interest or belittle it as *mere* character, because Shakespeare was entirely dramatic. Sometimes we can detect passages where Shakespeare indulged either his love of poetry or reflective philosophy; but Bradley thinks it impossible to find anywhere in the later tragedies where Shakespeare has followed an interest in character for its own sake, not connected to action. Bradley then mentions the novel *The Woman in White* as an example of a book where an interest in plot exists for its own sake, and says that Shakespeare had even less time for action not connected to character. There is 'plot' in the plays, of course, but it is woven in with other elements and subordinated to other effects, so we always feel, as a tragedy nears its final catastrophe, that the calamities and disasters follow 'inevitably from the deeds of men, and that the main source of these deeds is character'. Bradley thinks that the dictum that for Shakespeare 'character is destiny' is an over-statement, but one containing an essential truth.

Another question about the 'action' is whether we can define it more clearly by calling it a 'conflict'. Bradley explains that the idea of a conflict can be applied to two persons who are in conflict; and in more sophisticated forms this theory can either apply to two parties or groups of people, one of them led by the hero, or apply to the passions, tendencies, ideas, principles or forces these two conflicting parties animate in the drama. The examples are that Romeo's and Juliet's love is in conflict with their families' hatred, or that Brutus and Cassius's cause struggles against that of Caesar and his party. Bradley here suggests that the Macbeths are opposed by the representatives of Duncan. The 'conflict' theory divides the cast into two opposing groups, and sees the play as a battle ending in the death of the hero or leader of one of the groups.

Bradley accepts that there is this kind of 'conflict' in the tragedies, but thinks the theory leads to 'something a little external' in our way of looking at the play. He makes the point that in *Hamlet*, where there is a deadly conflict between the hero and Claudius, we are not fascinated by that conflict so much as by the conflict within Hamlet himself. This is the case with nearly all of the tragedies: there is an external conflict between people, but this is less interesting than the 'conflict of forces in the hero's soul'.

Bradley insists that the heroes of the mature Shakespearian tragedies, although they pursue their destined paths towards the catastrophe, are all, at some time during the action, 'torn by an inward struggle', which is often the time when Shakespeare is at his most powerful. Only Shakespeare's early tragic heroes, such as Romeo, Juliet, Richard 3 and Richard 2, actually fight against a hostile outward force, with their own souls largely 'undivided'.

The concept of conflict in general is not definite enough to describe this idea of both external and internal struggle. Bradley suggests the term 'spiritual force' to describe whatever forces, passions, principles, doubts, ideas and so on are acting in the human soul; and he says that in Shakespearian tragedy some such 'spiritual forces' are shown in conflict. The conflict between these forces gives rise to strife between people, and at the same time but less universally these forces disturb and create conflict within the hero's soul. The example is *Macbeth*, where 'treasonous ambition' collides with 'loyalty and patriotism', so there is an external conflict between Macbeth, and Macduff and Malcolm. But 'these powers or principles equally collide in the soul of Macbeth himself', which is the inner conflict. Bradley believes that neither of these conflicts would make a tragedy if it were by itself. Also, the idea of conflict underlines action as the centre of interest, while the struggle within the hero's soul reinforces the view that the action is essentially an expression of character.

Do the heroes themselves have qualities in common which make them tragic? Bradley regards the tragic heroes and heroines as exceptional in character as well as occupying high positions. They are not perfect or wildly eccentric people: they are made of 'the stuff we find within ourselves', but they are above normal people because of 'an intensification of . . . life' in them, and if we think about it we are unlikely to have met anyone like them. Hamlet and Cleopatra are brilliant. Othello, Lear and Macbeth are built on a large scale so their needs and passions have a 'terrible force'. In almost all of them there is a 'marked one-sidedness', a tendency in one direction and an inability to resist the force pulling in that direction. Bradley describes 'a fatal tendency to identify the whole being with one

interest, object, passion, or habit of mind' and calls this 'the fundamental tragic trait' in Shakespeare's tragic characters. This exceptional but 'fatal' gift, when joined with the other exceptional
qualities of the character, produces 'the full power and reach of the
soul' so its conflict fills us with 'not only sympathy and pity, but
admiration, terror, and awe'.

The exceptional quality or greatness of the hero means that Man
is not presented as a small or contemptible being, so we never react
to Shakespearian tragedy by feeling merely depressed. This greatness
of the hero also produces what Bradley calls 'the centre of the tragic
impression', which is an impression of waste. The passage in which
Bradley describes this feeling is worthy of quotation in full:

> We seem to have before us a type of the mystery of the whole world,
> the tragic fact which extends far beyond the limits of tragedy.
> Everywhere, from the crushed rocks beneath our feet to the soul of
> man, we see power, intelligence, life and glory, which astound us and
> seem to call for our worship. And everywhere we see them perishing,
> devouring one another and destroying themselves, often with dreadful
> pain, as though they came into being for no other end.

The fact that the hero who thus destroys himself is the highest form
of humanity in our view, makes us feel the value of what is wasted so
'vividly' that we cannot comfort ourselves with any tame reflections
about time or mutability.

If these great individuals are not the ultimate power in the tragic
world, what is that power? Bradley asks us to think of the hero
again, noticing that even the comparatively innocent heroes all have
some flaw or fault. These faults are all, in the final analysis, evil, and
they are decisive in bringing about the final disaster. So Bradley
observes that some 'ultimate power' is disturbed by, and fights
against, these faults or 'evil', and draws the inference that the
supreme power must be completely alien to all evil. This power
seems set on ruthlessly destroying the evil, and demands nothing
short of 'good in perfection'.

Bradley goes further: evil always shows itself as 'negative, barren,
weakening, destructive, a principle of death'; and it not only isolates

and destroys its opposite, but it is also self-destructive. When an evil man prospers and is successful, it is because of the good in him. When he is fully under the influence of the evil in him, it will kill other people through the evil man's actions; but it will also kill *him*. The evil man has been destroyed by the end, then, and what is left is 'a family, a city, a country, exhausted, pale and feeble, but alive through the principle of good which animates it'. There are also some people left. They are not as great as the hero who has died, but they are decent and we respect them. Since evil is shown to be incapable of existing in an order, and destroys itself, Bradley draws the conclusion that the 'inner being' or 'soul' of the tragic order must be goodness.

In the tragic world, these elements are at least as strongly marked as the ones that refer to the idea of fate. There is an order which has a 'moral' nature, different from any idea of fate or 'blank power', and which reacts out of its own necessary nature. It has a 'convulsive reaction' against any attacks, and against any person who does not conform to it. The audience does not feel 'rebellious or desperate' because we sense that the disaster is not due to something neutral like fate. We half-realise that the agony and deaths result from 'collision . . . with a moral power, a power akin to all that we admire and revere in the characters'. Realising this gives us a feeling like acceptance or willing submission; but it does not make us judge the characters, or lose our emotions of pity and terror, or our sense of waste. This is because we realise that the 'moral order' is not like a human being, but acts according to 'general laws' out of its own inevitable nature, so it is as 'ruthless' as fate.

Bradley finds that something still needs to be added to this idea. We can take it that the system, or order, which seems to be the ultimate power, is moral and acts morally in the way already described. However, it does not fit the plays to think that the dominant order is responsible, say, for the goodness of Desdemona, but that Iago is responsible for the evil in Iago. What we see in the plays is that the system or order has evil inside it. Indeed, it produces evil, it 'poisons itself' by producing evil, and although it violently cleanses itself in the action of the play, this still does not mean that evil was not within the supreme 'order' itself at the start.

Bradley returns to our idea of the tragic character. We do not think of Hamlet merely as not responding to the demands of some moral order, or of Antony as transgressing the rules, nor even does Macbeth simply attack order. What we feel is that in these exceptional people and their errors, the order is in conflict within itself, because it is led away from its natural tendency towards goodness. The system does eventually cast out these flawed people, because it must survive, but in doing so 'it has lost a part of its own substance, – a part more dangerous and unquiet, but far more valuable and nearer to its heart, than that which remains'. In Bradley's view, the characters like Fortinbras or Malcolm, who remain, are poor creatures in comparison to the exceptional hero. So, the tragedy is not that evil is cast out; 'the tragedy is that this involves the waste of good'.

Bradley then concludes the chapter:

> Thus we are left at last with an idea showing two sides or aspects which we can neither separate nor reconcile. The whole or order against which the individual part shows itself powerless seems to be animated by a passion for perfection: we cannot otherwise explain its behaviour towards evil. Yet it appears to engender this evil within itself, and in its effort to overcome and expel it it is agonised with pain, and driven to mutilate its own substance and to lose not only evil but priceless good. That this idea, though very different from the idea of a blank fate, is no solution of the riddle of life is obvious; but why should we expect it to be such a solution? Shakespeare was not attempting to justify the ways of God to men, or to show the universe as a Divine Comedy. He was writing tragedy, and tragedy would not be tragedy if it were not a painful mystery.

There are, according to Bradley, numerous intimations of something other than the tragic world. These include references to God or Gods, life after death, and a number of more or less romantic impressions which we may receive at particularly intense moments during the tragedy; but these are mere hints, and there is nothing consistent or definite about them. Shakespeare does not resolve the tragic world, then, nor does he suggest where there might be a solution. Instead:

We remain confronted with the inexplicable fact, or the no less inexplicable appearance, of a world travailing for perfection, but bringing to birth, together with glorious good, an evil which it is able to overcome only by self-torture and self-waste. And this fact or appearance is tragedy.[1]

By the standards of some more recent criticism, Bradley's meaning is not very precisely expressed. He has frequent recourse to italics for emphasis and tautological lists of adjectives, hoping to hammer home his idea. Sometimes he seems to be seduced by his own words, and loses touch with Shakespeare. For example, the part of his argument where he decides that the flaws in Shakespeare's tragic heroes are 'evil' does not convince me: it seems to be an unjustified leap and a gross over-simplification of the characters' weaknesses. It is unfortunate that Bradley deduces the 'morality' of his ultimate order or power from this weakest point of the argument. I am not able to agree with him about the involvement of morality or 'goodness' in this part of the tragic process, therefore. However brilliant or respected a critic may be, we are always entitled to make up our own minds in this way, disagreeing whenever we find that the critic's idea does not match our experience of the text.

There are important virtues in Bradley's analysis, however. His investigation of Shakespeare's heroes in Aristotelian terms, which leads him to re-define the concepts of *greatness* and *defect*, is illuminating, as are his remarks about *conflict* and his paradoxical suggestion of an order or system which is the ultimate power and reacts to protect itself from what it simultaneously creates.

Bradley's achievement, in particular, was twofold. First, his work helped to develop our ideas of character by pointing out that *conflict* exists both between characters and within them, and by recognising that the conflicts within the heroes are particularly fascinating. This insight focuses attention on the extraordinarily personal, or psychological, richness of the protagonists in Shakespeare's tragedies, which we examined in Chapter 3. Second, Bradley noticed that the

---

[1] From A. C. Bradley, *Shakespearean Tragedy*, 1904. All the quotations and extracts used in this summary have been taken from pp. 6–29 of the Macmillan edition, London 1965.

traditional concept of a 'blank fate' was inadequate to describe the forces dramatised at work in the world of the tragedies. He suggested a force which tended to goodness, yet engendered evil and suffered agony when purging the evil it had created. Bradley, then, noticed that there is a pattern in the way the Shakespearian tragic universe works. His theory was an early attempt to find and define this shadowy overall 'pattern'. G. Wilson Knight (our third critic) provides a later, more sophisticated example of this attempt.

*   *   *

The second critic we look at, Helen Gardner, writing in *The Business of Criticism* in 1959, suggests an approach she calls 'historical criticism' and tries it out on *Hamlet*. She begins by identifying a problem. On the one hand, Hamlet delays his revenge several times, and does not fashion the final denouement, bitterly reproaching himself for this lack of purpose. On the other hand, the tone of the play's ending is that Hamlet has lived well and has settled his scores in life. This paradox makes us feel that we may be missing something about the play that would make a solution to the problem obvious. Gardner does not agree with T. S. Eliot that Shakespeare was at fault, nor with Johnson that it is a weak plot, and answers Bradley's statement that the whole play turns upon the 'peculiar character of the hero' by pointing out that other heroes, with different characters, might equally have delayed their revenges. So, we should look at other comparable plays from the same period to see whether the problem we perceive was a problem in Shakespeare's time, or (possibly) a problem we have invented with our modern outlook, but in Shakespeare's time a reason for the play's popularity and success.

The essence of a revenge tragedy is that the hero is not responsible for the evil of the situation at the start of the play. The simple formula of tragedy being progress from prosperity to misery does not fit this kind of play, because the play begins with the hero in a situation which is horrible, but not of his own making. In Elizabethan revenge plays not only the situation at the start, but also the denouement, is initiated by some action of the villain's, so 'the revenger takes an opportunity unconsciously provided for him by the villain'. Gardner looks at Kyd's *Spanish Tragedy*, in which the villain Lorenzo provides the revenger Hieronymo with the perfect opportunity by inviting him to show a play to the court; Shakespeare's *Titus Andronicus*, in which Tamora is over-confident and thus provides Titus with his opportunity; and Tourneur's *The Revenger's Tragedy*, in which the villainous Duke asks the revenger to arrange a mistress for him, and himself arranges to meet at a hidden pavilion, sending his own servants away for secrecy, so that the revenger Vendice's opportunity could not be easier. In plays of this kind, then, it seems as if it was an expected part of the total effect that 'the villain should be to some extent the agent of his own destruction', and Gardner relates this typical structure of revenge tragedies to the moral satisfaction they produce:

> As initiator of the action he must be the initiator of its resolution. The satisfaction of the close included to a less or greater degree the sombre satisfaction which the Psalmist felt at the spectacle of the wicked falling into pits which they had digged for others. Here, obscurely, the hand of heaven could be felt.

After quoting Raleigh on the pageant of history, who observed that 'in the end' evil people will destroy themselves and 'purposes mistook' will fall on 'the inventors' heads', Gardner describes the passive or responsive kind of hero in these plays, using Vendice from *The Revenger's Tragedy* as her example:

> This conception of a hero who is committed to counter-action, and to response to events rather than to the creation of events, is very powerfully rendered by Tourneur in the exposition of *The Revenger's Tragedy*. The personages of court pass across the stage, while Vendice, holding in his hands the skull of his dead mistress, comments on the parade of vicious power and wealth. He is waiting for 'that bald Madam, Opportunity.'

There is, however, a significant difference between *Hamlet* and these other, lesser plays. The typical revenger waits for the opportunity

provided by the villain, and there is strong irony that the villain ini-
tiates his own destruction. However, when the opportunity comes,
these revengers take it without hesitation, and kill horrifically
without conscience. There is only mild irony in this, and these characters descend to the moral level of the villain without compunction.
Hamlet is different as both Claudius and Laertes are killed by their
own means (the poisoned sword and drink) as well as at their own
instigation. This intensifies the irony of their end. Hamlet, meanwhile, remains constant to his purposes and the 'fitness' of things,
and in both his revenge and his own death he stays 'most generous,
and free from all contriving':

> The tragedy of *Hamlet*, and of plays of its kind, of which it is the
> supreme example, does not lie in 'the unfitness of the hero for his
> task,' or in some 'fatal flaw.' It is not true that a coarser nature could
> have cleansed the state of Denmark, some 'Hotspur of the North'; 'he
> that kills me some six or seven of Scots at a breakfast, washes his
> hands, and says to his wife, "Fie upon this quiet life! I want work."'
> The tragedy lies in the nature of the task, which only the noble will
> feel called on to undertake, or rather, in the nature of the world which
> is exposed to the hero's contemplation and in his sense of responsi-
> bility to the world in which he finds himself. *Hamlet* towers above
> other plays of its kind through the heroism and nobility of its hero,
> his superior power of insight into, and reflection upon, his situation,
> and his capacity to suffer the moral anguish which moral responsi-
> bility brings. Hamlet is the quintessence of European man, who holds
> that man is 'ordained to govern the world according to equity and
> righteousness with an upright heart,' and not to renounce the world
> and leave it to its corruption. By that conception of man's duty and
> destiny he is involved in those tragic dilemmas with which our own
> age is so terribly familiar. For how can man secure justice except by
> committing injustice, and how can he act without outraging the very
> conscience which demands that he should act?

Gardner finally comments that she seems to have found a historical
answer to her own historical question: she has examined Elizabethan
revenge plays in order to find out how *Hamlet* would have been
received at the time; but it was the moral uncertainties and
dilemmas of the twentieth century that made her unable to see

Hamlet in terms of his failure or success in carrying out the Ghost's 'task' in the first place.

This does not destroy the value of having looked at *Hamlet* in comparison with its contemporary analogues, or the answers reached from that process:

> *Hamlet* is not a problem to which a final solution exists. It is a work of art about which questions can always be asked. Each generation asks its own questions and finds its own answers, and the final test of the validity of those answers can only be time.[2]

Helen Gardner acknowledges, in her final paragraphs, that she is using the 'historical approach' because the modern critic brings twentieth-century confusions and assumptions to the study of Shakespeare, and these need to be cleared out of the way before we can understand Shakespeare as his audience would have done. You may feel, after reading Gardner's argument, that the 'historical approach' and its benefits are rather self-evident. We should make ourselves aware of Elizabethan attitudes, to help us understand how the play was written and how it was received by audiences of the time. To achieve this understanding, simply read other literary and dramatic works of the time and compare them to each other. However, the 'historical approach' is a timely reminder that litera-ture is a historical study as well as personal appreciation; and it serves to illuminate the theme of fate in *Hamlet*, clearing away false assumptions so that we are ready to re-examine such knotty episodes as Hamlet and the pirates, Claudius's prayer and such statements as 'there is a special providence in the fall of a sparrow'. The approach has also led Gardner to describe the essential 'tragedy' of the play in a different manner: it lies in 'the nature of the task', 'the nature of the world which is exposed to the hero's contemplation' and 'his sense of responsibility' to that world. Rather than arising out of practicalities such as 'conflict' or heroic 'defects', then, the tragedy

---

[2] From Helen Gardner, 'The Historical Approach: *Hamlet*', in *Shakespeare: The Tragedies. A Collection of Critical Essays*, ed. Alfred Harbage, Prentice-Hall, New Jersey, 1964. All of the quotations and extracts in the above summary are drawn from pp. 61–70.

can be thought of as a philosophical whole – a condition of life. We will find this holistic approach justified in more detail by G. Wilson Knight.

Another noticeable characteristic of Helen Gardner's approach is its humility. Bradley sometimes decided that he knew better than Shakespeare, and describes 'faults' in the plays. He conveys the arrogant view that Shakespeare was a 'genius' but rather a careless 'artist', so we have to take the rough with the smooth in his works. Helen Gardner is reluctant to criticise Shakespeare. When a play shocks the modern reader, or does not satisfy our expectations, she makes an effort to overcome the problem by changing her own attitude 'historically', rather than by thinking that Shakespeare was at fault. Most recent criticism is of this kind: we assume the authority of Shakespeare, and our job is to reach an understanding. 'Critical' criticism has become less common.

*   *   *

Our next critic wrote *The Wheel of Fire* in 1930, almost thirty years before Helen Gardner's article appeared; but his argument is more all-embracing, so we look at him third rather than second. G. Wilson Knight discusses 'critical' criticism, and advocates seeing Shakespeare's plays as describable 'wholes'. He is led to suggest that each play has a poetic 'essence' which can be sensed by the reader and analysed by the critic, composed of the totality of all the elements in the play, such as character, symbolism, time and space, and 'atmosphere'. Further, he conceives of Shakespeare's tragic dramas as differing only in their individual emphasis or flavour. Together, they express a uniquely Shakespearian tragic 'vision' which Knight discusses in the second of the two chapters from which our summary is drawn.

In Chapter 1 of *The Wheel of Fire*, which goes under the title 'On the Principles of Shakespeare Interpretation', Knight begins by distinguishing between 'criticism', which assesses the value of a work of art and finally judges the work, or different parts of it, as either 'good' or 'bad', and what he calls 'interpretation', which accepts the work as a whole poetic experience and does not seek to pass judgement. 'Interpretation' analyses what happens in the work and when we read it or see it performed. Poetry is an imaginative creation producing a complex, intense reaction in us. 'Interpretation' is like translating the poetic experience into the slower process of logic and intellect. Some works are of such 'resplendent' quality that 'criticism' of them is pointless, and Shakespeare's tragedies are like this. So we should 'interpret' these plays, and our approach should include 'preserving something of that child-like faith which we possess, or should possess, in the theatre'.

Knight next distinguishes between the view of a play existing in time, with the events and the characters' actions and experiences following a set sequence, and an alternative view of the play which he calls a 'spatial' view. There are 'correspondences' between different elements of the play that operate on a level that is entirely separate from the time-sequence of the drama, and it is the totality of these 'correspondences' which operate together, forming a single thing Knight has called the play's 'atmosphere':

> Now if we are prepared to see the whole play laid out, so to speak, as an area, being simultaneously aware of these thickly-scattered correspondences in a single view of the whole, we possess the unique quality of the play in a new sense. 'Faults' begin to vanish into thin air. Immediately we begin to realize the necessity where before we saw irrelevance and beauty dethroning ugliness.

Knight believes that seeing the play in this 'spatial' way solves many of the problems we worry about when we are only thinking of it in its time-sequence. For example, episodes that many critics have argued about or found fault with, such as Gloucester's mock-suicide or Malcolm's detailed confession of crimes, are no longer a problem if we concentrate on their necessary correspondence to the prevailing 'atmospheres' of the plays in which they occur. Two modern plays, Sherriff's *Journey's End* and Chekhov's *The Cherry Orchard*, are good examples of plays which would seem trivial without the influence of their powerful 'atmosphere', which is perceived 'spatially' – that is, as a single, constant effect throughout the play. There is a difference between these plays and Shakespeare's, however, because they treat the sequence of the story and the dialogue as separate from the 'atmosphere' and set them off against each other:

> But with Shakespeare a purely spiritual atmosphere interpenetrates the action, there is a fusing rather than a contrast; and where a direct personal symbol growing out of the dominating atmosphere is actualized, it may be a supernatural being, as the Ghost, symbol of the death-theme in *Hamlet*, or the Weird Sisters, symbols of the evil in *Macbeth*.

When we analyse plays, it is natural for us to have in mind the events and developments of our own lives, which are dominated by time and ideas of 'past' and 'future', so we have been used to imposing this sequential view on the plays, because that is how we experience our lives. We are wrong to do this, since a play is a poetic whole, not like our lives even though it imitates them. Of course, since the play is a whole, it is artificial to draw such a rigid distinction between the 'temporal' and 'spatial' view of it; but Knight does not apologise as over-emphasis of the 'spatial' view is necessary to redress the balance. Criticism has been over-dominated by the 'temporal' view.

We should also avoid 'character', and particularly the kind of character-criticism that leads to ethical judgements based on analysing a character's supposed motives: for example, 'Shakespeare wished in *Macbeth* to show how crime inevitably brings retribution.' There has been an intense and fruitless search for satisfactory motives for Macbeth and Iago, which has been irrelevant. Ethical considerations cannot and should not be avoided altogether, of course; but it can happen that a person in the play acts in such a way that we are only aware of beauty, and 'a supreme interest'; yet what the person does would be morally intolerable to us if it happened in everyday life. Therefore there is a difference between our 'artistic' and our normal ethic, and as critics we should be true to the 'artistic' ethic. There are moral values in the way we respond to the play, but they operate on an instinctive level and always in connection with the 'aesthetic' of the play. For example, we like Cordelia better than Goneril, and our liking is partly based on moral considerations, but these should never be the prime aim of our judgement:

. . . ethical terms, though they must frequently occur in interpretation, must only be allowed in so far as they are used in absolute obedience to the dramatic and aesthetic significance: in which case they cease to be ethical in the usual sense.

Each play, then, should be regarded as a 'visionary whole' where all that we see at first, including the characters, and each suggestive symbol, 'radiates inwards from the play's circumference to the burning central core'. Most of the psychological analysis of Shakespeare's characters that has been carried out makes the mistake of travelling around the circumference and never approaching the core. Here are the main principles of 'right Shakespearian interpretation':

1. Before thinking about faults in the play, we must regard it as a visionary unit which only obeys its own laws. This means that we must remain absolutely true to our own imaginative reaction, however illogical or paradoxical it may be. We must beware of selecting the parts that are easy to understand, or fit together neatly, or we might forget the 'superlogical'.
2. We should be able to recognize 'temporal' and 'spatial' elements, so we can relate particular things we notice, either to the time-sequence or to the binding 'atmosphere' of the play. So the whole play is seen as an expanded metaphor in which the apparent things in the drama are only projections of parts of the original vision. This is the approach that allows many things that looked problematic on first sight to become 'coherent and, within the scope of their universe, natural'.
3. We should analyse poetic symbolism, minor symbolic imagery, and pay attention to recurrent images: when an image continually occurs in a certain connection, we should accept that the associative force is strong enough to give an associative value when the same image occurs alone. We should include aural effects such as discharge of cannon, trumpets, etc., in our analysis.
4. We should consider the place the play we are studying occupies in the development or 'sequence' of Shakespeare's works. Pay par-

ticular attention to what Knight calls the 'hate-theme', which
includes a 'mode of cynicism towards love, disgust at the physical
body' and dismay about death, particularly associated with the
limitations of life which are imposed by time.

We pick up Wilson Knight's argument again in Chapter 13, 'The
Shakespearian Metaphysic'. Knight discusses what he calls the 'hate-
theme', which is always related to love because it depends on 'the
failing of love's reality'. What happens is that the character in love
sees his ideal deprived of spiritual significance. As the spiritual
element of love is denied, the physical or bestial side of love looms
disproportionately large, and this brings, for example, the animal
references in Othello and in Lear's madness. The body becomes
unclean. Sex is foul. Men are seen as animals which falsely lay claim
to something they have no true right to:

> On the plane of (i) human intercourse, and (ii) sense-perception, the
> subject has no knowledge of his own reality apart from an object.
> Man cannot 'of himself' know his own qualities 'for aught' till he sees
> them reflected in others. . . . Regarding love as the supreme and most
> intense expression of (i) human intercourse and (ii) sense-perception,
> we find this dialogue to imply that the lover sees his own soul in his
> beloved. . . . The Shakespearian hero suffers an agonizing incertitude
> at the expulsion of his love or soul from its symbol.

This is what is meant by the 'hate-theme', so there are two primary
uses of 'soul' in Shakespeare. First, the lover can discern his 'soul'
reflected in the object of his love, and second, when evil has been
done to the protagonist, he sees that his own soul is an abysmal,
hideous vision of 'nothing'. If we accept that there is a dualism of (a)
soul or spirit, and (b) the actual world of the senses, then we can distinguish three kinds of Shakespeare's vision:

> We can say that good is love and exists when the actual burns with a
> spiritual flame kindled, or recognized, or supplied by the regarding
> soul; it tends to be immediate and intuitive. We can next observe that
> the Shakespearian hate, as expressed recurrently in what I have called
> the 'hate-theme', is an awareness of the world of actuality unspiritual-

ized, and shows a failure to body infinite spirit into finite forms and a consequent abhorrence and disgust at these forms. It tends to originate in a backward time-thinking, the recurrent plot-symbol being the failing of love's vision in the temporal chain of events. And, thirdly, the Shakespearian evil is a vision of naked spirit, which appears as a bottomless chasm of 'nothing' since it is unfitted to any external symbols; which yet creates its own phantasmal shapes of unholy imagination and acts of disorder and crime, making of them its own grim reality; which is concerned not only with the backward temporal sequences of manifestation as they normally appear, but looks forward and has forbidden knowledge of futurity, trades in half-truths and truths of prophecy; an inmost knowledge of the time-succession which, though not wholly false, is yet poisonous; a sight of that spiritual machinery which man cannot properly understand and into which he penetrates at his peril.[3]

The hero whose love-reality has failed may concentrate his attention either on the outer things he has lost, or on his own soul. In *King Lear* the disorder of these 'outer things' reacts on Lear and disrupts his mind, while in *Macbeth* it is the hero's mind that is in disorder and disrupts the state. So, Knight says, these plays present 'two aspects of a single reality', and the closest welding of these two 'aspects' occurs in *Hamlet*.

G. Wilson Knight's style can be over-rich: he favours words with '-tude' on the end, and often adds unnecessary epithets such as 'theme' or 'conception' which make his sentences stodgy to read. However, his 'metaphysic' is an obvious thought, since we assume that we can approach Shakespeare's tragedies as a group of plays, and since we are interested in defining 'the tragedy' in Shakespeare. We could re-phrase Knight's explanation of love- and hate-themes in more everyday language, thus: the hero gives his love but is somehow rejected or disillusioned; this experience is deeply disturbing and loosens the hero's grip on reality, disordering his perception of the world around him, and his own personality; the

---

[3] From G. Wilson Knight, *The Wheel of Fire: Interpretations of Shakespearian Tragedy*, London, 1930. All quotations used in the above summary are drawn from pp. 1–15 and pp. 262–9 in the Methuen edition, 1960.

disordered world, and the disillusionment he has suffered, give rise to cynicism, revulsion and disgust: hate.   Everyday language, however, loses much of the concrete force of Knight's writing, such as the concept of love 'embodied' in an external object, which is sensitively derived from Shakespeare's own metaphor-rich text.

Knight's distinction between 'criticism' and 'interpretation' and his preference for the latter, which begins our extract from *The Wheel of Fire*, is now the predominant view. It is also a helpful reminder for students. Our job is to analyse in order to illuminate the text; we are never expected to 'criticise' in the sense of finding fault with Shakespeare.

Knight's other distinction, between 'temporal' and 'spatial' analysis, however, is urgent and important. Many students learn to study characters, motives and actions very thoroughly, but remain caught within these bounds. It is important to move on, and consider the work you are studying as a whole, as a complete imaginative product, obeying its own internal laws. Any imaginative whole, whether a play by Shakespeare or a detective thriller by Agatha Christie, creates a world that works within its own confines. Some pretend to be close to reality, while others (such as *The Tempest*) are full of magic and other impossible, unnatural things. None of them are 'real' in the sense of being the same as life itself. Knight develops this insight, saying that we should look at Shakespeare's tragedies as if they were there in front of us, complete with every word and action, in one sudden moment. Then we will see the relationships between words, images and ideas in the play, wherever they occur in the text and whoever speaks them. Perhaps the clearest way to express this idea is that we should study a Shakespearian tragedy in the same way we would analyse a short poem. It is much more complicated and there are thousands more words, of course; but our effort to discern a 'pattern' of poetic expression and a 'core' of ideas and experience should be much the same.

*   *   *

We now turn to more recent criticism, taking our final sample from Terry Eagleton, writing in 1986. Before we do, however, we should be aware that many critics are now considered as belonging within 'schools' of criticism. This means that they have developed a theory about what is most important in literature; or they have chosen a particular angle of approach, and developed analytical methods that are designed to emphasise the preoccupation with which they approach their work. We may think that their views are bound to be more limited than those of the traditional critic, as a result. There is a danger that they will select what is relevant to their concern and ignore other parts of the text, so giving a distorted view of the whole. On the other hand, Bradley was preoccupied with character, and concluded that 'character in action' was the be-all and end-all of Shakespearian tragedies; and Knight was fascinated by his 'hate-theme', the story of disappointed love which he saw as the main-spring of tragic vision in Shakespeare. In short, these two critics had favourite ideas anyway. Perhaps such partial answers are inevitable, when any critic tries to explain something as many-faceted as Shakespeare's tragedies. Perhaps the modern critic, who declares his special interest at the outset, has the advantage of honesty: he does not pretend that he can explain the ultimate secret, the 'core' that defies description.

We should touch on two kinds of 'special interest' approach before moving on. There are 'feminist' critics, and there are critics who analyse in terms of 'cultural materialism'.

Feminist criticism examines the plays in terms of roles and con-cepts of 'masculine' and 'feminine', and adopts and makes use of analyses of family and social structures drawn from the sociology, social history and anthropology of the twentieth century. These produce a range of features and a critical method that can be thought of under an umbrella heading: feminist criticism focuses on 'gender issues'. The starting-point for much of this criticism of the tragedies is the undeniable point that the worlds they present on stage are dominated by men: all four heroes are men, the govern-ment consists of men, fathers rule their families, and so on. So Marilyn French (*Shakespeare's Division of Experience*, 1982) writes:

> The worlds of Othello, Lear and Macbeth, as well as the other tragic heroes, are utterly 'masculine'; they are dominated by men who place

supreme value on the qualities of the masculine principle and to varying degrees, slight, deny, or are ignorant of the value and importance of its complement. The kind of blindness to or rejection of 'feminine' values varies from tragedy to tragedy . . .[4]

and Kathleen McLuskie points out the misogyny of *King Lear*:

> . . . the narrative and its dramatisation present a connection between sexual insubordination and anarchy, and the connection is given an explicitly misogynist emphasis. The action of the play, the organisation of its point of view and the theatrical dynamic of its central scenes all depend upon an audience accepting an equation between 'human nature' and male power.[5]

These two 'feminists' differ greatly in their conclusions, however. Marilyn French analyses the 'feminine', distinguishing between 'inlaw' (love) and 'outlaw' (sex) femininity, and examines the heroes' relations to these and to their predominantly 'masculine' culture. She concludes that Shakespeare has provided a perceptive and radical analysis, a critique of the gender-values of his time and ours: 'Thus, the tragedies are among the most radical criticisms ever written of the values of Western society.'[6] Kathleen McLuskie, on the other hand, believes that the 'patriarchal' bias of *King Lear* is so powerful and unquestioned that it does not allow a feminine audience to relate to the play naturally. A woman watching *King Lear* finds herself and the feminine characters described and defined by a misogynist man, Shakespeare. The misogyny is in 'both the play and its hero'. The moment when these two critics part company is important: it is the point in their argument when Marilyn French distinguishes Shakespeare from his characters, and assumes that the poet can hold an independent, ironic view of his creation, and when Kathleen McLuskie insists that Shakespeare must be identified with

---

[4] From the chapter entitled 'The Late Tragedies', published as an extract in *Shakespearean Tragedy*, ed. John Drakakis, London and NY, 1992, p. 229.

[5] From 'The Patriarchal Bard', in *Political Shakespeare: Essays in Cultural Materialism*, ed. Jonathan Dollimore and Alan Sinfield, 2nd edn., Manchester, 1994, p. 98.

[6] French, *op.cit.* (see note 4), p. 229.

the patriarchal misogyny of Lear and Lear's society. In McLuskie's view, 'feminist criticism must also assert the power of resistance, subverting rather than co-opting the domination of the patriarchal Bard'.[7]

We have noticed that our first three critics were less and less likely to 'criticise' in the sense of finding fault with Shakespeare. Kathleen McLuskie (writing in 1985) argues strongly that Shakespeare's immunity from criticism should not continue.

The 'cultural materialist' critic is a product of two developments in thought which have closely identifiable aims. First, there is the historical materialism of Marx with its critical analysis of Western history in terms of feudal and bourgeois-capitalist eras. Second, there is the comparatively recent proliferation of cultural studies as a blend of 'history, sociology and English'.[8] This school of criticism is most interested in power, and analyses the means used by the powerful in a play or a society to dominate, exploit, subordinate or 'contain' any opposition. As with feminist criticism, this project can develop in two ways: either by analysing the plays to show Shakespeare's analysis of the power-structures he dramatises as the 'world' of a play, or by examining Shakespeare and his plays as supporting the dominant power. This latter, 'critical' attitude can be divided again. Some focus on the plays, criticising Shakespeare as a reactionary conservative writing what was essentially Tudor propaganda. This view suggests that the play's 'entertainment' is a cloak for a reactionary political message, making oppression palatable for the common in the audience. Others look at the position of Shakespearian drama in our culture, and criticise the way in which the establishment has adopted, and imposes, Shakespeare as a 'culture' idol, for example in tourism and education.

There are now many more 'schools' of criticism than these; and within these are many 'sub-schools'. Our brief description of two of the main recent developments shows that there is vast potential for argument both between critics and between a critic and Shakespeare, and will suffice for the present chapter. Now we can move on to

---

[7] McLuskie, op.cit. (see note 5), p. 106.
[8] Jonathan Dollimore, in *Political Shakespeare* (see note 5), p. 2.

Terry Eagleton (who could be billed as belonging in the 'post-struc-
turalist' school of criticism), and summarise his approach to *King
Lear*.

Eagleton begins by observing that Goneril's and Regan's insincere
declarations of love for their father start the play with 'a bout of
severe linguistic inflation'. Goneril declares that her love goes beyond
words and all other values, and this ironically reveals her 'more than
all' to be nothing. There is a distinction between something that
transcends meaning, and Goneril's love that has none. Regan's contradiction (that Goneril has defined her love, and fallen short)
negates her sister's negativity to create an even more inflated 'all'.
Since 'all' means nothing, Cordelia's 'nothing' is the 'only sound cur-
rency', and Lear is wrong to think that 'nothing will come of
nothing':

> . . . when meaning has been inflated beyond measure, nothing *but*
> nothing, a drastic reduction of signs to cyphers, will be enough to
> restabilize the verbal coinage. Only by a fundamental inversion and
> undercutting of this whole lunatic language game can the ground be
> cleared for a modest 'something' to begin gradually to emerge.

Cordelia is faced with the meaningless inflation of her sisters' declarations on the one hand, and the crass 'utilitarian exactitude' of
Lear's belief that love can be weighed, valued and paid for on the
other hand. She counters her sisters by being precise (she loves Lear
'according to my bond'), and she counter's Lear's error, later in the
play, with her forgiveness, which is creative excess. Lear is attempting
to clear away the 'referent', his real power and duties as a King, while
at the same time holding onto the empty 'signifier', the mere word,
when he says that he will retain 'the name, and all th'addition to a
king'. This is like his use of lines on the map to divide the kingdom,
since no map is the land it signifies. So Lear has 'struck his own title
abstract, divorced it from material life'.

Cordelia is excluded from the kingdom, and disappears into the
future of the play with France, who cannot overcome Lear's world of
exactly calculated imprecisions and must withdraw beyond the
bounds of the kingdom. With Cordelia and France gone, truth is

only found in inversions of Lear's statements: Cordelia is 'most rich, being poor' and, as Kent says, 'freedom lives hence, and banishment is here'. Eagleton then develops his analysis of the verbal paradoxes in the play:

> . . . the truth of a false condition can be articulated only in the dis-
> course of madness, in a language which raises political insanity to the
> second power, parodying and redoubling it so as to deconstruct it
> from the inside. There can be no straight talking, no bold gesture of
> unmasking, which will not be absorbed and reinflected by the nexus
> of delusion, becoming yet another mask and falsehood in its turn;
> only the coupling of two negatives can hope to produce a positive.

In breaking with Cordelia, Lear has cut his last connection with material bonds and so separates himself from his own physical life. In such a condition his body becomes nothing, because it is an 'insentient blank' ('this tempest in my mind doth from my senses take all feeling else'); and his mind, which has lost the constraint or direction it had when Lear cut it off from material reality, merely devours itself and is also therefore a form of nothing.

Gloucester wishes to release the connection between his mind and physical reality: 'Better I were distract; / So should my thoughts be sever'd from my griefs'; then his blindness thrusts 'the brute fact of his body into consciousness' and in the latter part of the play we hear references to combinations of senses and understanding in 'see feelingly' and the idea that he will 'smell' his way to Dover. The cul-minating event is his supposed fall. This is a rediscovery of the body that Lear also has to learn:

> To regain touch with the harsh materiality of things, to discover that
> one is nothing in comparison with all one had imagined, is in that
> very act to become something.

In the speeches on Dover Beach, Lear finds out his error, for 'To say "ay" and "no" to everything . . . was no good divinity', or is to say nothing at all – as Goneril and Regan did at the outset. Lear has 'smelt out' this truth.

Eagleton then describes Goneril, Regan and Edmund. These three he suggests are only a function of their own appetites, and Goneril and Regan are unable to continue hiding what they are, which has been determined by nature. Edmund is a 'self-creating opportunist' who can manipulate others' desires because he is so clearly aware of his own. The play thus makes a distinction between people who can submit to the needs of others and so 'creatively' surpass or transcend their own limit and their own nature (like Kent and Edgar), and those who are destructively passive because they only express and act on their own appetites.

This leads to a difficult dialectic which is the 'paradox' that *King Lear* explores: the creative element in humanity which leads people to transcend their physical limits, and thus the truth of an abundant surplus beyond any precise measure, is a 'natural' tendency; yet when this process goes too far it becomes detached from physical bonds and is thus destructive, not creative. So Lear's reply when the need for his retinue of knights is questioned, points out the tendency of humanity to demand more than physical life requires, because 'it is just structural to the human animal that demand should outstrip exact need', yet at the same time the opening of the play shows that the human capacity for lies makes humankind more destructive than other species. The 'surplus' is therefore a natural and creative human 'need', yet at the same time it creates a problem, so it is ambivalent. If we have too many material possessions they will wrap around us and prevent us from realising the misery of others. We then need to expose ourselves to 'feel what wretches feel'. This fellow-feeling would then move us to share the surplus with those who are poor in a re-distribution of wealth.

It is language itself that is the problem, that is excessive or superfluous about humanity. Eagleton suggests that language is constantly breaking out beyond the confines of the body:

> 'The worst is not,' declares Edgar, 'So long as we can say "This is the worst"' (IV, i, 28–9). By naming an ultimate limit, speech transcends it in that very act, undoing its own pronouncement by its own performance. Language is the edge we have over biology, but it is a mixed blessing.

Cordelia resolves the paradoxes of the play, both by her speech, which carefully constructs material truth (for example, her freely given but carefully divided love) beginning from the honest 'nothing' and consistently pitches itself at the 'elusive point between too much and too little', and by her 'combination of physical root-edness and freedom of spirit'. However, she dies. At the end of the play, Edgar enjoins all to 'speak what we feel, not what we ought to say'; and this could stand as a definition of Cordelia's practice and influence on the play; yet this will never be easily achieved or sustained:

> For if it is structural to human nature to surpass itself, and if language is the very index and medium of this, then there would seem a contradiction at the very core of the linguistic animal which makes it 'natural' for signs to come adrift from things, consciousness to overstep physical bonds, values to get out of hand and norms to be destructively overridden. . . . *King Lear* is a tragedy because it stares this contradiction full in the face, aware that no poetic symbolism is adequate to resolve it.[9]

Terry Eagleton, then, proposes a slightly different version of dualism. Bradley saw the hero and world 'order'; Knight saw the 'hate-theme' expressing the protagonist cut off from his soul, once embodied in his love. Eagleton distinguishes between language, or what he calls 'excess' and 'surplus', and physical reality or the 'limits of the body'. Eagleton's method focuses upon the use of language in the play, and he pursues this interest for what it can reveal about language. One of the most effective tools of his analysis is the linguist's idea that a word is a sign that represents something else – something real. He is particularly interested in how well language expresses its referent, or how far it can either fail to express anything or attempt to encompass that which cannot be expressed.

*　　*　　*

---

[9] From Terry Eagleton, 'Value: King Lear, Timon of Athens, Antony and Cleopatra', in *William Shakespeare*, 1986. All the quotations in our summary appear in the extract reprinted in *Shakespearean Tragedy* (see note 4), on pp. 389–94.

It is useful, before we end this sample of critical views, to bring together what the different critics have in common.

They all write about the tragedies in terms of paradox, dialectic, irony, contradiction, separation or breaking, ambivalence, conflict. Something cannot be 'resolved', it is 'irrational' or 'transcends meaning', and so on. These are all descriptions of a dynamic relationship between two elements in the drama that they see as fundamental in its world and its effect. They disagree about what these elements are; and the dualities they see, although all drawn from the same plays, do not greatly overlap. On the other hand, they all perceive that tragedy is a complex, ultimately insoluble dislocation between two forces or two principles. Our ideas from Part I of this book suggest that the tragedy lies somewhere in the irrational or 'absurd' relation between elements in the plays (such as order and chaos, appearance and reality, right and wrong, etc.), and that the 'absurdity' of these relationships renders them intellectually insoluble. The conclusions we have reached from our practical analysis of selected extracts, then, seem to be in the mainstream of critical attempts to describe Shakespearian tragedy.

Further Reading

Your first job is to study the text. There is no substitute for the work of detailed analysis: that is how you gain the close familiarity with the text, and the fully developed understanding of its content, which make the essays you write both personal and convincing. For this reason I recommend that you take it as a rule not to read any other books around or about the text until you have finished studying it for yourself.

Once you are familiar with the text, you may wish to read around and about it. This brief chapter is only intended to set you off: there are thousands of relevant books and we can only mention a few. However, most good editions, and critical works, have suggestions for further reading, or a bibliography of their own. Once you have begun to read beyond your text, you can use these and a good library to follow up your particular interests. This chapter is divided into 'Reading Around the Text', which lists some other works by Shakespeare and some by other contemporary writers, 'The Historical and Social Background', and 'Criticism', which will introduce you to the varieties of opinion among professional critics.

Reading Around the Text

Shakespeare wrote other tragedies apart from the 'Great Four'. Of these the most relevant are *Romeo and Juliet*, *Julius Caesar*, *Antony and Cleopatra* and *Timon of Athens*. The closest of them to the mature tragedies is probably *Antony and Cleopatra*; and reading *Romeo and Juliet* gives a sense of how far Shakespeare developed during the 1590s. *Troilus and Cressida* and *Measure for Measure* are two problem plays written during the same dark period in Shakespeare's work that produced the tragedies. It may also be useful to become acquainted with his comedies, starting, say, with *A Midsummer Night's Dream*, and his histories, beginning with *Richard*

3. Our discussion in Chapter 8 indicates *The Merchant of Venice* and *Henry 4 Part 1* as examples of later comedy and history plays respectively. A late 'romance' or tragi-comedy completes the picture: *The Tempest* is a fine example, although *The Winter's Tale* may be preferred, for its intense portrait of Leontes's destructive jealousy, if you are studying *Othello*.

Tragedy was a favourite form during Shakespeare's time. Among the finest contemporary tragedies by other playwrights are Webster's *The Duchess of Malfi*, Middleton and Rowley's *The Changeling*, and Marlowe's *Dr Faustus*. Two revenge tragedies are of particular interest in connection with *Hamlet*: Tourneur's *The Revenger's Tragedy* and Kyd's *The Spanish Tragedy*. We have discussed the 'Machiavel' character-type in Chapter 9. Bosola from *The Duchess of Malfi* and De Flores from *The Changeling* are particularly powerful examples.

The Historical and Social Background

The Elizabethan World Picture by E. M. W. Tillyard (Penguin, 1963) is regarded as naïve by many recent critics who believe that Tillyard took Elizabethan propaganda at face value, and that people of the time held conflicting views about the world. It is worth reading nonetheless, as it is a thorough explanation of *one side* of the 'order' question. The development of ideas and society in the Renaissance is, however, such a vast field that we will only mention two other works. Michael Mangan's *A Preface to Shakespeare's Tragedies* (New York, 1991) gives clear, readable and thoroughly informed discussions of contemporary society, ideas and events; and M. M. Badawi's, *Background to Shakespeare* (Macmillan, 1981) is also very informative.

Criticism

The critical works sampled in Chapter 10 are: A. C. Bradley, *Shakespearean Tragedy* (1904); G. Wilson Knight, *The Wheel of Fire: Interpretations of Shakespearian Tragedy* (1930); Helen Gardner, 'The

Historical Approach: *Hamlet*, from *Shakespeare: The Tragedies. A Collection of Critical Essays*, ed. Alfred Harbage (1964); and Terry Eagleton, *William Shakespeare* (1986).

Anthologies of critical essays and articles are a good way to sample the critics. You can then go on to read the full-length books written by those critics whose articles you have found stimulating. We referred to two recent anthologies in Chapter 10. *Political Shakespeare*, edited by Jonathan Dollimore and Alan Sinfield (2nd edn., 1994) is a collection of recent criticism with the accent on cultural materialism and feminism. *Shakespearean Tragedy*, edited by John Drakakis (1992) is an anthology of critical essays on the tragedies representing a broad spectrum of critical views. There are also anthologies devoted to the individual plays, such as *Macbeth: Critical Essays*, ed. S. Schoenbaum (1991) and *Modern Critical Interpretations: Othello*, ed. Harold Bloom, (1987).

The following full-length critical works may also be of interest and should be stimulating whether you agree or disagree with the writer's analysis: Richard Wilson's *Will Power: Essays on Shakespearean Authority* (1993), Stephen Greenblatt's *Shakespearean Negotiations* (1988), and Derek Cohen's *Shakespearean Motives* (1988) are all recent critical works on Shakespeare.

Finally, here is a jumble of more or less relevant reading, including some works that are about Shakespeare and some that are not. Aristotle, *The Poetics* (available in Penguin Classics); R. H. Tawney, *Religion and the Rise of Capitalism* (1926); John Middleton Murry, *Shakespeare* (1936); L. C. Knights, *Some Shakespearean Themes and An Approach to Hamlet* (1959); Ernest Jones, *Hamlet and Oedipus* (1949); Niccolò Machiavelli, *The Prince* (1514, available in Penguin Classics); George Bernard Shaw, *Saint Joan* (1924). As you can see, this is a very heterogeneous and personal list, including some which have no direct relevance to Shakespeare's tragedies at all. I mention them because they have contributed to the development of this writer's ideas. If you pursue your own thoughts and interests through reading, you will compile a similar list of your own, consisting of books about anything and everything.

Index